Conversations with Willie Morris

Literary Conversations Series

Peggy Whitman Prenshaw
General Editor

Books by Willie Morris

The South Today: 100 Years After Appomattox. Edited by Willie Morris. New York: Harper & Row, 1965.

North Toward Home. Boston: Houghton Mifflin, 1967.

Yazoo: Integration in a Deep-Southern Town. New York: Harper & Row, 1971.

Good Old Boy: A Delta Boyhood. New York: Harper & Row, 1971.

The Last of the Southern Girls. New York: Alfred A. Knopf, 1973.

A Southern Album: Recollections of Some People and Places and Times Gone By. Edited by Irwin Glusker, narrative by Willie Morris. Birmingham, Ala: Oxmoor House, 1975.

James Jones: A Friendship. Garden City, N.Y.: Doubleday, 1978.

Terrains of the Heart and Other Essays on Home. Oxford, Miss.: Yoknapatawpha Press, 1981.

The Courting of Marcus Dupree. Garden City, N.Y.: Doubleday, 1983.

Always Stand in Against the Curve and Other Sports Stories. Oxford, Miss.: Yoknapatawpha Press, 1983.

Homecomings. Jackson: University Press of Mississippi, 1989.

Good Old Boy and the Witch of Yazoo. Oxford, Miss.: Yoknapatawpha Press, 1989.

Faulkner's Mississippi. Birmingham, Ala: Oxmoor House, 1990.

After All, It's Only a Game. Jackson: University Press of Mississippi, 1992.

New York Days. Boston: Little, Brown, 1993.

A Prayer for the Opening of the Little League Season. San Diego, Calif.: Harcourt Brace, 1995.

My Dog Skip. New York: Random House, 1995.

The Ghosts of Medgar Evers: A Tale of Race, Murder, Mississippi, and Hollywood. New York: Random House, 1998.

My Cat Spit McGee. New York: Random House, 1999.

Photo credit: Hunter Cole

Conversations
with Willie Morris

Edited by
Jack Bales

University Press of Mississippi
Jackson

Publication of this book was made possible in part by
Harriet DeCell Kuykendall

www.upress.state.ms.us

Copyright © 2000 by University Press of Mississippi
All rights reserved
Manufactured in the United States of America

08   07   06   05   04   03   02   01   00   4   3   2   1
∞
Library of Congress Cataloging-in-Publication Data

Conversations with Willie Morris / edited by Jack Bales.
     p.   cm.—(Literary conversations series)
     Includes index.
     ISBN 1-57806-236-5 — ISBN 1-57806-237-3 (pbk.)
        1. Morris, Willie—Interviews.   2. Authors, American—20th century—Interviews.   3.
Journalists—United States—Interviews.   4. Mississippi—Social life and customs.   5.
Southern States—Intellectual life—20th century.   I. Morris, Willie.   II. Bales, Jack.   III.
Series.
PS3563.O8745   Z62   2000
813′.54—dc21   99-054749

British Library Cataloging-in-Publication Data available

Contents

Introduction

For over forty years, Willie Morris confronted the turbulent issues of his generation. As the controversial and bold young editor of the *Daily Texan* at the University of Texas in Austin, he quickly incurred the wrath of the institution's Board of Regents for his scathing attacks on censorship and segregation. While at the helm of the *Texas Observer* he courageously reported events that the mainstream press seldom bothered to cover, such as unsanitary and hazardous conditions in nursing homes ("A Dismal Study—The Aged in Texas" blazoned one headline), illiteracy, the social ineffectiveness of the death penalty, racial discrimination, and the political shenanigans and skullduggery of Texas legislators. As the youngest editor in chief in the history of *Harper's*, Morris aggressively transformed the stodgy, patriarchal magazine into one of the country's most exciting and influential periodicals.

"I have no alternative to words," Morris occasionally replied when asked about his far-reaching career. And driven by social conscience, he continued to speak out on matters that concerned him after he resigned his editor's position and left New York City, at various times writing with outrage, with humor, with sadness, and with affection—but always with passion and candor.

The author himself was as multi-dimensional as his writing. "Very few people really know Willie Morris," contended writer David Halberstam during the period the two men worked together at *Harper's*. A self-described "good ole boy," Morris—with his generous, adventurous spirit and self-effacing nature—captivated both friends and perfect strangers. Interviewers found him relaxed and affable, open to their questions, and forthright with his responses. Halberstam, however, believed that only Morris's closest friends also recognized him as a "very complicated, enormously sophisticated, strong man."[1] These few were probably not surprised if they had discovered that while he was working in New York City in the early 1970s, a study published in the social science journal *Public Interest* ranked him among "the seventy most prestigious contemporary American intellectuals."[2]

While Morris's public persona is readily apparent in the interviews and profiles that appear in this book, glimmers of his more thoughtful—perhaps even brooding—private side occasionally surface as well. For instance, in 1988 journalist Dick Polman managed to track him down at a lakeside cabin in McComb, Mississippi, where he had sequestered himself to write a novel. Polman spent an evening with him and several friends, during which the author talked emotionally about urban sprawl, politics, and racial integration in Mississippi. Morris remembered with chagrin that when he was twenty-one years old the White Citizens' Council in his hometown held a meeting, which was attended by his father and the neighbors with whom he had grown up. "If you love Mississippi," he sighed, "then it'll always touch your heart, because everything is complicated. We all love Mississippi, but sometimes it doesn't love us back."

Polman's article and these other literary conversations trace virtually Morris's entire career. In 1969, during one of his earliest interviews for a national publication, the young editor shared with Richard Cohen his plans for *Harper's* and presciently observed that television threatened the existence of his and other magazines. In later interviews he reflected on those years with a combination of wistfulness, pride, and fulfillment. While conversing with Nashville Public Radio's Rebecca Bain, for example, he recalled that although he was gratified to have published the works of many talented and well-known writers, he was most proud of "really being part of our American civilization of that period" and, he hoped, of "having shaped it somewhat for the better."

It was during this same period, shortly after he assumed the editorship of *Harper's*, that Morris published his first book, the autobiographical *North Toward Home*. In that widely acclaimed account, the author reflects on how many members of his generation—Mississippians who reached maturity in the early 1950s—have felt alienated from Mississippi but love their state and are still drawn to it. "The feelings are very complicated," Morris told Mary Jayne Garrard Whittington a year after the book's publication, "but the older I am the more [the South] means to me, the closer the ties." Throughout *North Toward Home* he struggles to understand his regional identity as he challenges the various social and cultural forces that characterized the nation from the 1940s through the 1960s.

During the three decades since the thirty-year-old Morris completed his "autobiography in mid-passage," he wrote seventeen additional volumes (including a second volume of autobiography) and attained national prominence as a journalist, nonfiction writer, novelist, editor, and essayist. He was particularly acclaimed for the many writings in which he compared his experiences and his complex southern heritage to America's own history. Yet, he did not consider himself a southern writer. "I am an American writer who happens to have come from the South," he often emphasized. "I've tried to put the South into the larger American perspective."

Morris was interviewed numerous times throughout his career, and although many of the dialogues concentrated on just-published books or other milestones, a large number touched as well upon his beloved Mississippi and the changing South. Robert H. Moore talked with him during the summer of 1970 soon after *Harper's* published Morris's lengthy article exploring how the forced integration of the public schools had affected his hometown (an article that appeared in book form a year later as *Yazoo: Integration in a Deep-Southern Town*). Moore's questions produced lively discussions of William Faulkner, *North Toward Home*, the autobiography as a literary form, and his article on school integration. During a book tour in May 1971, Morris and Mississippi newspaper reporter Lew Powell discussed how people from Yazoo City reacted to *Yazoo* and the difficulties the author faced while writing fiction.

Chatting with starry-eyed admirers, however, was probably far from Morris's mind as he signed copies of the just-published *Yazoo*. Two months earlier he had resigned from *Harper's* after becoming embroiled in editorial disputes with the publication's owner and moved to Bridgehampton, New York, a small town on the east end of Long Island. Refusing all the job offers that came pouring in, he decided to concentrate on his writing rather than edit another magazine.

The first project Morris completed after leaving New York City was *Good Old Boy*, an adventure-filled celebration of his youth that he wrote for his son, David Rae Morris, who had asked him what it was like to grow up in the Deep South. This book has since become a staple among teenage students in Mississippi and elsewhere, and for the rest of his life Morris regularly received fan mail from them, their teachers, and even their parents. "It is kind of a phenomenon," Morris told interviewer Jack Bales a few years ago, admitting that while he was writing the book, which features assorted practical jokes, boyish misadventures, and a daring rescue in a haunted house, "I never for a moment thought . . . that it would have such a fantastic effect on kids."

Morris followed *Good Old Boy* with his novel, *The Last of the Southern Girls*, and his combination biography and affectionate reminiscence, *James*

Jones: A Friendship. In 1979, soon after the publication of this tribute to his comrade-in-arms, Morris realized that it was important for him to have some proximity with his roots and the touchstones of his past. Late that year he moved to Oxford and in January 1980 began teaching classes in creative writing and the American novel at the University of Mississippi. "I wanted to come home," he explained simply to William Thomas a few weeks later. "I'm at a kind of juncture in my life, and I felt it was time."

Morris also told Mary Lynn Kotz how exhilarated he felt upon returning to his native soil and William Faulkner's hometown. Not only did he quickly ease into a comfortable lifestyle in Oxford, but as students flocked to his courses he assumed the same role as literary mentor and confidant with them that he had performed with writers and other companions in New York City. Kotz's profile, in fact, captures the essence of what several of Morris's intimate friends call his "great sweetness"—perhaps one of his most enduring legacies. As writer-in-residence and instructor at Ole Miss, he regularly encouraged aspiring young authors, particularly when he recognized exceptional aptitude. Furthermore, as he discovered the talents and sensed the innate goodness in his students, he inspired them to take advantage of those natural gifts and to build upon them. As he earned the trust of the young men and women in his classes they began confiding in him, talking of their plans, aspirations, and even their doubts and insecurities. He, in return, shared stories of his family, related anecdotes about his friends such as James Jones, and conveyed to this new generation his deep appreciation of southern history.

Throughout his life Morris demonstrated an acute sense of history, place, and family in much of his writing. "If there is anything that makes southerners distinctive from the main body of Americans," he remarked in 1975, "it is a certain burden of memory and a burden of history. . . . I think sensitive southerners have this in their bones, this profound awareness of the past. . . ."[3] A few years later he reminisced about his youth, childhood friends, living and long-dead family members, the Civil War, and race relations past and present in a perceptive and wide-ranging conversation with oral historian John Griffin Jones.

Morris also examined the complexities of race relations and racial changes in a previously unpublished interview with social historian Studs Terkel. The two writers met in the fall of 1983 on Terkel's Chicago radio show where they spiritedly discussed the multi-layered *The Courting of Marcus Dupree*, a skillful combination of sports reporting, historical analysis, and biography in which Morris recounts the madness surrounding the college recruitment of a talented southern black athlete. Morris and illustrator Barry Moser shared more lighthearted observations about sports with Wayne Pond in another heretofore unpublished interview, this one upon the 1995 publication of *A Prayer for the Opening of the Little League Season*.

I am fortunate to include other interviews in this book that have never before been published. Michael Feldman, host of Public Radio International's comedy/quiz show *Whad'Ya Know?*, discovered firsthand Morris's droll wit after the author repeatedly broke up the studio audience while a guest on the comedian's program in January 1996. PBS talk show host Charlie Rose invited Morris on his program for more serious discussions following the publication of several of his last books. In the interviews included here the two converse about *New York Days*, in which Morris reflects on his heady years at *Harper's* and how they mirrored the tempestuous 1960s, and *My Dog Skip*, his poignant tribute to the canine companion of his youth and memoir of a bygone era. New York public radio host Leonard Lopate rounds out the collection with a discussion of the 1998 volume *The Ghosts of Medgar Evers*, in which Morris combines an insider's view of Hollywood filmmaking with his characteristic eloquence and soul-searching about the South and racial healing.

After reviewing Willie Morris's *Homecomings* upon its publication, a *Boston Globe* writer concluded: "There's damn fine life left in this man's prose."[4] Some ten years later, readers of Jackson's *Clarion-Ledger* agreed, selecting Morris as Mississippi's favorite nonfiction author of the millennium.[5] Belying the words of one of the favorite authors of his youth, Thomas Wolfe, he clearly showed in recent years that, both literally and metaphorically, you *can* go home again. In the conversations that follow, while considering the significance of home, family, and even remembrance itself, he focuses on dozens of other topics that fascinate him, including sports, literature, the Civil War, dogs, politics, the 1960s, cemeteries, and the aging process. And, as a writer with such varied interests, Morris also passionately explores the paradoxical and complicated past of his native state, with its history of guilt and meanness and tragedy, but also of grace and courage and solicitude.

The twenty-five interviews and profiles in this volume span the years 1967 to 1998. As with the other books in the Literary Conversations Series, they are reprinted in the order in which each interview took place. In dating them I

have either relied upon the interviewers' statements and implications or upon
outside evidence. For example, Robert H. Moore's correspondence in the
University of Mississippi's library indicates that his discussion with Willie
Morris took place four years before its publication. Although published material is reproduced as it originally appeared, I silently corrected typographical
errors and obvious mistakes. Where appropriate, I have added explanatory
information in brackets.

I am grateful to Willie Morris for his enthusiastic interest in this book. In
September 1995 I wrote him what can only be called a "fan letter," asking
questions about *North Toward Home* and other works. His immediate reply
initiated a warm friendship, in which we exchanged hundreds of letters, numerous phone calls, several visits, and even one or two practical jokes (overnight guests were apt to find rubber snakes, spiders, and other assorted
creatures planted in their beds by the impish Morris, who often described
himself as the "oldest living sixth grader"). In November 1998 he and his
wife, JoAnne Prichard, visited me in Fredericksburg, Virginia, where he
charmed two audiences during public lectures and discussions at Mary Washington College. Literally up to the day of his untimely death, he generously
(and characteristically, as countless writers will attest) offered his advice,
cooperation, encouragement, and even his personal files. I am able to include
several interviews in this book—including at least two previously unpublished ones—only because he gave them to me. As broadcast journalist and
author Bill Moyers prophetically remarked more than a decade ago, "In the
end it will be the quality of his life that is the real contribution Willie . . .
made to our times."[6] The consummate lover of the written word, Morris
was—to use one of his favorites—ineffable.[7]

I wish to thank the interviewers, publishers, authors, and editors who
kindly granted me permission to publish these conversations. I especially
appreciate the patient guidance of Seetha Srinivasan, my editor at the University Press of Mississippi, and the continuous support of William M. Ander-
son, Jr. Carla Bailey, as usual, did yeoman service for me, as did Beth Perkins
and Linda Thompson. I also wish to thank Brandi Brinson, Shane Gong,
JoAnne Prichard, Lisa K. Speer, Anne Stascavage, Roy Strohl, Elizabeth
Young, and the Reference Staff of the Mary Washington College Library for
their inestimable assistance during the years I was working on this book.
Other persons who helped me include Jeff Abernathy, Dick Bales, Phyllis S.
Bales, Neal Biggers, William B. Crawley, Jr., Steven L. Davis, Donald R.
Eldred, John E. Ellzey, John Evans, William R. Ferris, Jennifer Ford, Mary

Grattan, Mary Jones, Larry L. King, Harriet DeCell Kuykendall, David Rae Morris, Barry Moser, Norman Mott, Midge Poyck, David Sansing, Carol Stabler, Steve Stewart, and Thomas M. Verich. This book is for Willie and JoAnne.

JB
August 1999

Notes

1. "South Toward Home," *Time* 95 (1 June 1970): 77.
2. Charles Kadushin, "Who Are the Elite Intellectuals?," *Public Interest*, no. 29 (Fall 1972):109–25.
3. Willie Morris, interview by Owen B. Caudill, 28 May 1975, transcript, University of Southern Mississippi, Hattiesburg, Miss.
4. Gail Caldwell, "Willie Morris' Southern Fire Is Still Burning," *Boston Globe*, 10 January 1990, 69.
5. Billy Watkins, "Mississippi's Favorite Writers," *Jackson (Mississippi) Clarion-Ledger*, 14 June 1999, sec. D, 1–2.
6. Bret Watson, "Having Headed South Toward Home, Willie Morris Brings a New Book North," *Avenue* 8 (December-January 1984):148.
7. Rick Bragg, "To a Beloved Native Son, A Mississippi Farewell," *New York Times*, 6 August 1999, sec. A, 10.

Chronology

1934	William Weaks Morris born on 29 November in Jackson, Mississippi, the only child of Henry Rae Morris and Marion Harper (Weaks) Morris; family moves to Yazoo City, Mississippi, six months later
1946	Begins writing sports stories for the *Yazoo Herald* newspaper
1951–1952	Editor of Yazoo High School newspaper, the *Flashlight*, during senior year
1952	Graduates class valedictorian in the spring of 1952 and is voted "most likely to succeed" by classmates; enters University of Texas in Austin that fall and joins staff of student newspaper, the *Daily Texan*
1955–1956	Editor in chief of *Daily Texan* during senior year
1956	Publishes first article for a national magazine, "Mississippi Rebel on a Texas Campus," *Nation*, 24 March 1956; elected to membership in Phi Beta Kappa honor society and graduates from University of Texas in the spring with a B.A. degree in English; matriculates at Oxford University's New College as a Rhodes Scholar
1958	Associate editor of *Texas Observer* in the summer; marries Celia Ann Buchan on 30 August; father dies on 31 August
1959	Receives B.A. degree in modern history from Oxford University; son David Rae Morris born in England on 1 November
1960	Takes graduate courses in American and British history at Oxford University; returns to *Texas Observer* as associate editor in July
1961–1962	Editor in chief and general manager of *Texas Observer* from March 1961 to November 1962
1962–1963	Sits in on graduate courses at Stanford University in Palo Alto, California

1963–1965   Associate editor, *Harper's* magazine

1965   *The South Today: 100 Years After Appomattox* (editor)

1965–1967   Executive editor, *Harper's* magazine

1966   M.A., Oxford University

1967   Awarded honorary Ph.D. from Grinnell College; first book, *North Toward Home*, is published and receives Houghton Mifflin Literary Fellowship Award for Nonfiction; appointed editor in chief of *Harper's* magazine; excerpts 45,000 words from William Styron's *The Confessions of Nat Turner* in September issue

1968   Receives Carr P. Collins Award from Texas Institute of Letters for *North Toward Home*, which recognizes the best nonfiction book by a Texas author or about Texas; publishes Norman Mailer's "The Steps of the Pentagon" in March *Harper's*; awarded honorary Ph.D. from Gettysburg College

1969   Willie and Celia Morris divorce

1970   Publishes Seymour M. Hersh's "My Lai 4: A Report on the Massacre and Its Aftermath" in May *Harper's*

1971   Publishes Norman Mailer's "The Prisoner of Sex" in March *Harper's*; resigns from *Harper's* that month (along with most of the contributing editors) and moves to Bridgehampton, New York; *Yazoo: Integration in a Deep-Southern Town*; *Good Old Boy: A Delta Boyhood*

1972   Receives Steck-Vaughn Award from Texas Institute of Letters for *Good Old Boy*, which recognizes the best book for children by a Texas author or about Texas

1973   *The Last of the Southern Girls*

1975   *A Southern Album: Recollections of Some People and Places and Times Gone By*

1976   Writer-in-residence at the *Washington Star* newspaper from January to March

1977   Mother dies on 15 April; friend James Jones dies on 9 May and Morris completes last several chapters of *Whistle* (1978), final volume of Jones's World War II trilogy

1978   *James Jones: A Friendship*

1979–1980   Returns to Mississippi in December 1979 to accept position as writer-in-residence and instructor in University of Mississippi's English Department. Begins teaching courses in creative writing and the American novel when classes start in January

1981   *Terrains of the Heart and Other Essays on Home*

1983   *The Courting of Marcus Dupree*; *Always Stand in Against the Curve and Other Sports Stories*

1984   Receives a Christopher Award for *The Courting of Marcus Dupree*, which recognizes those "who have achieved artistic excellence in films, books, and television specials affirming the highest values of the human spirit"

1988   Multimedia Entertainment, Inc. films *Good Old Boy* in Natchez, Mississippi, and The Disney Channel broadcasts motion picture in the fall

1989   *Homecomings*; Public Broadcasting System televises *Good Old Boy* as part of its *Wonderworks* series; *Good Old Boy and the Witch of Yazoo*

1990   *Faulkner's Mississippi*; Mississippi Library Association selects *Homecomings* as best Mississippi nonfiction book of the year; marries JoAnne Shirley Prichard on 14 September and moves to Jackson, Mississippi

1991   Resigns as writer-in-residence from University of Mississippi in February

1992   *After All, It's Only a Game*

1993   *New York Days*

1994   Mississippi Institute of Arts and Letters selects *New York Days* as best nonfiction book of the year

1995   *A Prayer for the Opening of the Little League Season*; *My Dog Skip*

1996   Awarded third annual Richard Wright Medal for Literary Excellence at Natchez Literary Festival; "A Prayer Before the Feast," introductory essay to the *Official Souvenir Program* of Atlanta's Centennial Olympic Games

1998   *The Ghosts of Medgar Evers: A Tale of Race, Murder, Missis-*
            sippi, and Hollywood; Alcon Entertainment begins filming *My*
            Dog Skip

1999   Dies on 2 August of heart failure and buried in Yazoo City,
            Mississippi; *My Cat Spit McGee* published posthumously; War-
            ner Bros. releases motion picture *My Dog Skip*

Conversations with Willie Morris

Authors & Editors

Roger H. Smith / 1967

From *Publishers' Weekly*, 192 (9 October 1967), 21–22. Reprinted in *The Author Speaks: Selected* PW *Interviews, 1967–1976*, 314–15. New York: R. R. Bowker Co., 1977. Reprinted by permission of *Publishers Weekly*.

Thirty-two is generally regarded as a tender age for writing autobiography. Nevertheless, Willie Morris, editor of *Harper's* magazine, has written his autobiography at the age of thirty-two, and Houghton Mifflin will publish it, *North Toward Home*, on October 23. Already it is one of the most talked-about nonfiction books of the season (*Saturday Evening Post* ran a ten thousand-word chunk of it in its October 7 issue), and John Kenneth Galbraith seems to have summed up the general pre-publication reaction: "No one at thirty-two," he said, "should write his memoirs; Willie Morris is the only exception."

Fiction is the expected medium for thirty-two-year-old writers. "For a long time, I worked on this material in fictional form," Mr. Morris told *PW* in an interview the other day. "Then I decided: Why not tell it like it really was?"

The result—"like it really was"—is a book about three places: Mississippi (Yazoo City, where Mr. Morris was born, grew up, was a "big wheel" in high school); Texas (Austin and the University, where he was a splendidly controversial editor of the student newspaper); and New York City (where, like so many literary outlanders before him, he was initially rebuffed by the literary "establishment" and subsequently became one of its ornaments).

What's so unusual about growing up in Mississippi? "Small-town life in the Mississippi Delta upsets me and probably always will," Mr. Morris said. "There's the heaviness of nature, the overwhelming sense of the past, the emphasis on storytelling, the courtliness and violence. Once you have it, it's always with you. The older I get, the more it talks to me." Mr. Morris said he had no idea how the book would be received in Mississippi. "I hope," he said, "that a few people there will see the book for what it is: an act of love." He had no comment about whether Mississippi now is a better or a worse place than it was when he was growing up there in the 1940s and '50s. "After the Supreme Court's school desegregation decision in 1954, Mississippi went

1

through an almost criminal period," he said. "More recently, there has been recognition that racial sickness is a national thing; it belongs to us all. The South, at its best, could lead the country out of this social madness."

Mr. Morris said that his next major writing project probably will be fiction ("though not any time soon") and that he plans to write, probably a long essay, about the fourth major place in his life, not covered in *North Toward Home*: Oxford, where for four years he studied as a Rhodes Scholar. "Oxford," he said, "is a great place. It gave me four years to think. But in this book, I skipped it consciously; I wanted this to be a book about America."

Meanwhile, except for a book promotional trip or two, Mr. Morris's basic concerns these days are with the editorial direction of *Harper's*, where he has been editor since July 1. "We're going to be doing a lot more with book material," he said, pointing to the current issue, which excerpts fifty thousand words of William Styron's *The Confessions of Nat Turner* (Random House). "And we're going to be looking conscientiously for opportunities to publish new, good writers."

Willie Morris, All-American

Leslie Cross / 1967

From the *Milwaukee Journal*, 22 October 1967, sec. 5, 4. © 2000
Journal Sentinel Inc., reproduced with permission.

Everybody calls him Willie. We arrived early for a 2:30 appointment at *Harper's* magazine the other afternoon in New York, and the dark-haired receptionist in the trim red dress said she would see whether Willie was in. Another girl, from an inner office, came into the anteroom just then and said that Willie hadn't got back from a late lunch.

But our wait was a short one. In a few minutes the receptionist was able to assure us that "Willie will see you now."

Willie Morris is a well-knit, fair-haired, personable young man who at thirty-two is the youngest editor that *Harper's* has had in its 117 years. He is also the author of what is certain to be one of the most discussed books of the year, *North Toward Home*. Officially, it will be published by Houghton Mifflin tomorrow, but hundreds of thousands of readers have already seen generous excerpts in Willie's magazine and in the *Saturday Evening Post*.

It is the story of Willie's life in small-town Mississippi and in Texas and New York, and John Kenneth Galbraith, who read it in proof form, let himself be quoted: "No one at thirty-two should write his memoirs; Willie Morris is the only exception."

"I tried very hard to make this an American book—one that would give the reader a sense of place and a consciousness of belonging," Willie told us. "In an urban environment, it isn't always easy to come to a realization of who we are and where we came from. I wanted the book to reflect the experiences of my generation, which came to maturity in the early 1950s. But I've had many letters from people of earlier generations who read the magazine pieces and said they recognized their own youth and childhood in them."

Most of Willie Morris's boyhood recollections are affectionate, but he does not hide the less pleasant aspects of Mississippi life, such as its racial cruelties. For a while he worried about how the book would be received in Yazoo (he calls it "Yazoo City"), where he was born and grew up. He had fifty advance copies of the book sent to a store there, and waited for the reaction. It came immediately and was overwhelmingly favorable.

3

"They sold out in an hour," he related. "A friend wrote me, 'This is the biggest thing that's hit Yazoo City since the Civil War.'"

Morris started the book as fiction, then decided it would be better to tell his experiences as they happened. "I tried to use the techniques of fiction, though," he explained. "I wanted the book to be a work of imagination as well as fact, with a steady narrative flow." He regards autobiography as a virile American art and would like to see *North Toward Home* on a shelf near such books as Mark Twain's *Roughing It* and *Life on the Mississippi* and Ernest Hemingway's *A Moveable Feast*; Twain, especially, was an influence, he said.

In a future book, Morris hopes to write about his years at Oxford, where he was a Rhodes Scholar after he left the University of Texas. Those years are only lightly touched upon in his present book, but he considers them highly important; "Oxford," he has remarked, "gave me four years to think." Before that book is written, he plans to complete a novel on an American theme. He intends to call it *Chaos of the Sun*, a phrase from Wallace Stevens's poem "Sunday Morning."

If *North Toward Home* has woven into an American whole the strands of childhood reminiscence with those of a Texas editorship and literary and intellectual discovery in New York, he thinks that is as it should be.

"This problem of roots, of finding identity in American diversity," he said, "is something that affects us all as a people. The feeling isn't particularly southern. Recently I got a letter from a New York banker who said he came from Aurora, Illinois, and that what I wrote about Mississippi reminded him of his old home there. Letters like that are reassuring."

Morris now lives with his wife, Celia, who was once a fellow student at the University of Texas, and their son David, seven, in an apartment on the upper west side of New York. Every weekend, though, they drive out to an old farmhouse north of Brewster in New York state; they bought it a few years ago, and part of it was built in 1780.

And they plan to get back to Mississippi for a visit before too long.

Willie Morris

Mary Jayne Garrard Whittington / 1968

From *Delta Review*, 5 (October 1968), 53–54, 60. Reprinted by permission of Mary Jayne Garrard Whittington.

By now practically everyone knows Mr. Morris is the editor of *Harper's*, a magazine almost four times his age, and that he is the author of a book *North Toward Home*. Aficionados know his dog was Skip and his wife is Celia. Trivia experts know his boyhood idol was the *Memphis Commercial Appeal* sportswriter Walter Stewart. Yet he has puzzled alike many of those who knew him when, and most of those who know of him now.

Why did a southerner call the book in which he deplores New York and disparages New Yorkers *North Toward Home*? Why did his venerable magazine give unprecedented and prestigious attention to Norman Mailer's "The Steps of the Pentagon" by printing it in its entirety? [March 1968 issue] Why would a man who holds his distinguished position in the world of letters choose to be known (mastheads, dust jackets, and all) as Willie, a name most Williams shake as frivolous? Why these paradoxes from a man not in the least enigmatic in appearance, far more candid than opaque in conversation?

"I hadn't thought the book's title would be all that puzzling," said Willie Morris. "Certainly I don't feel alienated from the South, far from it; the feelings are very complicated, but the older I am the more it means to me, the closer the ties. This is very usual, I think, of southerners. More so than it is of those from other regions. The title was chosen in a way for its irony."

So the seeming contradictions of Willie Morris turn out to be clues rather than riddles. This unassuming man, serious though he is about *Harper's*, writing, writers, and their relation to (and obligation to) society, simply does not take himself so seriously that he feels he should become other than what he's always been, Willie Morris. It seems, in fact, that the distinguished editor from Mississippi is somewhat ruefully amused at his lot, as readers of *North Toward Home* may have judged from his impulse to pick up the amber phone, while seated at the President's desk in the White House, and shout, "It's Willie Morris from Yazoo City, Mississippi."

Repeated references to the Morris book as an autobiography have annoyed purists who quibble that inaccuracies preclude its being so called. Of this dispute on semantics the author says, "It's true the Mississippi section of the book is more an evocation of a time, a place, and its people; reflections on a composite picture of what it was like at home, the good and bad that's always a part of a person, or a place." Mr. Morris himself evokes that section, its subtle courtesies, obvious good humor, and flair for telling a story.

"It's the obsession for storytelling, I think, that accounts in part at least for southern writers—there are many fine ones working now, Robert Penn Warren, William Styron, Walker Percy. No, the novel is not dead, far from it; and I don't see newer forms replacing it. Very good writing is coming in to us. With the editor it's not only a question of seeking good work, it's a matter of selecting it from the great total that comes in."

To the contrary, in the April issue of *Harper's*, novelist William Styron spoke of allegedly "eyeball-oriented" youth, which reads little but black humor and is perfectly capable of identifying Thomas Wolfe as "The Tangerine Streamlined Whatever-it's-called guy" ["The Shade of Thomas Wolfe"]. And the same month in *Commentary*, novelist Edward Hoagland wrote, "We go to the movies now, or read the lyrics on the back of the Beatles' record album. . . . We writers are told that the novel is dead, that we're working in a dead language" ["On Not Being a Jew"]. Thus prepared for the wake, readers and would-be writers alike should be cheered to hear that fiction is alive and in tiptop condition.

"It's not easy to say how young people who want to be writers should go about it," said the thirty-three-year-old author-editor. "The individual shapes the answer. In general I don't think classroom work is so very important, a great amount of reading is, so is moving about, knowing different places and the people in them." Willie Morris then added, "Writing has been called correctly 'a very stern discipline.' I don't know that I'd want my son to be a writer."

Even so, I wouldn't mind if my daughter married one; I know the family pretty well. Still it's always surprising to see the considerable poise shown by writers when their work is misconstrued or misunderstood. Willie Morris's reaction has been one of regret, rather than dismay or anger, when readers have taken *North Toward Home* to be denigrating Mississippi. The book has been widely and favorably reviewed, many of the letters that have come in to the author have compared him to Mark Twain; yet there have been readers who have been indignant, even hurt. Of them the author says, "I hope in time they'll see the book for what it is, an act of love."

Those who have read *North Toward Home* will recall a passage in which the author says this country badly lacks "a truly national magazine, unidentified with any intellectual clique or with any region, or city, or slice of a city, willing to fight to the death the pallid formulas and deadening values of the mass media," a magazine "to reflect the great tensions and complexities and even madnesses of the day, to encourage the most daring and inventive of our writers, scholars, and journalists—to help give the country some feel of itself and what it is becoming." Possibly *Harper's* well may become that magazine, for its editor has said, "It's not the point how *Harper's* or its readers felt about there being the march on the Pentagon last October. The significant thing is there *was* the march. It's important, I think, for every American to take a long look at it, and Norman Mailer's book [*The Armies of the Night*, 1968] is a way to do that."

Readers of *North Toward Home* are wondering if its author will write now about his years as a Rhodes Scholar in England. Very probably, I think, but my guess is he will write sooner or later, again about the South, for there is in Willie Morris more than a faint echo of Tom's closing soliloquy in Tennessee Williams's poignant *The Glass Menagerie* [1945]. Tom, having left his handicapped sister, Laura, and his gallant impoverished mother, Amanda, says in the closing lines of his reverie, "Oh, Laura, Laura, I left you behind, but I am more faithful than I intended to be."

Harper's Willie Morris

Richard Cohen / 1969

From *Women's Wear Daily: The Retailer's Daily Newspaper*, 19 August 1969, 38–39. Reprinted by permission of Fairchild Publications.

The scenario of the life of Willie Morris, editor in chief of *Harper's* since 1967, takes a crucial turn in the fall of 1952. He is seventeen. We see him hoisting his grips aboard a big, square Southern Trailways bus, and we follow it in a long, high, tracking shot as he leaves his hometown, Yazoo City, Mississippi, and heads west to matriculate at the University of Texas across the flat, black Delta which spreads out before us as the camera continues to ascend. The bus picks up speed and the voice of Mississippi John Hurt, lining out a lament for home, rises from the soundtrack while we glimpse Morris's life as an All-American small-town boy in a series of quickly cut flashbacks: high school valedictorian; smiling teenage radio sports announcer; bugler at American Legion funerals; the flashing thighs of the county's sexiest drum majorette prancing by Morris, who stands on the curb watching as their eyes lock briefly.

As the bus grows too small to follow we hold the sun in soft focus for a long moment and then dissolve to another bus speeding along the Pulaski Skyway in New Jersey. It is a much newer bus, streamlined and with chrome. As we track in, we see Morris by the window searching out the New York City skyline as it rises from the mists of the Jersey meadows like concrete outcroppings of the Manhattan schist.

Morris is older by fifteen years than when he boarded the first bus and in another series of quick cuts, over the jazz-rock sound track of Blood, Sweat and Tears, we flash back to what's happened to Morris between buses: editor of the student newspaper in a confrontation with the president of the University of Texas; lying under a tree reading poetry to a campus beauty queen who wears a Phi Beta Kappa key; the same two, an infant's pram between them, lolling on the Oxford Backs; editor of a journal of dissent, *The Texas Observer*; passing around a bottle of bourbon with a group of beefy Texas politicians in an Austin hotel room; the neon-lit, drive-in pizza stand; wrecked auto-yard desolation of El Camino Real in Palo Alto, California.

The flashbacks go by as the bus curls down the ramps to the Lincoln

Tunnel and emerges into the terminal. Morris descends. He jostles his way
through the crowds, becoming part of the myth of the small-town boy come
to the Big Apple (the Big Cave, he calls it) to hack out his niche.

We dissolve to a large corner office on Park Avenue. The room is furnished
in contemporary nondescript—salt-and-pepper carpet, desk and chairs of
vaguely walnut ancestry, framed covers of *Harper's* of other eras on the
walls.

A desk calendar is open to August 1969. Morris is behind his desk, a big
fleshy man with a round, smooth face. On the desk is a half-consumed bottle
of Coke. Morris is wearing the smartly cut six-button blazer of the man-
about-New York, but he stuffs a grossly swollen wallet into the hip pocket of
his britches, small-town style. His voice is still rich with Mississippi, and, as
we close in, Morris, thirty-four, in the noon of his life, is speaking.

"An editor has to live in New York City. New York is America writ large.
It feels all the pressures of change; an editor has to be pushed around a little
by the forces of his day.

"It's the most exciting city in the world. When I first came here, I hated
the city. But I've grown to love it. It's a great place to bring up a child, a
great place to grow to maturity. My son, David, who's nine, lives here with
his mother. We were divorced a few months ago. Most of the people you're
talking to in New York are from North Carolina, or Massachusetts, or Ore-
gon—somewhere else. The city's always been the great magnet.

"You bring to New York your old provincial fears, and if you're tough,
you bring to it a lot of your strengths.

"Yet, if *Harper's* ever became a New York institution it would cease to
have any important role to play—there are too many intellectual hazards.
Harper's must continue to be a national institution.

"*Harper's* has not only survived—it's 116 years old, America's oldest
magazine—but it has retained its influence. The primary reason it's been able
to do that is because it has always changed with the times. I want *Harper's*
to continue to reflect the American experience. As a magazine it must show
the outrages, the faults, the failures of American society. For if America
doesn't make it, the whole human race isn't going to make it.

"We want to be a liberal magazine with uncommitted liberal writers who
know a lot about this country, who can capture something of the feeling of
the country right now. We're a plastic society; we lack a sense of history.
Harper's is trying to reflect that. We'll be publishing more writers who are
writing about real events.

"We're organizing our own group of writers, most of them, like me, men in their thirties, products of the Eisenhower years—David Halberstam and John Corry whom we got from the *New York Times*, Marshall Frady, and Larry L. King, southerners. True, there is a danger—an intellectual danger—in having a confluence of voices, but the advantages outweigh the disadvantages.

"We—writers and editors—know this country, we come from different parts of the country. We have a strong feeling for America. We're fascinated by details of the country. We share this feeling that if America isn't what it ought to be, that we can show where the country's going. And to do it while maintaining a literary tradition in its broadest sense, and to have a feeling for the language.

"Language is almost a set of values in itself. It reflects the deepest impulses of our people.

"What the editor does in all this is to set the tone and character of the magazine. You can't run a magazine as if it had a personality of its own. You have to have a purpose. When you're dealing with writing and journalism, the role of the editor in chief is to have the pretension to greatness.

"You work with editors whom you trust and encourage writers to write to the highest level that they can. There's a natural hostility between writers and editors—you can't do anything about that."

Recent issues of *Harper's* provide some concrete examples of what Morris has been talking about. Through them run the two strains that make up the texture and tone and the myth of America. The hard-pan reality of a nation in social and political convulsion and as a counterpoint, the other America of home; of newspaper trains arriving in the misty morning and screen doors slamming in the dark; of life quiet and sweet; of other times fondly remembered.

The July *Harper's*, which Morris is particularly proud of, leads off with a harsh exegesis of the life and career of McGeorge Bundy, President of the Ford foundation, arch-establishment figure, written by Pulitzer Prize journalist Halberstam, as a paradigm of the failure (in Halberstam's view) of liberal establishment activism.

There is a piece on a rock group by a young journalist, Sara Davidson, in which the group's music and life style are perceived as a significant aspect of American culture today, an account by *Harper's* managing editor Robert Kotlowitz of the intricacies of making an example of our time's greatest art form, a movie, reporting how Janos Kadar, the Czech director, goes about

transferring Bernard Malamud's "The Angel Levine" from page to film with
Zero Mostel and Harry Belafonte; and a warm and nostalgic reminiscence
refined by her finely honed sensibility by critic (of everything) Elizabeth
Hardwick.

The last is one of her childhood home, Lexington, Kentucky, a "Going
Home to . . ." series that Morris has commissioned. Home, not only as a
place to be from, but the mythic quality of home, the tangled memories of
birth and death, of loss and longing that home evokes—as with Proust's
madeleine—has a powerful hold on Morris. The title of his autobiography,
written at thirty-two, is *North Toward Home*. The word surfaces repeatedly
in his conversation; it cropped up in a review Morris wrote recently for the
Sunday *New York Times Book Review*; one of the first questions Morris puts
to a visitor is: "Where were you raised?"

"Getting on that bus that took me away from Yazoo City when I was
seventeen was as real a turning point in my life as any. I had to go to Texas
to become a liberated human being.

"Tom Wicker (associate editor of the *New York Times*) who's from Hamlet,
North Carolina, and I often talk about the qualities that make a southerner
distinct from other Americans. In some ways, we white southerners are not
complete Americans. We have always viewed American society as outsiders.
We grew up—the brightest of us—at the edge of U. S. existence. We constantly judge America as outsiders; we are constantly judging the country as
southern boys. I suppose that's why the concern with home is exaggerated
with me.

"I still go back to Yazoo City. My mother and grandmother are there. I can
still walk down the main street and tell you who died in every one of the
houses on that street since 1938. I took Norman Podhoretz (editor of *Commentary* and husband of *Harper's* executive editor, Midge Decter), down
there not long ago. He had a fine time and said, 'Those are the warmest,
friendliest, most hospitable people in the world—until the fourth drink.'

"The number of southern boys in publishing is of a piece with southern
literary traditions. Much of it is derived from our involvement with language.
We grow up with storytelling—and we start writing.

"Southern intellectuals have an adaptability, and in our crazy ways we
respond well under pressure and are skilled administrators in a human sense.

"Many of my friends are southerners of both races—but not only southerners; some of the New York intellectual-literary circle—the people Norman

Podhoretz calls The Family—are my friends. I think an editor ought to meet all kinds of people.

"Magazines these days are responding to the challenge and impact of television. The mass circulation magazines are already appraising what their role is in American life. Magazines are better than ever, yet it is ironic, for example, that *Life* and *Time*, which have been symbols of the American conservative establishment, have become responsive to American society at a time when their editorial content is being challenged by the immediacy of television journalism."

Morris's judgments on the confrontation of television and the mass circulation magazines skims the profound changes now taking place in American magazines. For the gusts of changes are blowing through their editorial offices. They are always blowing, of course, in this most competitive of art forms, but the closing years of the decade appear to mark one of the recurrent watershed periods in the life cycles of American magazines.

Seemingly impregnable institutions are shuddering and threaten to topple, while new contenders thrust up and long-dormant magazines spring back to life.

The end of small-town, rural America brought down the magazines that served it: first *Collier's*, and finally the *Saturday Evening Post*. Television's capture of the mass audience for entertainment now threatens the magazines that offered the quick view at the world. *Look*, which first among the establishment press paid attention to the nation's social concerns, and mighty *Life*, which brought photo journalism to its highest peak of accomplishment, have futures so uncertain that *Life* staffers at a recent Manhattan party spoke flatly of its agonies as terminal.

The struggle, mano a mano, of the newsweeklies *Time* and *Newsweek* is one of the wonders of journalism; it has seen the once amiable doormat, *Newsweek*, rise up to smite testy, omniscient *Time* and force it to transform itself from a mountain of arrogance (to both readers and staffers) to a publication of decent human concern. Even peerless *New Yorker*, premier of them all, hustles to reverse declines in advertising and stagnation in circulation.

But some magazines with strong identities prosper. *National Geographic* was never healthier. *Playboy*, which codified hedonism, continues to make like crazy.

Of all of them, *Harper's* has turned hot in the past year or so—"hot" being that elusive quality a publication acquires when it gets talked about, quoted, paid attention to.

Harper's acquisition of hot can be dated at its publication of Norman Mailer's Pulitzer Prize-winning account of the siege of the Pentagon by citizens opposed to the Vietnam War ["The Steps of the Pentagon"]. It appeared in the March 1968 issue, ran ninety thousand words (Morris believes it is the longest magazine article ever published) and marked Mailer's emergence as a journalist of unique power and gifts and Morris as an editor to be reckoned with. Morris recalled the origins of Mailer's masterpiece:

"I found out on the Monday after the Pentagon confrontation that Mailer was in jail and was thinking about writing about the story of the whole Pentagon weekend. I was on the phone all day with a lot of people, trying to line up the piece.

"At the end of the day I had met somebody for a drink and I was walking up Sixth Avenue in the forties when, in one of those inexplicable coincidences, I ran into Mailer. We talked about his doing the piece for *Harper's* and he said, 'I'm going to Provincetown and write it.' Midge and I went to Provincetown to read the pieces. It was a memorable occasion. It's one of the genuinely gratifying things in life for an editor to read a manuscript like that.

"We also published Norman's reporting from the 1968 political conventions ["Miami Beach and Chicago," *Harper's*, November 1968], and after that I had lunch with Norman and one of his advisers and we talked about an idea I had that he ought to write an article on the Apollo moon shot. The adviser knocked the idea as being unworthy of Norman's talents, and we came to no agreement about it.

"Then, some weeks after that, I got a call from Norman who said, 'I wanted to tell you before you read it in the papers that I've signed a contract with *Life* to report on going to the moon.' No, I wasn't annoyed. I think I was a little saddened by it. *Harper's*, including our book division, could have paid a very good price for the piece, but nothing close to what he'll get from *Life* and Little, Brown, which Time, Inc. also owns.

"I've found the better the writer the easier he is to work with. All the great writers have to live continuously with their guts on the table. They have to deal with their own insides. Almost all the fine novelists are deeply anguished human beings.

"I feel myself very much part of a tradition here. Sometimes I come into the office on a Saturday and just pull down a volume of the magazine from, say, 1890, and start to read.

"I became editor of *Harper's* at thirty-two. What a marvelous opportunity that is. It's not true that the institutions of power are closed to the young. I don't feel the professional life of an editor ought to last a whole lifetime—ten years is long enough. I don't know what I'd do after that. Write, probably. No, not another autobiography. Autobiography is for the young and the old, not for the middle-aged."

The Last Months at *Harper's*: Willie Morris in Conversation

Robert H. Moore / 1970

From *Mississippi Review*, 3, no. 3 (1974), 121–30. Reprinted by permission of *Mississippi Review*.

This exchange occurred while Willie Morris was editor in chief of *Harper's* magazine, but was withheld from publication in the context of Morris's differences with his publisher which culminated in his resignation in March 1971. During 1973 Morris reviewed the transcript of our exchange and consented to its publication after making minimal substantive changes for the sake of clarity. [*Editor's note*: Moore's correspondence and original transcript are in the Willie Morris Collection, Department of Archives and Special Collections, J. D. Williams Library, University of Mississippi.]

Willie Morris's career has frequently been controversial. His resignation from *Harper's* set off a tumultuous series of events highlighted by the resignations of contributing editors David Halberstam and Larry L. King, among others, and by extraordinary appeals to *Harper's* publisher for Morris's reinstatement from a group including Arthur Miller, William Styron, John Kenneth Galbraith, Gay Talese, and Tom Wicker. Morris's first novel, *The Last of the Southern Girls*, published in the spring of 1973, attracted wide attention for its portrayal of a young woman whom many have seen as modeled on Washington socialite Barbara Howar.

In the reminiscences which follow, Morris discusses the work of William Faulkner, James Dickey, Bill Moyers, and Albert Murray, and provides illuminating comments about his first two books, *North Toward Home* (1967) and *Yazoo: Integration in a Deep-Southern Town* (1971). His remarks also revealingly reflect his state of mind during his last months at *Harper's*.

Occasional editorial emendations and notes are provided to fill in details pertinent to the discussion.

Q: Would you comment on what people in Yazoo City had to say about Faulkner when you were growing up there in the 1940s and early 1950s?

Morris: To all the people down in Yazoo City at the time, Faulkner was out for the Yankee dollar. He was some incorrigible eccentric who lived up the road in Oxford, and he was making a very fine living writing for the outlanders. I remember that somebody in Yazoo once told me when I was a boy, "Do you know he would get naked, get drunk, and climb trees. He's crazy! He's crazy!" They would ask, "Have you ever tried to read any of his books? He's crazy!" They would try to read *The Sound and the Fury* [1929] and they would say, "Anybody who'd go and write all that gibberish!" They were saying that about Eudora Welty too. My most memorable association with Faulkner's work in those years was when I was sixteen or seventeen and they were filming a Hollywood movie in Faulkner's hometown, and that was all very exciting. This film, *Intruder in the Dust*, is the only Faulkner movie I've ever seen. It was good, a marvelous movie. I saw them filming the scenes outside of the old jailhouse. But at that time—I don't remember what I said about this in *North Toward Home*—I had not read any of Faulkner's work.

Q: You were in Oxford on a high school trip as I recall?

Morris: Yes, at a convention for Mississippi high school editors. I was the editor of the Yazoo High School *Flashlight.*

Q: At what point did you begin to read Faulkner?

Morris: I started reading Faulkner when I was at the University of Texas. I was just starting to read on my own. I had an English teacher from Jackson, Mississippi, named Frank Lyell; he went to Millsaps and is an old friend of Eudora Welty. He was my freshman English teacher. He started talking about Faulkner in class. I was making something like fifty dollars a month writing sports for the *Daily Texan*, and I took my fifty dollars and I'd go over to the University of Texas Co-op and buy books, mostly Modern Library editions. I was going to do what Marilyn Monroe wanted to do. I was going to buy the whole Modern Library. I was going to read straight on through and I started with Faulkner.

Q: I understand that you know Jean Stein. Would you comment on her interview with William Faulkner? ["The Art of Fiction," *Paris Review*, Spring 1956.]

Morris: It's an interesting interview. It's my impression that Faulkner wrote most of the interview. He and Jean Stein were very good friends, and Faulkner just typed that interview out himself. In fact, a couple of years ago Jean gave me the first manuscript page of the interview which Faulkner had typed out on her typewriter.

Q: One of the most interesting aspects of *North Toward Home* is your desire to demonstrate the complexity of your innocence as a young boy in

Mississippi. Would it be fair to call it an intricate part of your narrative strategy?

Morris: I think innocence, the idea of innocence, in writing is an effective literary device. I don't have anything against it. I think some of Mark Twain's early work uses this device, if one can call it that, very successfully. For instance, his descriptions in *Innocents Abroad* [1869] and in *Roughing It* [1872] had a great influence on me in writing *North Toward Home*. I think the first half of *Roughing It* is splendid.

Q: Your concern with the loss of innocence is particularly reflected in the New York section of *North Toward Home*. In this regard, I have the impression that you feel that many of the southerners you know in the city are people who are tougher, intellectually, than the natives. And that this is in part because they have the advantage of a more complicated cultural background than most New Yorkers.

Morris: Well, I think so. No doubt about it. You can have an unusual time in this city being a southerner. You can sneak up on them.

Q: In *Time*'s recent article on you and on "Yazoo . . . Notes on Survival," your friend David Halberstam is quoted as having said you are a very complicated person and that "very few people really know Willie Morris" ["South Toward Home," *Time*, June 1, 1970; "Yazoo . . . Notes on Survival," *Harper's*, June 1970]. Don't you think *Time*'s emphasis is as much a comment on New Yorkers' presuppositions about southerners as it is about you?

Morris: I'd go along with that. People in New York tend to have the old ingrained suspicion against anybody who has a southern accent and they are always surprised if a person with a southern accent has brains. There is certainly a tendency among many easterners not to take people with a southern accent seriously. That's all right with me. And when you know that in 99 percent of the cases that you are at least as smart if not smarter than they are and that you're tougher also than they are and that you have more experience with humanity and with the world, you know you can cope rather well. And the fact is that we had the greatest fighting men in the field in the history of warfare, even though our machines failed us. But we can sure catch up with them in other ways. (Morris laughs.)

Q: What kind of mail have you gotten at *Harper's* as a result of *North Toward Home* and more recently, "Yazoo . . . Notes on Survival"?

Morris: The mail I've gotten on the book and on the piece in *Harper's*—

the mail on the two put together—has been absolutely fantastic. I have a file of letters. I have a Negro secretary and a Jewish secretary who keep a file on them all. On the book alone I'd imagine I've gotten two thousand letters. And they run the whole range of reactions. I've probably gotten about four hundred letters so far on the piece in *Harper's*. This volume of mail is deceptive because it is not like my friend Styron sitting up in Roxbury writing great novels. I'm accessible because they know I'm editor of *Harper's*, so they have an address to write to and they know that I'm sure to be there. This is one of the reasons that I get so many. Some memorable letters, some will tear your heart out, some beautiful letters. And then a lot of hate mail.

Q: A lot of hate mail?
Morris: Oh, yes, considerable hate mail.

Q: What kinds of things do they accuse you of having done?
Morris: Selling out the South (from the southerners), being a traitor to the South, pandering to the northern establishment. That kind of thing. They are ashamed of me because . . . (Morris pauses for thirty seconds). And the title of *North Toward Home* confused them, I suppose. And then you get letters from people outside of the South who call you a racist. I got quite a number of letters from people who call me anti-Semitic.

Q: For what?
Morris: For one phrase. It's about my grandmother Mamie. I said if there was one last fried chicken wing in the world, she'd give it away to whoever needed it—white, black, or Jew.

Q: In "Yazoo . . . Notes on Survival" you wrote that a well-known New York writer and his wife at a dinner party on New York's Upper East Side indicted you for being an unreconstructed racist because of a story you told at the party about Mamie, who on her deathbed was kept company by Viola, a Negro woman who had worked for Mamie's family for more than a generation.
Morris: You know a writer named William Manchester? That was William Manchester and his wife.

Q: That scene at the dinner party is reminiscent of incidents in *North Toward Home*, and in many respects "Yazoo" reads like a postscript to the book. Did you reread any sections of *North Toward Home* before you wrote the Yazoo piece?

Morris: I haven't looked at the book in about two years.

Q: What impressions have you gotten about how widely the book has been read?
Morris: The book has been read. It surprises me. It must have struck some kind of chord in its readers. Especially southerners, but not necessarily so.

Q: Don't you think that the turmoil which the book reflects of you trying to sort out your life invites both the hostile responses you have described in the letters while at the same time it attracts readers who identify sympathetically with your own struggle for meaning?
Morris: Yes, I think that's true. So many people are groping around and don't know what to believe.

Q: How did you begin to write *North Toward Home*? Did you start out to write an autobiography?
Morris: Well, I started it as a novel. I took, as I recall, a leave of absence from the magazine for six months and I had to go to the bank to borrow money. And I started it as a novel and I got into it—oh, I guess, seventy or eighty pages, something like that, but a lot of hard work and really thinking hard about it—and I realized that I was writing an intensely autobiographical novel. I didn't like too much what I was writing and I finally decided just to go ahead and try to tell the story of my life. I decided to use real places and real names and everything else and risk what I knew would be inevitable, what was going to happen—that a lot of people would say that here is this egocentric thirty-one-year-old writing the story of his life. Who in the hell does he think he is? But I made that decision and it was the most basic decision of all and I'm glad I did it. I don't think I'll ever do it again because I have a feeling that autobiographical work like this is either for very young men or very old men. I may be wrong; I may change my mind. I'm going to write a novel in the next two or three years. *North Toward Home* has its autobiographical form—and I'm speaking from experience—the autobiographical form has its limits but it also has its strengths. Its limits are that you don't have the emotional freedom to go all the way. At least I didn't feel I did. Its strengths are that you can root around for things that actually happened and you have considerable latitude in a rather tangible way. You don't have to tell the complete truth. It's like what Mark Twain said, sometimes in writing work like *Roughing It* and *Life on the Mississippi* [1883] occasionally one has to lie to tell the truth. I've lied on and off in *North Toward Home* to

tell the truth. It's not a literal form of writing. You can take great freedom, great liberties, with time itself and chronology. It's a good form. It's a very sturdy form in American literature.

Q: How would you account for the fact that so many American writers have been drawn to the form of autobiography in the last ten years?

Morris: Well, I think this kind of writing is flourishing now and this kind of nonfiction form is stronger in America today than it ever has been. And I think magazines today such as *Harper's,* the *Atlantic,* and the *New Yorker* have had a great deal to do with this flourishing. I think that *Life* magazine, for instance, is probably better today editorially than it has ever been, even though it probably won't survive. But fiction may be the most difficult art form of all. It will endure.

Q: What kind of writing are you most interested in publishing in *Harper's?*

Morris: I don't really care much now for any strict compartments. The lines are so blurred today between various forms of writing. What I'm interested in is the work itself. I think Norman Mailer's work has had enormous influence in this regard. A lot of the work we publish are projects we commission for the magazine. Bill Moyers, a very impressive man, is going all over the country for us right now, traveling thousands of miles, listening and talking to people. If what he writes is good enough we'll devote a good part of an issue to it. (The December 1970 issue of *Harper's* was primarily devoted to Moyers's "Listening to America," which was subsequently published in expanded form in 1971.)

Q: How did Moyers happen to leave his job at *Newsday?*

Morris: He was disinherited by Harry Guggenheim when Guggenheim sold the paper to the *Los Angeles Times-Mirror*. Probably in the long run it will be better for Moyers that he got out of that job.

Q: You have also published a lot of work by relatively unknown people. Writers like Albert Murray for instance.

Morris: Yes, we have. How did you like that writing on Faulkner that Al was reading at lunch?

Q: I thought the Faulkner material was very good and I was really fascinated by his account of himself and Ralph Ellison and other undergraduates at Tuskegee Institute who were reading Faulkner's books as they were being published in the thirties.

Morris: I got him to go home and do some writing for the magazine, and he has turned it into a book called *South to a Very Old Place* [1971]. He's got it all written except for the last ten pages. What he read us at lunch was from that book, and I thought his section on Faulkner was marvelous.

Q: What is Al's background? What has he published other than *The Omni-Americans* (1970)?

Morris: That's his first book. He was a major in the Air Force for twenty or twenty-five years and he ended up teaching Air Force ROTC at Tuskegee, but he was based all over the place. He knew James Dickey. He and Dickey were in the Air Force together. Al was a captain and Dickey was a first lieutenant and they'd get together in the officers' bar in Keesler Field in Biloxi. I wonder if Dickey saluted.

Q: What are your feelings about the apparent difficulties many writers face in choosing a form that they find congenial for writing about their chosen subject matter?

Morris: I think these are very arbitrary considerations. If a man is going to write, he is going to write. And he is going to write about the things that mean the most to him. And if he has any talent, he is going to write in whatever form he is best suited to. And the process of choosing form is very intimately involved in the process of writing about the things that mean the most to him. It can be intensely painful, both in the deeply personal way and sometimes painful to the people one loves. But if you have a faith in your talent, you have to press ahead. Sometimes you're going to have to hurt people that you love or once loved. That's always been the case with good writing and it always will be. There is a terrible price that you pay. I say this both as an editor and as a writer. I would be a much happier human being and much more secure if I didn't have any ability to write at all. I'm the editor of America's oldest and most distinguished magazine, but I'm torn between running *Harper's* for a long time and doing my own work, and it's a very real tear. You can't do both. You can make an effort, but that's about the best you can hope for because the two roles are not complimentary. On the contrary, they're antagonistic.

Q: How much time did you spend on "Yazoo . . . Notes on Survival"?

Morris: Well, I spent a lot of time working on that, but I wrote it in two weeks. I had it organized in my mind. But that also is deceptive because two weeks of writing something that profoundly matters to you is really the equivalent of about four months of work. You can't run a magazine and be a serious writer at the same time today. The people who were running these magazines a generation or two ago could get by with it. But you can't do that anymore. It's not so much a matter of time; it's emotional commitment. What drives me crazy over at *Harper's* is that goddamn telephone. That's why I have the most unusual office hours of any editor in history. Most of the time you spend on the telephone is a waste. But these men a generation or two ago who could run their magazines and do their work didn't have the frenetic pace of life to cope with that an editor of a magazine in New York has today. So what do you do? You've got to ultimately decide over a period of time which one means the most to you and go with that. But you remember what one of our masters said about writing—"Moments of passion remembered in periods of tranquility." A man must have some reasonably peaceful and tranquil circumstances in order to do his own work. Let no one tell you otherwise.

On Being the Famous Writer Willie Morris

Lew Powell / 1971

From the *Greenville (Mississippi) Delta Democrat-Times*, 16 May 1971, sec. 1, 5. Reprinted by permission of the *Delta Democrat-Times*.

"I've got this son who's eleven years old, whom I care about very much. I've been on some TV, and during this whole *Harper's* magazine business and the book coming out, I had my picture in *Newsweek* and the *New York Times* and all this stuff.

"He asked me the other night—and it touched me right down to my heart—'Do you think I'll ever grow up to be as famous as you?' This just took me off my guard. 'Well, David, I don't think any kind of fame is worth the effort. Fame is nothing. I just want you to grow up to do what you really want to do, what you enjoy doing and what you think is important in your life and to hell with fame.' "

—Willie Morris

The author of *North Toward Home* and ex-editor of *Harper's* magazine has a new book out [*Yazoo: Integration in a Deep-Southern Town*], and he was in town Friday autographing copies for admirers at the local bookstore.

Willie Morris also found time during his visit to this "remarkable, civilized river town" (from his book) to talk about himself.

Mostly, he was gracious enough to talk about being famous and being a writer, because that is mostly what I asked him.

What are you working on now? A novel?
Yes.

About what?
I don't really want to talk about it.

What kind of reaction did you have to the book when you went back to Yazoo?
Well, they had a big book-signing party at a gift shop on Main Street. I didn't really want to go, but my editor persuaded me to, and it was marvelous. A huge outpouring of people, just totally nice. Sold a whole bunch of copies

23

of the book. Sold out in two hours and had about 100–120 copies of it. It was good.

Are you on tour now?
Yeah, I got to go to Atlanta in the morning. TV programs. And I have to go to Richmond, Virginia.

Do you hate it?
I don't like it very much. It's the last time I'm going to do it. I figure this book is about Mississippi, and this is where I ought to be when the thing comes out.

What effect has being a celebrity had on your life?
Oh, God. In the first place, I don't consider myself a celebrity. But if I am, I don't really enjoy it all that much. It's such an artificial thing.

It's really funny, because I just suddenly realized in the last three or four months that I'm recognizable and I don't particularly enjoy it—especially now that I've made a big break in my life and I'm pretty much leaving public things like running a magazine.

I just want to spend the rest of my life as a writer. It's terribly lonely. That's a reverse side of the coin, of course, but it's so goddam lonely. I just want to live somewhat quieter.

Being a celebrity is something you care about when you're twenty-one years old, but not when you're thirty-six, if you have any kind of balance about you.

I don't know how these movie stars deal with it, the intelligent, sensible ones. I know a few up there, and you'll go out to dinner with somebody like Lauren Bacall, who's a very good friend of my girlfriend's, and people just keep flocking up to her. You don't have any privacy. It's the privacy loss that I care about.

The change from the public life of *Harper's* to your relatively private life now—do you think it's going to be permanent?
Yes, I do. I think—these are things one really shouldn't even talk about—but I think for me it's got to be permanent, because my whole life is wrapped up in my private work.

I've been living in New York City for eight years and ran this magazine which I think was a truly great one—the best magazine of our day—but now that that's really behind, all I want to do is to do my work. That's what I've always wanted to do—to tell stories and everything—and the most gratifying thing in the world to me is my own writing. It's not much fun to do it, but it's immensely gratifying, and I do want to spend the rest of my life at it—and I'm going to. I don't ever want to work for anybody or any other institution again if I can make a living at this. If I can't make a living at it, I'll try to beg money off rich people.

Do you expect to ever again get the stimulation you got from *Harper's* the first couple of years?

It was great stimulation. I loved it, because you'd come out with an issue of your magazine every month and you knew it would be read by just about everybody in the country you wanted to read it.

But living in New York City and being an editor of a magazine like *Harper's* is an intensely public existence. I think it had to be. I might have made it that way, but I think it had to be, for our kind of magazine. It's almost too much stimulation.

I know New York City pretty well. There's this whole strain in our literature—people from the provinces going to New York and either being successes or getting to know the cultural capital well. And I feel very much a part of this strain.

I might be getting old prematurely, but I'm thirty-six years old and I really couldn't have taken too much more of this. There was too much public life, too much enthusiasm and all the time too much exposure in a very frenetic kind of social life.

It's great for a young person to be there in that fantastic city, but I just could never live the rest of my life that way.

If you consider yourself in your heart and your guts to be a writer, at some point you've got to confront the fact that you have not only got to be your own person, but you have to live in relative isolation. At *Harper's*, I worked with some of the best writers of our day—Norman Mailer, William Styron, Arthur Miller, Robert Penn Warren, people like this—and I've grown to really respect writers and the calling they have chosen for themselves. It's not easy.

It does involve loneliness, but I respect fine writers probably better than anybody else. I know what they go through. It is a process of having your guts on the table a lot.

Have you done any fiction before?

Never.

Is it something you've always wanted to do?

Yes. I think it's the most difficult art form. You're just drawing on your imagination the whole time, and this is extremely painful.

I asked my friend James Dickey, who's a marvelous poet. Dickey's now forty-seven, and he came out with his first novel last year—*Deliverance*—great novel, I think. He's writing another one now.

I asked him, "Dickey, what kind of advice can you give to people who turn to fiction, to the novel, relatively late in life?"

Dickey said, "Willie, don't *ever* lose sight of the fact that the basic and most historic function of us writers is to be entertainers."

He's a great man. We got thrown out of the bar at the St. Moritz in New York once. Dickey was quoting his poetry—he loves to read his poetry out loud and get other people to read it. I don't blame him; if I were a poet, I probably would, too.

The maitre d' came over. "I want you gentlemen out of here right now!"

Dickey said, "I beg your pardon?"

"I want you out of here!"

"Do you realize you're throwing out of this restaurant America's second greatest poet and the editor in chief of *Harper's* magazine?"

The maitre d' said, "Out!"

Whenever he comes to New York City, he goes wild, but that's what New York City is for. It's like what Greenville is for people from Hollandale, I guess.

Do you have a fear of failure with the novel?

I don't even think about it. I really don't even want to talk about it. I just know that I love writing so much and I've written a lot and I've come out with these two books and I know I can write.

If I can't deal with my own imagination in a serious, extended way, then I'll just spend the rest of my damn life writing non-fiction. It's not a bad form.

But I don't have a fear of failure. I do have a fear of not satisfying myself. I look back on my first book, *North Toward Home*, and I can see the flaws in that book.

It's a splendid book up to about halfway through. The section on Mississippi, if I even say so myself, is a work of art. Parts of what I described about Texas are damn good. But at some point, it starts falling apart, and I know now why it does—because I was just too damn close to the things about myself and about the people I know and the places I know—too close to it. I believe very much in having one's imagination funneling through a period of time, and I know the Mississippi part of that book is going to *endure*. I just *know*. I have that much of an independent judgment on it. I also know that one can fall in pitfalls as a writer. When you're working, you may think you're doing something great, and you're not.

Willie Morris Comes Home Again

Marjorie Hoffman / 1973

From the *Austin (Texas) American*, 25 May 1973, 4. Reprinted by permission of the *Austin American-Statesman*.

Willie Morris sat at a table in Scarbroughs book department drinking coffee, smoking Viceroys, and dashing off autographs for friends and fans, most of whom shyly kept a respectful distance from the table stacked with his latest book, *The Last of the Southern Girls.*

"I like Austin," he said, lamenting that his promotional tour allowed him only a few hours in Austin Thursday. "I consider it my second home."

Morris, who now lives one hundred miles from New York in Wainscott, Long Island, made his home in Austin while a student at the University of Texas during the 1950s.

"I had to come from Mississippi to Texas to get liberated," he laughed.

He arrived on the bus twenty years ago from Yazoo City, not exactly taking the giant anthill by storm. Not yet.

"By my sophomore year, though, I started thinking about being editor of the *Daily Texan.*" Which he did, of course, in his senior year at UT. He recalled that year fondly and still stands by the issues he fought in student editorials with no trace of apology for the fervor of his attacks on "the conservative hierarchy that ran the state" and influenced the school.

One might expect that the man who was at the helm of *Harper's* for several years would dismiss these idealistic outpourings with a wave of the hand and to say, "Oh, I was just a kid then."

But Morris is respectful of the student newspaper. "I believe in it," he said. "I hope it survives."

He also has "great admiration" for the *Texas Observer,* which he edited before his jump to *Harper's.* "The *Observer* is a unique phenomenon in Texas and a great forum for young writers, a good place to learn how to write."

And since his controversial resignation as editor in chief at *Harper's* in 1971, that's basically all Morris has been doing. It's obvious, of course, that Morris already knows how to write some of the best nonfiction on the market. *North Toward Home* and *Yazoo* are exhibits A and B. But fiction, which *The*

28

Last of the Southern Girls is, is another matter. Especially for a journalist who has been trained to deal with facts.

"There were some difficulties (in switching to fiction writing)," he said. "But then I'm a natural born liar," he added with amusement.

"I tend to dwell in my dreams and memories a lot and I call on my impressions of things. Fiction draws on a different part of your brain."

At first he was "upset" that Barbara Howar's book *Laughing All the Way* [1973] came out at the same time his did and that critics considered the two the same tale.

"I don't care if people think it's about Perle Mesta, Martha Mitchell, *or* Barbara Howar," Morris said with an emphatic note that could be mistaken for caring.

Despite what reviewers tend to think of the book, Morris believes it's a durable one, "a strong, sturdy work that is going to last," and there is talk of making it into a movie with maybe Faye Dunaway in the principal role.

He just wants to live next to the ocean and spend the rest of his life writing fiction.

Right now, though, he stands and greets the visitors that edge toward the table—an English teacher who "just discovered *North Toward Home*," an author-friend who has him sign Barbara Howar's book, and a hefty southern belle with gray hair.

"Hello, Mr. Morris," she said. "I'm one of those cotton-pickin' southern girls from Yazoo . . . ."

Willie Morris:
Fiction Still Alive in U.S.
William Delaney / 1976

From the *Washington Star*, 19 March 1976, sec. A, 1, sec. F, 12. Re-printed in *Authors in the News*, edited by Barbara Nykoruk. Volume 2. Detroit: Gale Research Co., 1976, 204–05. © 1976, the *Washington Star*, reprinted with permission of *The Washington Post*.

Willie Morris, who last week completed a stint as the *Washington Star*'s writer-in-residence, was editor of *Harper's* magazine from the mid-1960s until 1971. His books include an autobiography, *North Toward Home*, and a novel, *The Last of the Southern Girls*. He was interviewed by *Washington Star* staff writer William Delaney.

Question: Who are the giants in American fiction-writing today?

Morris: I think mainly you have to consider the Jews and the southerners. For a couple of generations in America, their writers have existed sort of along parallel lines.

Q: How so?

A: Because I think they both write from a common sense of loss. I'm simplifying, but I mean a feeling of loss, of the complexities of the past, which quite often involve families and history, a real sense of history.

Q: Which writers, specifically, do you regard as the best?

A: I don't think I'd even want to name them. In a society that takes litera-ture seriously, at any given moment there are never really more than a handful of truly distinguished novelists. But no, I really wouldn't want to name them, get into that.

Q: For the past dozen years it's been almost a cliché that fiction-writing in America has succumbed to journalism—that no novelist could possibly in-vent what in fact happened to the Kennedys, to Nixon. Established novelists like Norman Mailer and Mary McCarthy turned to journalism. But you, an established journalist, turned to autobiography and finally fiction. Do you or did you see yourself fighting a "fiction-is-dead" syndrome? If that indeed existed?

A: I think it was an attitude that existed, but primarily in the 1960s, which coincided with my editorship of *Harper's* magazine. We were getting some of the best novelists in America, not only publishing their fiction but getting them to turn to nonfiction.

Q: Encouraging this, you were?

A: Yeah, when there's someone like William Styron between books, to do nonfiction things for us. And I was also lecturing a lot on the campuses during the sixties and early seventies and it was one of the constant questions that you were asked; students had been led to believe by a lot of proselytizers that the fictional form was dead in America. And I believe more strongly now that that's nonsense. All you have to do is look at the best works of the six or eight or ten truly fine novelists in America in the last generation to see that the novel in America is anything but dead—it's flourishing. A lot of people, I think, have detracted away from fiction for self-serving purposes. And this is something I deplore. I think fiction is deep in the blood of the human race, as is poetry. They were drawing pictures on the walls of caves many thousands of years ago, telling stories and making up stories.

Q: Fiction is far from dead in America, then?

A: It's very much alive and it's a crucial form. It's much more difficult than journalism because it draws, I think, in a very profound way, on a different part of the brain. I know when I wrote my first book I was a young man—thirty or something like that—and actually started it as a novel. The more I got into it the more I realized I was only barely changing the names and addresses. I decided at a certain point to take an enormous gamble and, as a young man, to write it straightforwardly as an autobiographical narrative, which I did. But I think the autobiographical form is either for very young men or very old ones. And I'm intrigued by the fictional form, and I'm going to commit the rest of my life to it, for better or for worse.

Q: As writer-in-residence at the *Star* you had to produce three nonfictional columns a week. Was it harder or easier than you had imagined?

A: Well, I knew it was going to be hard when I came down here. Because I was out of practice in this form. I did it all the time when I was in my middle twenties or my late twenties and I knew it was going to be a very difficult thing to do and a challenge to the soul. But I just decided I was going to do it. I know Washington, but I don't know it the way a native knows it or the way someone who has lived here for ten or fifteen years. I have a deep feeling for Washington, for the surfaces of it. And I concluded that I was not going to see any of my old buddies over in Georgetown, that I was going to lead a different kind of life from the life that I have had in Washington off and on in the past.

Q: You lived here for a time, didn't you?

A: I spent a lot of time in Washington, say, three years ago, living in Georgetown, and I developed a great feeling for the city and I didn't realize, until in retrospect, just how dismally unhappy I was. I was a terribly unhappy man, as if I didn't even know where my life was going. And this quite often happens to a writer when you live on your own resources and your life is—although it has to be one of tremendous discipline—it's essentially an inchoate life because it deals with memories and emotions and dredging up these old things from one's past, which can be quite painful. But coming down here this time, I thoroughly enjoyed being with an institution like the *Star* in its time of great excitement. I've taken the writer-in-residence job seriously, to try to write some good things. It has been difficult, but I'm glad I did it. I'm ready to go home, to get back to my book.

Q: You say you're going to devote the rest of your life to fiction. What are you working on now?

A: Well, now I'm working on a novel, which I've been working on off and on for about ten years and just settled down to it in a serious way for the last two years, and it's been a very difficult thing for me. The title I have is *The Chimes at Midnight*, which is from Shakespeare's *Henry IV, Part 2*, and most of the narrative takes place in Oxford, England, in the late 1950s.

Q: When you were there as a Rhodes Scholar.

A: Yeah, and in Europe, among a group of young Americans and southerners and their first confrontation with the great European culture. A culture of great guilt and a sense of the past at a time when the dollar was riding high and the big green passport might have brought a lot more than it does now. But I've had a hard time writing about that subject because Oxford University was such an exotic experience for me. And I've always had a difficult time trying to relate it to the stream of my whole life. Because you're there in the place, you're living in what amounts to a work of art. The college I lived in when I got there was built in 1386; living in a little room there across from the old city wall, which was eleventh century, with the embattlements and the slots for arrows. That takes a lot out of a good ol' American southern boy. But I just realized when I started this that I was finally ready to devote myself to those experiences and I have the novel I think, I hope, pretty much under control and I just want to go back home and see it through.

Q: Back home is what, Bridgehampton, Long Island?
A: Yes.

Q: Where you live in sort of physical communion with several other writers, like James Jones. Does that help you, having other writers around, as opposed to the isolation of, say, Faulkner in your native Mississippi?
A: I think that serious writers go through different phases in their lives on this thing you mention. We don't have anything approaching a writer's community up there. There are a lot of close friends who happen to be writers up there and who would be the first to spurn this concept. Jones is like a brother to me and I learn a great deal from him. We don't talk about writing all that much. Capote's up there and we're very good friends. John Knowles, Peter Matthiessen, and that's really about it for the year-round residents who write—Jean Stafford is up there. It becomes a completely different place in July and August. I've never known an area to change character so drastically, say, from what it is now—a very quiet little village close to the ocean—and what it becomes in the summer when you get all the New York people and a lot of people from Washington who come up to have the same parties they'd had on the Upper West Side or Georgetown with the same people, and it changes character so much that it begins to grate on you in the summers because you develop a sort of proprietary set of emotions about it. But it's one of the most beautiful terrains in America—ocean, potato fields—and it's a damned good place to work. And you have people that you can talk to at night when you put your work aside.

Q: Talk a little about writing, as work.
A: I guess one of my heartfelt feelings about writing is that, especially fiction, which is just a horrendously difficult form, is that you do have to devote pretty much your whole life to it and the actual writing itself is so often the tip of the iceberg because it embraces the totality of a man's experience, and you have to move slow and treat it with great respect or it can destroy you. It's not an accident that many of the great writers and artists are somewhat nuts, as indeed they should be. I'm talking about the really good ones who are never more than a few at any given time. But it's just something you have to dedicate your whole life to. And I think one of the things—I

haven't completely thought this out—but just being down here for two months writing these pieces three times a week on all sorts of people and things in the Washington area, it's given me more of a sense of my own work and of the absolute necessity of privacy, in the deepest human sense, that I've never had before. I mean, you must arrange and organize your whole existence around this one piece of talent that the good Lord has given you and treat it with great respect and don't allow yourself or any other creature to trespass on this little private part of yourself.

Q: You mean like not answering the telephone when you're writing?

A: Yeah, but those are the minor distractions which can be taken care of very easily, by not answering the telephone, which I rarely do. I think I'm going to put up a no trespassing sign in my front yard when I get back up there. I think it's something deeper than minor distractions—an attitude of mind which tells you that nothing should get in the way of what you have. Not the little third-rate book reviewers on Manhattan Island who are so full of venom and envy; not the major distractions of life, the ones such as wanting to travel around and all the rest. But just settling in, and doing it, and dedicating yourself to it.

Willie Morris Comes Home Again to the Delta

James Dickerson / 1978

From the *Greenwood (Mississippi) Commonwealth*, 4 April 1978, 2.
Reprinted by permission of *The Greenwood Commonwealth*.

Willie Morris had come home again.

But this time there was a difference. Instead of the threats of violence that had greeted the Mississippi-born author at other homecomings—the result of *Yazoo*, a book about school desegregation in his hometown of Yazoo City—there was now a showering of affection.

The former editor of *Harper's* magazine (1967–1971) and the author of *North Toward Home* and *The Last of the Southern Girls*, had come to Greenwood to participate in the city's annual Arts Festival. He would spend a day and a night, deliver a speech, then drive to Yazoo City, where he would spend a week before returning to his home in Bridgehampton, New York.

Sitting in the upstairs room of a stately house on Grand Boulevard the afternoon before he was to address a literary seminar, he was the picture of contentment. His eyes wandered, taking in everything. At forty-four, there is still a boyish glimmer in his eye.

"I see I have my own pool table," he said, spotting one across the room. His head nodded with approval. He was dressed in a knit shirt, that type worn by golfers, and he had the look of someone who had just stepped from a car after suffering a two-hour confinement on the roads of Mississippi. He had been in Greenwood for less than thirty minutes.

"My flight down was like a Greyhound bus. We made five stops between Richmond and Memphis. Are the dogwoods in bloom here yet? I saw dogwoods on the way from Memphis. Not here yet? They'll be in bloom here within four days. Just wait and see."

Morris said he had returned to Mississippi last summer for *Time* magazine to cover President Carter's visit to Yazoo City ["Yazoo City: South Toward Home," *Time*, August 1, 1977].

"I stayed in a Yazoo motel," he said. "I was the only civilian there. I was surrounded by Secret Service people. Before that the last time I had come home was when my mother died. I had to close down the old house where I grew up. It looks like I'm coming down more and more. I'd like to spend more time here."

Morris said that his home in Bridgehampton, one hundred miles due east of New York City, was located in a rural area that reminded him of the Mississippi Delta.

"I'm surrounded by all these potato fields," he said. "They have the same growing season as cotton and they look a lot like cotton. The only difference is the potato fields don't have the resonance of the Delta. Whenever I go into New York, my palms start getting sweaty along about Babylon."

Since the publication of *Yazoo* in 1971, Morris said he had been "a little bit out of touch" with developments in the civil rights movement in Mississippi.

"I do get the impression that the public schools have held their own," he said. "What I've seen in the Deep South over the last decade is an element of civility between the races in public that is quite marked. That wasn't true when I grew up. They seem so polite to each other now.

"When President Carter went to Yazoo City, I think he went out of his way to say how he was speaking in a brand new high school building that was the product of a bond issue that passed overwhelmingly. Obviously the public is willing to support public schools."

Social commentators in the state, he was told by a reporter, are now beginning to speak in terms of political alliances between "rednecks" and "blacknecks." They say the direction of change in Mississippi in the 1980s will be determined by the state's poor whites and the blacks. And they say their political goals will be identical.

"I saw a glimmer of that when I was working on *Yazoo*," he said. "Of course, the populist movement that started in the 1880s showed the beginnings of a working alliance between blacks and poor whites.

"If true, it portends immense change. It depends on the leaders—certainly it's not surprising that blacks have turned on their white, liberal benefactors. That's in the nature of the human beast. I don't know where it's headed, but I do know this: the state of Mississippi is a hell of a lot more integrated than the state of New York.

"Mr. Faulkner knew. He knew it in his bones. Read 'Delta Autumn.' Tell people to read that, the answer's in that."

The Last of the Southern Girls (1973), is Morris's first published novel. But he said he's hard at work on a second novel called *Taps*.

"It's set in a Mississippi town during the Korean War period," he said. "It's based on the experiences of two teenage boys who are playing 'Taps' at a military funeral. I put it aside to write a story about James Jones."

Morris explained that before Jones—a close friend and neighbor—died, he asked him to complete the last three chapters of his novel *Whistle* [1978], the final volume in his trilogy about World War II. Morris said that by using Jones's notes and the tape recordings he made while in the hospital, he was able to finish the book in about three weeks. He described the book as one of the "great books" in American literature.

"After that I wrote a long memoir about my friendship with Jones for the *Atlantic Monthly*," he said. "Then I expanded that into a full-length book, which I just finished. It's about Jones, but it's also about the life of a writer. It's coming out, I think, in October, the magazine story in June."

After leaving the editor in chief's chair at *Harper's* magazine in 1971 over a dispute with publishers, Morris has steered clear of other magazines and newspapers. Instead, he has devoted his time to writing fiction.

"I don't miss the organized publishing world at all," he said. "I don't miss New York either. Its fashions come and go as if the length of female skirts had anything to do with the enduring female anatomy—I wouldn't want to have anything else to do with a national magazine."

Morris, who said he tries to write five or six hours every afternoon, described writing as a "universal, private calling."

"The written word, when done well, is one of the few endeavors of the human race that lasts and matters," he said. "If you write something good, it's going to last—it's that simple.

"On my first novel I learned something that's almost impossible to put into words. I learned about the discipline of fiction. I learned a lot about dialogue and I learned how very, very tough the writing of fiction is. With the exception of high poetry, it's the most difficult of the art forms. It draws everything out of me. You do it, and you just see what happens. You have to stick with it.

"I'm just a writer, always will be. I'll stick to fiction. That's what my life is."

"American fiction is alive and flourishing," he said. "I don't see any decline at all. You often hear (the opposite) from people who can't write fiction. The old sturdy rhythms of American fiction are there and always will be. At any given time there haven't been all that many good writers at work. Now

we've got William Styron, Walker Percy, Truman Capote, Norman Mailer—
it's a good group.

"And there's James Dickey, who is working on a big novel set during
World War II. He's a wonderful poet. He's in the tradition of the old traveling
bard. That's good as long as he does his own work, which he does. I'm not
saying a writer should do this constantly."

Morris the editor, the newspaper reporter, possibly the last of the great
southern writers with ties to the pre-suburbia South, is filled with questions
about the Mississippi Delta. He asks about the mood of the people in the
Delta. He asks about friends such as Philip Carter, editor of the *Delta Democrat-Times* at nearby Greenville, and his brother, Hodding, now an assistant
Secretary of State in Washington, D.C. He asks about people who have come
and gone. He wants to know everything.

"I'm so attuned to this land," he said. "You never get it out of your blood.
You have all these memories associated with it. It haunts me to see some of
these old landmarks. Coming into Greenwood I saw things that hadn't
changed much since I was a child. That Billups service station at the edge of
town was there when I was four. I played a lot of baseball at a field near
there. Where is that field now? Is it gone?"

Willie Morris arrived at the W. M. Whittington Playhouse a few minutes
late to address a capacity crowd of nearly two hundred. Dressed in a blue
suit, blue shirt and striped tie, he did not appear as relaxed as the day before,
but, still, there was no trace of tension: he had come home again to be among
friends.

Yazoo City newspaper editor Norman Mott introduced Morris, a friend of
many years.

Speaking of Morris's book *Yazoo*, he said it was the story of "how Willie's
hometown dealt with the integration crisis of 1970."

"Willie's account stood up," said Mott. "He has a tape recorder ear—he
is a literary historian. Last week I reread *Yazoo*. It is a masterpiece of in-
depth reporting."

When Morris rose to speak, he said he was "deeply touched that (his)
friend came up from Yazoo."

"It's good to be here during the Delta springtime," he said. "God, these
Delta parties. I'm out of practice. It touches my heart to see old friends from
the past. There's no place like our good ole Mississippi Delta, especially after
dark.

"I'm proud to be a Mississippian, to be from the same state as William

Faulkner, Eudora Welty, Hodding Carter, Betty Carter. My God, that's the first team. The power of southern literature comes from those qualities of caring about people. Caring for a place. The power of remembering—I hope we never lose those things."

With both hands clutching the top of the lectern and one foot crossed over the other, Morris told the story of how he had come to complete James Jones's novel, *Whistle*. He told of writing the memoir about his friendship with Jones. He described it as a "kind of a sequel to *North Toward Home*."

Then he read from the soon-to-be-published memoir.

Morris was sitting in a neighborhood bar, he said, when he looked out the window and saw James Jones drive up and park his car behind his own car.

"He came up to me," Morris read. " 'Your mother just died,' he said. 'I'm sorry—I've been looking all over for you. Come home with me—you don't need to be alone.' "

Morris, his voice showing emotion, said that the two "great presences" in his life were his mother and James Jones. He told of the pain of returning to New York after burying his mother, only to find Jones near death in a New York hospital.

Months later, he said, while going through Jones's papers, he found this note scribbled on the margin of a manuscript page: "April 15, 1977. Willie's mother died in Yazoo today."

The death of the last surviving family member, Morris said, "tortures one with the mysteries of living."

Question from the audience: Mississippi has had an unfavorable image in the past. What can we do as Mississippians to convince the Northern press that we live in the twentieth century down here?

"To hell with the image," said Morris. "F—- the Yankees! I don't think the state of Mississippi should do anything to improve its image. It's obvious to any perceptive observer that what has happened here in recent years has been momentous.

"I sure as hell wouldn't concern myself about what the people in the Bronx think about Mississippi."

Question from the audience: If you like it so much here in the Delta, why don't you live here?

"Being a writer, the place where one lives doesn't matter," said Morris. "I don't live here on a day-to-day basis because I love it too much. I suffer too much in the physical setting, and over the time setting. I don't feel I have to live here."

Question from the audience: What is the responsibility of the writer?

"Writers are the custodians of the memory of being a human being," said Morris. "Especially now with television—it's diverting a number of young people away from the written word. Television will go. When it does, they'll still be writers. As long as there is a human race, there will be literature."

Hampton Life Interviews
Willie Morris
Mary Cummings / 1978

From *Hampton Life*, 4 (October 1978), 10–11. Reprinted by permission of Mary Cummings.

Since most people read first and travel later, they carry with them to faraway places certain unshakable literary baggage. They take it to Paris where, at the Ritz, the ghost of Fitzgerald dares them to be reckless, hell-raising, brittle, and beautiful. In London they hear echoes of erudition and civility in the streets of Bloomsbury and sense that deep, troubling mysteries dwell behind each heavy door.

And with the accumulation of literary associations, the setting becomes more familiar and at the same time less real. Having passed through the lens of another's perception, the place has emerged somehow larger than life. And though people undoubtedly continue to live there, walk dogs, scold children, and drink beer at twilight, the air that they breathe is not the same air that we breathe and these people are different from us.

It is strange, then, to pick up a copy of one of the last legitimate literary magazines in America and to read of such a place where two writers are bound by a friendship. A brief introduction explains that the two men were brought together by "a love of books, the South, drink, pranks, history, rural life, storytelling; by a sense of what counts and what doesn't." In the words of one of them, it is "a rural place with a quiet village life," a place where "there are hauntingly beautiful days in the autumn when you feel you do not want to be anywhere else on the Lord's good earth."

What is strange is that we'll never be able to make a pilgrimage to this magic place. We will never walk through these quiet streets, look upon these open fields and dunes, gaze overhead at flocks of Canadian geese and say to ourselves that the place where we live is pale by comparison.

It *is*, in fact, the place where we live. We rediscover it in Willie Morris's prose; we admire him for finding the words to describe what we love and for taking the trouble to tell us just why it is beautiful. We know this place intimately. The faces which fascinate him are the faces of friends or neighborhood fixtures; the "country dogs with big friendly faces" are the local mutts, perhaps even our own. His perception has endowed us with an added dimension.

Willie Morris lives in Bridgehampton. It is in Bridgehampton that he wrote *James Jones: A Friendship*, and it is from this book—to be published in October—that the excerpt in June's issue of the *Atlantic Monthly* was taken.

Both men lived in Bridgehampton. They first met in New York in the sixties and by the time Morris left the city, seven years ago (following an "unhappy experience" as editor of *Harper's*), they were friends. James Jones was working on *Whistle* [1978], the book he considered the work of his life, and living in an old farmhouse with his family. Willie Morris thought it a good old house, dubbed it "Chateau Spud," and spent many hours in its large kitchen lingering over good food, good talk, TV, and poker. In the summer of 1977, the friendship ended when James Jones died. *James Jones: A Friendship* is Willie Morris's account of the novelist's last days.

Also the author of an autobiography, *North Toward Home, Yazoo*, and a novel, *The Last of the Southern Girls*, Willie Morris is a writer whose reputation spares him the kind of hustling untried authors must often endure to get published. There is apparently no need for constant city forays to keep himself in the forefront. Born in Jackson, Mississippi, in 1934, he was an only child and no family remains there to call him back home. A son, David, is in college and Willie Morris could probably live anywhere in the world. What made him choose Bridgehampton?

WM: I lived for ten years in the city. I was editor of *Harper's* and that ended, as often happens, in a big dispute. I have all these roots in the South. But the question is—where does a writer live? He can live almost anywhere. In the sixties, when I was living in the city, I came out here and when I saw it I just thought—this is for me. I was in Wainscott as first, in Georgica with a friend. East Hampton was my town then. I drank at Cavagnaro's. Then gradually, almost unconsciously, I gravitated towards Bridgehampton. It's the most unpretentious village in the Hamptons. It has a genuine community on a year-round basis. As Lyndon Johnson said, "People care when you're sick and they know when you die." They know each other's children and dogs and they truly do give you your privacy.

Invading Willie Morris's privacy would never be easy. By his own admission, he "rarely" answers the phone. A much better bet is to track him down

at the end of the day at one of his neighborhood haunts—Bobby Van's, Mel-
on's, or Rick's—where he is a regular. A friendly Labrador outside the door
is an excellent sign. It's very likely Willie's dog, Pete, a celebrity himself.

WM: I'm doing a book right now, a children's book with some other
writers for Rolling Stone Press. It's about my dog Pete, the Mayor of Bridgehampton. Everybody knows him. He has friends all over town. My agent told
me to send the piece to the *Reader's Digest* and they took it ["Pete, 'The
Mayor of Bridgehampton,' " *Reader's Digest*, December 1978]. Their photographer was out here all day taking pictures of Pete. He loved him. Pete
was perfect, did everything right, except for trying to eat the flies.

Morris is also collaborating on a book with his son, David, now eighteen.

WM: It's called *The Sounds and the Silences*. David's a fine photographer.
He studied for three years at the International Center for Photography and
he's studying photography in college. It's about the people, the land, and the
changing seasons out here. What we're trying to do—with his photos and my
text—is to show the stresses of an area such as this, which is physically and
spiritually threatened. We're trying to capture that marvelous quality of
beauty it still has.

HL: Do you think we will lose it? Will it all have disappeared in twenty
years?

WM: The question is really whether all regionalism will disappear in the
whole of America, destroyed by television and the rest.

HL: Do you ever consider fleeing to some place like Maine for the
crowded summer months, or during the dead of winter?

WM: Well, yes, I've thought of that. July and August get tougher and
tougher as the years go by. I think, though, my choice would be to divide my
time between the South and here—New Orleans, maybe Mississippi. I still
have a lot of friends in Mississippi. I've gone away almost every winter. Not
this winter because I was working on the book. Around here in the dead of
winter you almost have to be into something that's very important—a book
or *something*. I go to Mississippi a lot.

HL: Is the South still home for you?

WM: Yes, it's still home. Well . . . there and here.

HL: Is there something that both places have in common, something that
attracts you to both places and makes each feel like home?

WM: That's a good question. I've been thinking a lot about that and I think they do share great similarities. It is probably true that I am profoundly attracted to Bridgehampton because it reminds me of the South. The flat land looks like the Mississippi Delta, potato plants even look like cotton plants during part of the year, and there is a haunting, brooding quality to both places. The black people here are like the black people of Mississippi, the people in a small town in the deep South. There are real local people with colorful eccentricities. But there are differences too. Mississippi is so isolated. They're still a little bit—very much more indigenous.

I'm working on a novel now that's set in a small Mississippi town during the Korean War. It's based on real things. They activated the Dixie Division of the National Guard when I was in high school. The division was decimated. A friend and I were the two best trumpet players in town and we took turns playing "Taps" and the echo for all those funerals.

HL: How do you work? Are you one of those writers who keeps a rigid schedule—up early, writing all morning?

WM: No. I work in the afternoon. I sleep until noon. Then I follow Pete, the Mayor, around town. The work ebbs and flows.

HL: You've always made your living either directly or indirectly from writing. A lot of people would like to be in that position. Do you actually enjoy writing?

WM: I don't like it when I'm doing it. I like it when it's finished. I can't think of any writers who do really like it. But after a while you have no choice. It's such an expression of yourself. Like so many writers I know, I feel I have no choice.

HL: You seem to know just what's next when you wind something up and even to have more than one thing going at once. Don't you ever get down at the end of a project and wonder what to do next?

WM: For the last three or four years I haven't had any problems like that.

HL: You are at the point where you are able to do just what you want in a place that you love. You know you'll be published without major problems and your words will be read. It's an enviable position.

WM: I guess so. But that's not to say there aren't hazards. It's very lonely. You're spending the best hours of your day alone, dealing with memories and emotions that most people don't deal with.

Others have spoken of the writer's vocation as both gift and curse and sounded foolish, romantic, affected. When Willie Morris says the probing is painful, the life lonely, it is a simple statement of fact.

Willie Morris is an unpretentious man. An admirer of simplicity, he seems to value people and places on that basis. In the place where we live he has found people of character and places of beauty where others might have looked all their lives and missed them.

Willie Morris: "I Will Forever Consider This My Home"

Melissa Baumann / 1978

From the *Jackson (Mississippi) Clarion-Ledger / Jackson Daily News*, 8 October 1978, sec. G, 1- 2. Reprinted by permission of *The Clarion-Ledger*.

Near a corner on North Jefferson Street, behind a Tote-Sum store and across from a Jitney Jungle, Willie Morris's magnolia tree still stands.

Not as grand as some, and lopsided where a telephone wire has knocked out some of its branches, it is inconsequential to the drivers competing at the intersection there. But Morris recalls how thirty-four years ago, on his annual summer visit to his Grandmother Mamie's house, he carved "Willie M." in block letters in the bark.

"It broke my heart when they tore the house down to put in a parking lot," Morris said, seated in a Holiday Inn hotel room in Hattiesburg.

"But the tree's still there, with my name on it. I carved it there when I was ten years old." [*Editor's note*: A photograph of the carved "Willie M" appears on page 12 of Susan Puckett's *A Cook's Tour of Mississippi* (1980). A caption indicates that "during the summer of 1980, a vandal cut the name from the tree, although the tree still stands."]

Morris, down from his Long Island home for a conference at the University of Southern Mississippi on *A Sense of Place* here, stares out his hotel room window, his blue-grey eyes seeming to fetch memories from his Mississippi boyhood.

The bed is unmade but he tells the cleaning woman to "skip it" and return later.

He smokes continually, his short fingers holding the cigarette halfway down. His reddish, wavy hair is slicked back. His turquoise LaCoste shirt hangs out over his blue serge pants, but his loafers are polished.

Something outside, beyond the hot top and the highway, keeps begging for his attention.

"Oh, Jackson's changed," he said with a melancholy that befits the landscape of his Delta youth, a childhood tenderly embraced in his memoir *North Toward Home*.

His voice is gentle, with just the trace of a southern accent.

"The view you get on Highway 55 coming in—it's a beautiful piece of terrain but now it could look like Cleveland, Ohio, with all the franchise housing, the pizza joints and the hotels.

"Jackson when I was growing up was really quite a sleepy capital city," he said. "We'd take these long walks, with forests of crepe myrtle everywhere and old ladies sitting on their front porches asking you in for iced tea.

"But I scarcely recognize any of the neighborhoods any more."

Morris, who left the state more than twenty-five years ago to attend the University of Texas, Oxford University, and then to work at *Harper's* magazine in New York, returns to Mississippi four or five times a year for university seminars and to visit his friends.

He can't write here, he says, because he feels "dislocated, with too many nerve endings alive," so he stakes out with Pete, his black Labrador retriever, and sometimes his son David in an eighteenth-century house a mile from the Atlantic. His neighbors, a comfortable distance away, are other writers. Among them, until last year, was James Jones, the late author Morris calls his best friend and the subject of Morris's latest book—*James Jones: A Friendship*—to be released by Doubleday this month.

Jones, as Morris details in the memoir he calls "a sequel to *North Toward Home*," died in the spring of 1977 shortly after Morris's mother passed away in Yazoo City. Morris came home then to close up the family homestead and bury his last kin in the state.

"All my people came from Raymond, they founded Raymond," said Morris, a history buff and a Rhodes Scholar in history at Oxford.

"My great-grandfather—George W. Harper—was the editor of the *Hinds County Gazette* there," he said. "When the Yankee troops came through they dumped his printing presses in the town well. He later reopened and then became one of the first white men during Reconstruction elected to the legislature.

"But I don't have any relatives here now," he said, "not since my mother died. She taught four generations of kids piano in Yazoo City."

Morris sold her piano to the Methodist Church when he went home to pack up the home where he lived as an only child.

Like many southern small towns hiding outside the reach of time, Yazoo City hasn't changed much since the days when Morris hunted in its woods, harassed its old school marms, played baseball, and lingered in one of his favorite hangouts, the town cemetery.

"Growing up there, there was always the feeling of time standing still," Morris said, his gaze still fixed outside the window.

"And one of the things I remember," he said, "we were always playing tricks over there in Yazoo. It had to do with a sense of fancy. There wasn't too much going on over there in the summer—this is before the TV and the big expressways—and we had to do something in a place where the intellect wasn't much accepted.

"You had to work out your imagination somehow," he said, "so the one-shot practical joke was the thing. Like putting my dog, Skip, on the dashboard of the car and ducking my head under the steering wheel. And going by the Dew Drop Inn about ten miles an hour, with the old men whittlin' and chewin' tobacco shouting, 'Look at that ole dog drivin' a car.'

"I suspect they knew after a time who it was."

On visits to Yazoo City now, Morris said, he stays in the Yazoo Motel.

"And I spend about half my time in the cemetery," he chuckled.

"I have to go back there and find out who has died since my last trip home."

Half of the action of the novel Morris is currently writing, to be called *Taps* and set during the Korean war, occurs in that cemetery, Morris said.

"The Dixie Division of the National Guard was activated and sent boys into Korea," he said. "They were decimated, and I remember a period of months when the boxes started coming home. A friend and I would always play 'Taps' at the military funerals. We'd flip a coin to see who'd play at the grave and who'd play echo. Playing at the grave was not too pleasant."

Memories, Morris is convinced, are the sustenance of literature; they are also the prerogative of southerners, particularly Mississippians.

"We have a unique past," Morris said. "There's a genuine sense of community, a communal awareness of what we all share. I will forever consider this my home. Yet can this communal awareness survive the almost relentless American urge toward uniformity, the destructive urge for everything to be similar and everyone to be the same?

"I think it can, for Mississippi has such a dark, contorted, and complicated history," he said. "With the sense of community, the feelings toward the past, and words, the tremendous oral tradition, it's no accident that Mississippi in the twentieth century has probably produced the greatest writers— William Faulkner, Eudora Welty, Walker Percy—the list goes on."

Although he speaks of his book on Jones, his fifth book, with much enthusiasm, (Morris is generally modest about his work); he mentions Faulkner, however, with awe.

"I started reading Faulkner when I was eighteen," Morris said, "not before. Everybody in high school told me he was out for the Yankee dollar. One fellow told me he got drunk and got naked and bayed at the moon up there in Oxford, where they called him 'Count No 'Count.'

"Only later did I realize how profoundly he affected me," he said. "The landscape here is sad, it fills me with sadness. Faulkner wrote about it, about the violence, and the blood and the guilt. Mississippi's a violent place, a place of extremes."

And Morris, apparently, can't let go of that. Long Island, he says, is "much too civilized." New York City, where he spends as little time as possible since resigning as editor in chief of *Harper's* in 1971, has a frenzied tempo and is "a terrible place for a writer."

Morris's home in Bridgehampton, Long Island, though, reminds him somewhat of the South—the town is 40 percent black and the agrarian touch is there in a potato field that stretches from his house to the sea.

Photographs of Yazoo are up on the walls of the room where Morris writes in the afternoons, starting then because he sleeps until noon. In between parties and movie-going, Morris and his son David, a photography student at Hampshire College in Amherst, Massachusetts, are planning a picture book on Mississippi.

Morris has memories of New York, of the days at *Harper's* when editors and publishers fought it out with "ideological switchblades," of the time Ted Kennedy mistook him for the bartender at a posh party on Central Park West, of the hours spent at Jones's bedside helping him make tapes to finish *Whistle* [1978], his last novel, before death claimed him.

But the best memories, Morris said, come from childhood, a bank of experience that Morris treasures for his art's existence.

"Literature is the great expression of memory in the human race," he said, facing his listeners this time.

"The phenomenon of memory is the hallmark and requisite of a serious writer—not just one's own memory but the collective memory of a people.

"But I think," he mused, "even if they pave over the Mississippi Delta and make it one vast parking lot all the way down from Memphis, the southerners will always retain their literature.

"The changes in the land here, this new spirit of acquisitiveness, has got to affect the spirit. But I don't think it matters where a writer lives past a certain age—because the memories are there."

Willie Morris, Home Again

William Thomas / 1980

From *Mid-South*, the *Memphis Commercial Appeal* magazine, 2 March 1980, 6, 8–10. Reprinted by permission of *The Commercial Appeal*.

As soon as his writing class is over, Willie Morris drives home, across the University of Mississippi campus in Oxford, Mississippi, to pick up his dog, Pete, and take him for a walk in the cemetery where William Faulkner is buried. Morris, who has returned to Mississippi thirteen years after the publication of his bittersweet southerner's autobiography, *North Toward Home*, has been taking the dog to the cemetery almost from the first day he arrived in Oxford and went out to see where they'd put down "Mr. Bill."

The cemetery—St. Peter's—is one of those shimmering southern places with a great, spreading magnolia tree off to one side and a circle of cedars planted long ago by one of the town's more prominent families. The second-most-famous person in the cemetery is L. Q. C. Lamar, who drafted the Mississippi ordinance of secession in 1861 and, after the war, became known as the Great Pacificator. The cemetery is full of history and myth and grim tales of yellow fever victims. It's exactly the kind of place where Morris, who is working on a novel called *Taps*, would choose to walk his dog.

The dog is a big, black Labrador retriever that Morris brought with him from his northern place in Bridghampton, Long Island. A town of about two thousand in the winter, it is in the middle of the potato country, where Morris has lived for years, working and hobnobbing with some of the country's leading literary figures. It is also the town where he met Pete, who is no ordinary Labrador retriever.

"Pete is the Mayor of Bridgehampton," Morris says. "He pushes open the doors of the bars there with his nose and goes in. He is famous. He has been in the *Reader's Digest*" ["Pete, 'The Mayor of Bridgehampton,'" *Reader's Digest*, December 1978].

Pete, who is nine years old and in spite of his bloodline too lazy to play fetch, was waiting for Morris when he arrived home after the class. The dog met him just inside the door of a white frame house on the University's Faculty Row where Morris is living during his one-semester teaching assignment.

The house, built in the 1930s when land was plentiful, sits on a big, rolling lot studded with shade trees. However, the rooms are small and sparsely furnished. About the only object of interest is a large, pine worktable in the dining room. The table is stacked with paperback books that Morris uses in his classes. In the middle of the table sits a battered typewriter that has not been much used lately.

"I've sort of put my novel aside while I'm here," Morris says. "It was deliberate. I wanted to concentrate on these classes I'm teaching. Also, there is a juncture in the book and I thought it would be healthy to put it aside and then come back to it. It's set here (in Mississippi) a generation ago, during the Korean War. The actual place is Yazoo. But Oxford is close enough to soak up some impressions."

The novel is based on Morris's experiences as a young, hometown bugler who played "Taps" at the funerals of the Korean War dead as they came home for burial. Consequently, walking through cemeteries is part of the writer's soaking-up process.

Morris looks through the house until he finds Pete's leash. Then he leads the dog out to a skinned-up, 1975 white Plymouth Valiant that had belonged to his mother in Yazoo City. Morris's son, David, calls the car a (Ya)zoo-mobile.

Pete, the dog-mayor, jumps into the car and lies down on the back seat. Morris gets behind the wheel, backs out of the driveway and heads for the cemetery a few miles away. It is a winter day and the kudzu along the road is brown and lifeless. But the sun is bright and the air warm and Morris is in high spirits.

"I haven't been this happy in a long time. It's the sensual texture of things here. It's the wood smoke that's in the air on a dreary winter day. It's the chicken and barbecue that they sell in little stores and service stations. It's the conversations about people from the past with old family names that intertwine. I drive out to these small, courthouse towns and look at the people—and it's Yazoo City of a generation or two ago."

Morris looks at the hills on both sides of the road and says this is what makes the difference between Oxford and Yazoo, some sixty miles to the south. "Although Yazoo is half hills, it faces the Delta, and I've always been a Delta boy. But the people are the same and so it feels like home."

And that's why Willie Morris came.

"I wanted to come home. It's no more complicated or simple than that. I'm at a kind of juncture in my life, and I felt it was time. Besides, my nerve ends come alive when I cross the Mississippi line. I'm not exaggerating. It's got to have something to do with that whole business of the burden of memory—the memory that serves one's imagination as a writer."

Morris, who has written of the almost tropical vegetational density of Mississippi and of the prolific green creeping vine that comes right up to the highway, looks at a great curtain of brown kudzu going by and says he can't wait for springtime. Then he goes on:

"I have no doubt but what this business of coming home is stronger for southerners than it is for any others in the country. And, among southerners, the feeling is strongest in Mississippi. Why? Because there's just something about Mississippi that's different . . . different than any other place . . . absolutely different. It is something profound in our emotions."

Coming home is an experience that Morris has had any number of times since he first left Mississippi at eighteen to go away to college. Until now, however, he has never come back for any sort of extended stay. He just kept moving north. It is a journey that started in 1952, when he went to the University of Texas and became editor of the student newspaper. Four years later he graduated with honors and went to Oxford, England, as a Rhodes Scholar. He still tells funny stories of the Oxford days when he was studying history:

"My first tutorial was on the Reform Act of 1832. I stayed up all night working on the paper. The next-to-the-last sentence read, 'Just how close the people of England came to revolution in 1832 is a question that we shall leave to the historians.' When I read this to my tutor, he said, 'But Morris, we *are* the historians.'"

When he came back from England, he went to Austin, Texas, and edited the *Texas Observer*. Then he went to California for graduate courses at Stanford. A Greyhound bus took him to New York—the Big Cave, he called it—where he joined the staff of *Harper's* magazine. In five years, he became the youngest editor in chief of the oldest literary magazine in the United States. He stayed at the top of the heap until 1971, making all kinds of literary friends. Then, crash. . . .

"I went through an unhappy experience running the magazine," he wrote later, "and resigned."

Things didn't get any easier.

In April 1977, his mother, a piano teacher in Yazoo City, died. She was his last blood-and-kin tie to the town where he grew up. He sold the house and wrote a moving scene about the way it ended:

The moment came that I stood alone in the empty house. Did I know then how it would grow to haunt my dreams and nightmares? In the gloom of it that day I strained to hear the music again, my father's footsteps on the porch, the echoes of boys playing basketball in the backyard, the barks and whines of Tony, Sam, Jimbo, Sonny, Duke, and Old Skip. I locked the front door and did not look behind me.

A month later, his best friend and Long Island neighbor, James Jones, the novelist, died before finishing the wartime trilogy that he had begun with *From Here to Eternity* [1951]. He was three chapters short and knew it. In the final, slow days of his death, Jones went over the material for the last chapters with Morris—and asked him to complete it for him.

After the funeral, Morris went up into Jones's attic, where the writer had written the bulk of the book, and began "organizing the notes" for what was to be the end of the novel, *Whistle* [1978].

Nobody was better qualified. Not only had Morris been one of the brightest editors in the country and understood exactly how Jones wanted the book to end, but he had firsthand knowledge of Memphis, where much of the book takes place. Morris handled the ending with grace and intelligence. Then he wrote a warm memoir titled, *James Jones: A Friendship*.

The deaths of his mother and his friend weighed on Morris for two years. Then he decided to try coming home.

"I was speaking to the Delta Arts Council in Greenwood, Mississippi, about a year and a half ago," he says, "and I told a good friend, Larry Wells, who runs the Yoknapatawpha Press in Oxford, that I'd like to come and be a sort of writer-in-residence at Ole Miss. So Larry and Evans Harrington, the chairman of the English department, got things organized for me—and that's how I happen to be here."

Morris drove down in January with his son, David, who is twenty, and his son's Yankee friend from Amherst College in Massachusetts. "They were drooling all the time they were here," Morris says. "Ole Miss still has more beautiful girls than any university in the country. The boys kept finding excuses to walk the dog."

When they weren't on the campus they were out in the country looking at small, out-of-the-way places with strange, Mississippi names.

"We went to Vardaman, Tupelo, Caulhoun City and Bruce. Then we went down to Greenville and had dinner with Betty Carter, 'Big Hodding's' widow and 'Little Hodding's' mother. And just before the boys left to go back to school, we went to Yazoo City incognito. We only had about two hours and I didn't want to see anybody. If you go back to a place where you have a lot of friends, you can't see one—you've got to see them all."

The trips were enough to convince Morris that Mississippi has undergone some significant changes.

"To see it, I think maybe it takes someone who is from here but who has lived removed from it. I doubt if people living here on a day-to-day basis are aware of the extent of the changes. But be advised that the changes are extraordinary. The biggest one, I think, is in public circumstances—there is courtesy between the races. Real courtesy.

"It tends to prove, I think, that once Mississippians got the albatross of race off their necks, once the guilt and the brutal parts were removed, then the good ole state of Mississippi could go on being what it always was, which is the most complicated, histrionic, craziest, most colorful and kindest state in the union. You take a place like Ole Miss. I feel it is a place of distinction, like all places that have suffered through their own fault, their own guilt, their own cruelty, and through the misunderstanding of outsiders."

There are other changes, Morris says, some very close at hand. "I live right across the street from the Director of Black Studies," he said. His name is Cleveland Donald and he is a brilliant, distinguished historian with a Ph.D. from Cornell University in New York. He is also a man of courage. He was the second black student at Ole Miss, James Meredith being the first. And he's my neighbor."

Morris is so sensitive to what he calls "the new courtesy" that when his son attached a Confederate flag to the antenna of his car he quickly removed it for fear it would hurt the feelings of the man across the street.

"By God, this may sound like a cliché," Morris says, thoughtfully, "but it's this simple courtesy among people in the South that's unflagging. You just run into somebody in the supermarket and start talking and something happens that doesn't happen anywhere else. It doesn't happen on Long Island, and I love the place. It's hauntingly beautiful and I have my best friends there. But it's not the same. In Bridgehampton, there's a great bar where the writers go. In Mississippi, it's more personal: people go to one another's homes."

Morris drives through the gates of the cemetery where William Faulkner is buried and parks the car and lets Pete out. The weather is almost balmy.

"Right now, it's very severe and bleak in Bridgehampton," Morris says. "The wind comes whipping in off the ocean and it's the best time to be away

from there. Of course, there's a sense of homecoming to it when you go back.
But it's not as intense as coming home South and all that's here."

Morris yells at the dog, who pays little attention to him, and then continues,
pursuing the thought:

"That doesn't mean Mississippi is all good," he says. "When you go out
to the hamlets in the Delta you still see incredible poverty—the shacks and
all the rest. That hasn't changed and it always gets to you. Something has to
be done about that. But the big change I'm talking about is in public civility.
So much of the cruelty—physical cruelty and cruelty in the public dis-
course—is gone. And thank God it is. It is a marked change."

Morris collars the dog and then heads down the hill toward William Faulkner's grave.

"Mississippians have done bad things, but it's getting better. You can't
turn your back on your heritage, even the bad parts, especially if you're a
writer. Miss Eudora (Welty) and I would agree on that, as, I am sure, would
Walker Percy and Mr. Bill if he could come down from his grave and sit with
us and sip a little bourbon."

William Faulkner's grave is located at the base of a small hill. For writers,
Faulkner is an ever-present force here.

"The whole aura is very much Mr. Bill. It pervades this town. I like that.
I enjoy the pleasure of the aura of Mr. Bill hovering over Oxford. I like
moving around in the things and the places that he wrote about. At twenty-
five, it would have scared hell out of me. At forty-five, I know that I write
very differently than he did and it doesn't scare me. We all learned from
him."

As it so happens, Morris's closest friends here are Faulkner folk: Mrs.
Dean Faulkner Wells, who was Faulkner's niece, and her husband Larry, who
has published a number of Faulkner items, most recently his poems.

Morris spends a lot of evenings at the Wells house, south of the square,
drinking bourbon and branch water and talking about writing and Faulkner.

"One time, I was sitting on the couch talking to Dean Wells's mother,
Miss Lucy, who was William Faulkner's sister-in-law. 'Willie,' she said, 'this
is a very interesting town.' And I said, 'Miss Lucy, I fully agree. It is so
interesting, in fact, that I think somebody ought to write about it.' We both
laughed."

At the cemetery, Morris and Pete are walking back to the car when Bill
Appleton, the superintendent, appears and wants to know who they are. For
just a second, it seems that Appleton, a former policeman, might be about to

lay down the law. But, as it turned out, he is just being friendly. He knows a lot about the cemetery and enjoys talking about it.

"People have come here from all over the world," he says. "This is a very historic place. That stone step you see over there is the one that the Yankee officers used to dismount from their horses. And all those small, plain stones mark the graves of yellow fever victims who were buried alive. There are a lot of Faulkners buried. They were all fine people, except for that William Faulkner. Now he was something else."

Driving home with Pete in the back seat, Willie Morris thinks about all the stories that Bill Appleton would have to tell about the people in the cemetery where Faulkner is buried.

"It's good to be back," he says.

Willie Morris

John Griffin Jones / 1980

From *Mississippi Writers Talking,* II (Jackson: University Press of Mississipppi, 1983), 75-118. Reprinted by permission of the University Press of Mississippi.

I left a message with his maid for him to call me at the Gin Restaurant in Oxford when he awoke from a late afternoon nap. I was playing shuffleboard with a friend when the call came an hour later. Willie Morris sounded refreshed, downright jaunty, on the telephone. "Hurry on over," he said, "and tell the Mayor we'll be down as soon as we finish the interview." At his house on Faculty Row I was greeted by his old dog Pete, an overweight black Lab who wheezed and managed a few indifferent woofs to welcome me, and by Morris, the wayfaring Yazoo boy, looking fit and happy in the appropriate campus clothing: knit sports shirt with "Ole Miss Rebels" printed over the pocket, slacks and penny loafers. The three of us repaired to his sparsely furnished den—a photo of Miss Welty was all that adorned the walls—and there we sat and talked for almost two hours. Afterwards we headed to the Gin where the Mayor was saving us two seats, and late into the night I watched as the author of *North Toward Home* talked with students and locals, signed napkins for sorority girls, and immersed himself in the lively atmosphere of Faulkner's town at the end of a college semester. "You know," he told me just before we parted, "I'm so glad to be back. Just keep your eyes open; there's so much to see. 'South Toward Home' is coming."

Jones: You say for the last couple of days you've been in Jackson and Yazoo City?

Morris: Yes. Larry Wells of Yoknapatawpha Press in Oxford brought out a fancy reprint of a children's book that I did in about 1970, called *Good Old Boy.* So we were in Yazoo City signing books at the library. And then we went out and had a historic occasion in Belzoni in the Delta. It was the first time an author had ever signed books in Belzoni.

Jones: They don't have a bookstore, do they?

Morris: No, they don't have a bookstore in Belzoni, but they do have a library. Thank God for that.

57

Jones: And you saw Bubba Barrier?

Morris: I saw my old friend Bubba. I grew up with Bubba, who's your cousin. He was the best man in my wedding.

Jones: Was he?

Morris: Yes, in Houston, Texas, many years ago. The marriage didn't last, but Bubba did. I've known Bubba since we were both about—well, it goes back before memory—since we were about one year old. My first memory of Bubba is a long-ago afternoon. I was killing ants on the sidewalk with a hammer. Bubba said, "The Lord ain't gonna like that." And I guess He didn't.

Jones: Some of my favorite parts of *Good Old Boy* and *North Toward Home* were when you talked about driving around in his red—what did he have, a Model T?

Morris: He had a Model T, yes. One of those old models with a rumble seat. Of course, when we were growing up in Yazoo City, we all started driving when we were about twelve or thirteen. I think Bubba started driving when he was eleven. He'd borrow the family car—his parents didn't know it—and come down and pick me up, and we'd drive all over Brickyard Hill and out into the Delta. I do think Bubba was eleven or twelve then.

Jones: Is Muttonhead Shepherd still alive?

Morris: At last report he is. I sure hope so.

Jones: Where is he?

Morris: Someone told me he's teaching school and coaching up in North Carolina.

Jones: And Honest Ed Upton?

Morris: Honest Ed Upton is a Methodist preacher.

Jones: Where?

Morris: Out in Dallas, Texas. And Big Boy Wilkinson—I saw him the other day in Memphis. He's a very successful dentist in Memphis. So the group seems to be doing okay.

Jones: Did you keep up with them through the years?

Morris: Well, off and on, sporadically. Since I've come back down here to live a good part of the year, I hear a lot about them. So it's an expression of keeping in touch.

Jones: Do you still have family in Mississippi?

Morris: No, I don't. All of my family is dead, except for my son David, who just turned twenty-one. My mother died about three years ago. She was an only child. My grandmother died about six years ago.

Jones: Harper?

Morris: Yes, she came from the Harper family at Raymond. Her father, my great-grandfather, was George W. Harper, who was the editor and publisher of the *Hinds County Gazette* in Raymond. It was one of the distinguished newspapers in the pre-Civil War period. He was one of the first white men reelected to the Mississippi State Senate.

Jones: During Reconstruction?

Morris: Yes. George W. Harper married Anna Sims, from Port Gibson. My grandmother was the youngest of seventeen children, and she was the last one to die. She's buried in the old section of the cemetery in Raymond, which is crumbling now, and all grown over with vicious weeds. Her grave is about fifty yards from where the Confederate dead are buried. But all my Mississippi people are gone. I've got some relatives up in Tennessee on my father's side.

Jones: Did your father have brothers?

Morris: Yes, he had one brother and three sisters. One of his sisters is still alive. My father was from Camden, Tennessee, which is in Benton County about eighty miles north of Memphis. His parents died when he was a little boy and he was brought up by relatives. His father served in the Tennessee State Senate with Cordell Hull. He was a Tennessean. But my Mississippi roots go back very far. Cowles Meade, who was one of the early territorial governors, was related. So was Henry S. Foote, who was a governor and senator before the Civil War and then in the Confederate Congress.

Jones: He left the Confederacy.

Morris: Yes, toward the end of the war. There's a letter that exists from Lincoln to Grant telling Grant to let ex-Senator Foote come through the lines in Virginia. He became an emigré. He went to Canada after the Civil War.

Jones: So somehow you're connected with Shelby Foote.

Morris: You know, most of the older families in Mississippi are related one way or another. Shelby and I've got to be distant cousins, I would think.

The other day in Memphis I met probably the most beautiful girl I've ever met in my life, Lynda Lee Meade Shea, who was Miss America from Ole Miss in about 1962, I suppose. I was signing books in a big bookstore, and she appeared from nowhere—a brief apparition.

Jones: Where's she from?

Morris: She's from Meadville and Natchez, I think, and so we must have shared this same great-great-uncle Cowles Meade, Meadville was named after Cowles Meade, so we have to be about twentieth cousins. She was so beautiful she frightened me. Baudelaire once wrote a poem many years ago in Paris, describing his fortuitous meeting with a girl so beautiful she frightened him. Why did she scare him so much, he asked in his own poem. She frightened him about the possibilities of his own capacity for love, he said to himself, and all the complexities of such things. Then, suddenly, in the bookstore in Memphis, this girl vanished for me, like a pebble in a pond. Just as well. We're still cousins, I'll bet. Anyway, I'm not really sure she was there. She was a dream, that's all. It was a Mississippi thing, even in Memphis.

Jones: A vision. Did your daddy come down here to work because your mother wanted to be near her family?

Morris: No. They actually met in Jackson. My daddy came down here during the Depression and went to work for Standard Oil in Jackson. That building still stands—that old office building right across from the War Memorial. Anyway, my mother and father met in the late '20s. They moved to Yazoo City when I was about six months old, in 1935.

Jones: I was reading some of the newspaper clippings on *North Toward Home,* and I read where some Yazoo Citizen wrote in: "Why doesn't Jackson claim Willie Morris? He was born there."

Morris: That Yazoo person didn't want me, I guess. Many people in Yazoo City were upset when *North Toward Home* came out. I knew they would be, but they're not anymore. I think they were mad at me for about five or six years. But this always happens in America with writers. In your home town they get a little disturbed at first when a book comes out that deals with people there, whether it's fictitious or not. *North Toward Home,* of course, was an autobiography. Then they calm down about it. This happens time and again. They grow rather proud of you, in a curious way. It certainly happened here with Faulkner. Lord knows, Sinclair Lewis in Sauk Center, Minnesota— they wouldn't let him back for twenty years.

Jones: They told Thomas Wolfe they'd lynch him if he ever came back to Asheville.

Morris: That's right. Now the tourists all go to his gravestone with the angel on top. I was once in Sauk Center, Minnesota, and I made a point to go to Sinclair Lewis Boulevard. The sign there on Main Street is not just "Main Street," it's "The *Original* Main Street."

Jones: I remember my mother gave me *North Toward Home* when I was fifteen or sixteen, and I read it and thought, "What a wonderful book." I talked to my relatives in Yazoo City about it soon afterwards—not the Barriers—and I was interested to see them look away and half-smile. They said, "Well, you know Willie could've come back here, but he didn't. He should've had the courage to write it living here." That sort of thing.

Morris: Well, I think I probably couldn't have written it living there. It's that old question of where a writer feels he should live. I couldn't live in Yazoo City. You know I love Yazoo City, I have many friends there, but I don't think I can ever work there. I know it too well. And they know me too well. Too many ghosts for all of us. This is the perfect compromise for me, living here in Oxford, with Old Miss here. Oxford is a hill country town, but there're great similarities between Oxford and Yazoo City, so this is a healthy modus vivendi.

Jones: At the time you were working on *Yazoo: Integration in a Deep-Southern Town*, had the town accepted you again, were you able to move freely in the white community?

Morris: Very much so. I talked to anybody I wanted to, from John Satterfield, the lawyer, former president of the American Bar Association, to William Barbour, a friend of mine who probably represents the moderate-conservative establishment in Yazoo City. Of course I had this entree with the blacks, which was necessary.

Jones: At the time you were growing up in Yazoo City, did you have any sense that what you wanted to do was write?

Morris: I think it was a feeling that grew on me over a period of time. I don't think I ever said to myself explicitly, "I want to be a writer." But I was always writing. I had a little portable typewriter I got when I was twelve or thirteen years old, and I started writing sports for the *Yazoo Herald* and for the school paper, and I never stopped. I once quoted John Keats's "Ode on a Grecian Urn" in my description of a basketball game between Yazoo City and Satartia. I guess—it's hard to remember these important things—it was at the University of Texas when I was editor-in-chief of the *Daily Texan*, which I think by then was almost without peer the greatest college newspaper in the country. It might have been then that I decided, or maybe it was when I got to Oxford, England, to Oxford University, which I call now the "other Oxford," that I began to have the feeling that I was going to be a writer. I know I started a novel over there in Oxford. I started it after my son David was born in Oxford in 1959. I would stay up all night, and my son was just beginning to crawl. He'd be crawling around the floor of this old Victorian house we lived in, and I'd be writing away on this novel. But I didn't get anywhere with that novel. I burned it.

Jones: Set in Yazoo City?

Morris: Well, set in the Delta, as I recall. I did get a few little things from it here and there in *North Toward Home*. But I think I wrote three novels that I burned over a period of time.

Jones: During what point in your writing life?

Morris: Ten or fifteen years ago. Sometimes you have to burn them in self-defense. I know a lot of good writers who burned their words. Of course, I wouldn't do that now. Time is too precious. If you burn a manuscript at age forty-six, you'd just as well be a staff writer for *People* magazine.

Jones: Did you destroy these after *North Toward Home?*

Morris: I think one was before, and one was after, when I left *Harper's* magazine in 1971, and moved out to the east end of Long Island to a little town called Bridgehampton. That's been almost ten years.

Jones: Was there anybody in Yazoo City that influenced you in your writing life, that was an intellectual mentor for you in Yazoo City?

Morris: Well, I had a great high school English teacher, Mrs. Omie Parker. I saw her yesterday, as a matter of fact. I dedicated this new edition of my children's book *Good Old Boy* to her. She was a marvelous high school English teacher, and a genuine taskmaster who opened up to me the whole world of language and its possibilities. She got us to reading good books, literature, and poetry. Then I guess the *Yazoo Herald* under the Motts was always good to me. But in general I think it was the whole atmosphere of growing up in a town like Yazoo City, half hills and half Delta, and all crazy, that must have brought out certain impulses.

Jones: When did you get your political education, become aware politically?

Morris: At the University of Texas. There's a fellow out there named Ronnie Dugger who had founded the *Texas Observer,* a really great little paper. It was a weekly at that time. I came under the influence of Ronnie, who was a politically active, brilliant young man several years older than I. I'd never been political before. I do remember I wrote an editorial in the Yazoo High *Flashlight* in 1948 endorsing the Dixiecrat ticket—Strom Thurmond and Fielding L. Wright, the Mississippi governor. But I became rather political there at the University of Texas running the highly controversial student newspaper, the *Daily Texan.* I then went off to Oxford, England, for four years and then came back and took over the *Texas Observer.* a political and literary journal. I think for a writer the best thing about that experience was moving about among different kinds of people, and traveling around Texas and writing a lot of words under a deadline, thousands of words every week. That was probably the toughest job I ever had, the *Texas Observer.* After my tenure running that, I was exhausted. It was a lot harder than running *Harper's,* because at *Harper's* I had good people working with me, and it was a monthly. You had the great writers contributing. But the *Texas Observer* was a marvelous experience, writing constantly about that vast and unusual state.

Jones: As editor of the *Daily Texan* as an undergraduate, did you think about returning to Mississippi and getting into journalism?

Morris: As a matter of fact, I remember some thoughts I had along those lines in Oxford, England, later. I expected to stay there two years and I ended up staying four. I got married in my third year. But I remember I wrote big Hodding Carter with the Greenville paper during my last months in England asking him if he had any jobs. He didn't at the time. I did come back to this country in the summer of 1958 and worked with Ronnie Dugger on the *Texas Observer.* Ronnie was getting tired, and he asked me to return from England and take over the paper from him. Subsequently I did that. But I certainly did have strong temptations to come back to Mississippi after England.

Jones: I've heard you say that you thought for a time about coming back and entering Mississippi politics.

Morris: Well, I think I did have some thoughts about that. I guess if I'd done that I would've come back to the Ole Miss law school and would've had quite a different life. But I don't know. I eventually stayed with the written word, and I don't have too many regrets about that.

Jones: Was Mississippi something that you felt you needed to leave at the time that you left it?

Morris: I don't think it was that conscious. One can look back over one's life and give a rationale to things that I don't think often exists in reality. You know, in retrospect you can give some kind of coherent pattern to your life, but the big decisions are often so—not haphazard—but often the creature of accident. It depends so much on the moment. But I'm glad I went back to Texas after England. I wouldn't take anything for that experience on the *Observer* and an atrocious one several months later in a place called Palo Alto, California.

Jones: Doing what?

Morris: My ex-wife had a Woodrow Wilson Fellowship and was doing graduate work in English.

Jones: At Stanford?

Morris: Yes. As I recall she had a choice between Stanford and Columbia, and we decided that we'd go out to Stanford because we'd never live on the West Coast in the natural course of things. I had a suspicion that we were going to end up in New York City anyway. I remember we were sitting at the breakfast table in Austin, Texas, one morning. I was running the *Texas Observer,* and I'd been doing some writing for *Harper's* when John Fischer was the editor. Suddenly with the morning mail came this letter from Fischer, editor of *Harper's* for a number of years. I must have been twenty-five years old, maybe twenty-six, and here was this letter from John Fischer saying quite frankly that he was looking for a successor, that he was getting tired and he liked my writing, liked the *Texas Observer,* and wondered if I would come up to New York and take a job as associate editor, and then if I worked out I would be his successor. That's a very unusual letter to get in the morning mail in Austin, Texas, when you're twenty-five, twenty-six.

Jones: Why haven't we, your readership, heard more about your experiences in Oxford?

Morris: I have down in the basement of this house a pretty good segment of a novel set in Oxford, England, about between 40,000 and 50,000 words. Actually I'm under contract now for two novels with Doubleday. One of the

books is a novel set in Oxford, England. I hope I can find the cardboard box
it's in. The other is the one I'm working on now, called *Taps.*

Jones: *Taps.*

Morris: I think what I'll do when I finish *Taps* is go back to that Oxford
book, because I like it. It begins in Chapel Hill, North Carolina. I have a first-
person protagonist who's a North Carolinian, and one of the characters is
somebody from the Mississippi Delta. It begins as a love story. My title is
The Chimes at Midnight, which is from Shakespeare. It's from a conversation
between Falstaff and Master Shallow walking along the old city wall at midnight when all the bells start ringing. Oxford is such an exotic experience for
young Americans. There have been many talented Americans at Oxford University over the years, some splendid writers. I once asked Red Warren—
Robert Penn Warren—if he'd ever written anything based on his years in
Oxford, and he said he'd never been able to get even a short poem out of it.
You go there and you're thrown into another world. My college, New College, was founded in 1386. You're living in a museum. You're overwhelmed
with this horrendous sense of the past, and then all of a sudden you're back
in your own country to make your way, and it's immensely hard to work all
that in. When I was writing *North Toward Home* I did try to bring Oxford in.
I divided that book into three parts: "Mississippi, Texas, New York." I probably should've had another section called, "America Abroad," or "America
From Abroad," or some such, and I should've tried to wrench something
about Oxford out of me for that. But I didn't do it. Maybe I'll get this novel
done. Anyway, it's one of those things.

Jones: Robert Penn Warren was a Rhodes Scholar?

Morris: Red's from Guthrie, Kentucky. I'm trying to get him down to Ole
Miss this spring with his best friend, William Styron.

Jones: I saw you and William Styron at Millsaps [College] with the governor last spring. That's where I met you for the first time. What were you
doing over there at Oxford, studying to get a master's?

Morris: Yes, I got a B.A., but at Oxford if you get a B.A., it automatically
becomes a master's after several years.

Jones: Why did you spend four years there?

Morris: Well, I think toward the end I was looking for a scholarship with
a built-in retirement plan.

Jones: With a pension.

Morris: You get so lazy over there. Nobody ever tells you what to do. I started out in a program called Philosophy, Politics, and Economics: PPE. I didn't like that too much. I couldn't deal with the British linguistic philosophy; it drove me quite mad. It didn't seem to make any sense to me. At first I thought I was dumb, then decided otherwise. So I switched to history. I always loved history. The core of history at Oxford was British history, with a touch of European history. I did a deeply intensive special course in American history covering the decade before the Civil War, which fascinated me.

Jones: The decade of the 1850s.

Morris: Yes, with Arthur Link who had the Harmsworth chair there. Herbert Nicholas, the British historian, was in charge of it. That awakened me to the history of my own country. So I spent another year there officially doing a graduate degree in American-British diplomacy in the ten or fifteen years before World War II.

Jones: Must have had A. J. P. Taylor.

Morris: No. I had Herbert Nicholas. But that was an excuse for me to stay on for another year and read anything I wanted to. The very year I got married the trustees of the Rhodes scholarships voted to allow third-year Rhodes scholars to get married and have their money. So my timing was bad. I borrowed some money from my parents. The warden at Rhodes House, a wonderful man named E. T. "Bill" Williams, who had been General Montgomery's chief of intelligence in World War II, got me my Rhodes money. I was there for my fourth year, and he called it my third. I was reading books and starting a novel that year.

Jones: You came back to Austin one summer during your study and heard from Ronnie Dugger that he was getting tired?

Morris: Yes, that was the summer of 1958. I came back that summer, worked for Ronnie, and got married. So I had a fairly good idea that I'd go back and take over the *Observer* from Ronnie.

Jones: That's a real interesting thing to happen to someone so young. Did you ever consider teaching at that time in your life?

Morris: When I left the *Texas Observer,* I was becoming immersed in American history. When we were out at Stanford, I met the distinguished American historian, David Potter. One of my heroes among the historians was C. Vann Woodward.

Jones: A great Southern historian.

Morris: I later got to know C. Vann Woodward pretty well, a wonderful man. I think for a while I conceived of myself as sort of a C. Vann Woodward of my generation. But I wouldn't have lasted in academia. I have very mixed feelings about academia.

Jones: The other voice you might hear on this tape will be Pete, Mr. Morris's black Lab who talks from time to time.

Morris: He's damned articulate, Pete. He's considerably more articulate than some of these Ole Miss coeds. Aren't you, Pete?

Jones: So you returned to the *Texas Observer*. I'm interested to ask you this: here was someone who'd grown up in Yazoo City, Mississippi, certainly a good example of the conservative Deep South, going to work on this muck-raking periodical that was certainly concerned with liberal causes; how did you make that leap?

Morris: That's a good question. I think it started at the University of Texas, running the *Daily Texan*. I could argue that the roots of Southern liberalism are deep. The *Observer* was a muckraking paper in the sense that we used investigative reporting, which Lord knows Texas needed, and still does. But it was more than that. The *Observer* had a strong literary side to it. As an editor I don't think I was as political as Ronnie Dugger. It was during my tenure on the *Observer* that I became more and more interested in the human aspect of things. There's a danger when writers get too deeply im-mersed in politics. This is not to say that writers should not be on the side of civilization, civilizing values, and all the rest. But there is a subtle danger to it, when you involve yourself too much in it. A writer, by the nature of the calling, has to be somewhat detached from himself and from life. You have to have that quality in your perception that makes you a stranger to the things and places and people you care for most. You have to be something of a stranger to the things you love the most. It has to be that way.

Jones: As editor of the *Observer* you had seen the causes come and go and had taken sides?

Morris: Yes. I was very much involved in that. There were aspects of Texas that repelled my Mississippi soul: the terrible extremes of poverty and wealth and the callousness of the oil and gas culture would offend any south-ern boy from the Delta, believe me. It was a rapacious society. I don't think it's any accident that the poor old state of Mississippi, which is ranked fiftieth in the United States economically—I was reading in the Jackson paper recently some statistics which said that Mississippi is not only fiftieth, it's so far beyond Arkansas that they say it'll never reach forty-ninth—but, to continue my thought, I don't think it's any accident that Mississippi with a population of two and a half million has produced more fine writers than the state of Texas, say, with its immense wealth and its hustling, go-getting entrepreneurial atmosphere, and its many, many more people.

Jones: Much less Arkansas.

Morris: Exactly.

Jones: At that time did you come to know Larry L. King and Larry McMurtry and all those Texas writers?

Morris: I didn't get to know Larry L. King until he was with *Harper's*. He spent considerable time in Washington as administrative assistant to a Texas congressman. I got to know Larry in Washington before I became editor-in-chief of *Harper's*. I also met McMurtry in Washington. He was writing books and running a bookstore. He owns a bookstore in Georgetown. I think McMurtry's best book is *In a Narrow Grave: Essays on Texas* [1968]. The best writer Texas has produced was Katherine Anne Porter, who was born and raised there. She was from Indian Creek, a little west of Austin. When I was an undergraduate at the University of Texas Frank Lyell from Jackson, one of Eudora's closest friends, taught me English—a wonderful teacher, a literary person in the best sense: he lived for literature. Katherine Anne Porter was coming in to give a lecture. Frank Lyell was to meet her at the airport; she was flying down from Washington or New York. I went with Frank and we met her at the airport and we were heading back toward the university, and she saw the state capitol, a beautiful building, all illuminated against the horizon, and she said, "Frank, do we have time to stop in the capitol for a minute?" We went into the rotunda, and there were tears coming down her face. Frank said, "Katherine Anne, what's wrong?" She said, "My Daddy brought me to this building when I was ten years old, and it was the first real building I ever saw."

Jones: What year did you take over the *Observer?*

Morris: I came back from England and took it over in '60.

Jones: Did you believe in John Kennedy?

Morris: I liked Kennedy. I really did like him. I liked his brother Bobby, too. I never met Jack Kennedy, although I have a number of friends who

knew him well, but I did get to know Bobby in New York. Bobby grew
tremendously.

Jones: But did your paper support Jack Kennedy?

Morris: Oh, yes, sure. Of course, that's when Lyndon Johnson was making
his serious bid for the presidency, in 1960.

Jones: Did you support Johnson?

Morris: Not for the nomination, no. The *Observer* was not representing
the liberal wing of the Democratic Party, but we certainly believed in the
things that the liberal wing of the party did. Johnson and Sam Rayburn were
the adversaries within the party. When Johnson was elected vice-president, I
made some gestures to heal the wounds. It didn't work on either side; there
were antagonisms between the establishment of the Democratic Party and the
liberals that went back many years. I liked Lyndon personally. He was a
complex man. That was before the genuine rise of the Republican Party in
Texas and the rest of the South. Many of the conservative Democrats were
siphoned off by the Republicans when they started moving. But Lyndon
Johnson was a vital presence in Austin. You'd always see his big old car
zooming around the streets at night, and you'd see him at the Mexican restaurants and at Scholz's. He was bigger than life. My friend Bill Brammer,
William Brammer, wrote a wonderful political novel with an unfortunate
title: *The Gay Place* [1961]. Bill Brammer, who's now dead, didn't know
what "gay" meant. He was just an old Texas boy. He took the title from a
poem by Scott Fitzgerald, and he wrote a fine political novel with a character
based on Lyndon Johnson. I'm a character in it: Willie England, running a
weekly newspaper in the state capital of the unidentified largest state in the
Southwest. I had just gotten back from England, and I told Brammer, I said,
"Brammer, at least Thomas Wolfe changed the names and addresses."

Jones: Lyndon Johnson was the moving force in Texas politics throughout
those years?

Morris: Yes, he was. He and Sam Rayburn. I don't think Johnson would've
ever been elected president had he not come in the way he did. I don't think
the country was ready for a southerner as president. Johnson was more of a
southwesterner, I suppose, but he sure sounded southern. He was a good
president. He got mired in the tragedy of Vietnam. But some of those pieces
of legislation he got through in the months after Jack Kennedy was killed . . .

Jones: The Civil Rights Act of '64 and the others?

Morris: They changed the face of the nation, especially the South.

Jones: Did you write every day with the *Observer?* Did you have an editorial in every paper?

Morris: Oh, more than that. We were a weekly, and I'd write long articles, sometimes ten to fifteen thousand words. There were never more than two of us on the paper. But we had some excellent people: Bob Sherrill, Bill Brammer, Larry Goodwyn, and, of course, Dugger, who was the guiding spirit of the *Observer,* and a number of others. I remember I'd end up every week out at the print shop, the Futura Press on South Congress Street, and stay up all night. We not only had to write everything, we had to make up the paper, proofread, headlines, all of it. I'd set up the typewriter next to the linotype machine and hand in my copy page by page. It was a tough job. I got a lot of nonsense out of my system, I guess. I hope so, having written that many words a week.

Jones: How did you move from a more political scope in your journalism to a more literary or artistic scope as editor of *Harper's?*

Morris: Well, I'd always loved literature. I went to work at *Harper's* as associate editor in 1963. I'm going to have to write a memoir about this. I hope that someday I'll do a sequel to *North Toward Home* called *South Toward Home.* But I want to wait awhile. I want to have a large section in there on New York City and my time at *Harper's,* with all that it symbolizes and represents for me. I joined a staff of several distinguished people who were much older. I think *Harper's* had gotten quite stodgy. I joined the staff with this understanding from John Fischer, whom I did like—he's now dead, too. I disagreed with him on a lot of things. But I did have this understanding that I would take over from him, which I eventually did. I was actually running the magazine without the title of editor for a long time. Jack Fischer would leave the country a great deal. I really wanted to get *Harper's* back to its roots, its traditions. It's the oldest magazine in the country. I wanted to return to its literary traditions by drawing on the best writers. I thought it was going to take a long time, but it didn't. I found it unexpectedly easy. The truly fine writers were ready to have a magazine like that. And I think from the point of view of the readers, a lot of Americans wanted a magazine that drew on the best literary traditions of the United States. And we did it. There was that old continuing problem with the ownership, you know: who owns the mimeograph machine? The people who did own the mimeograph ma-

chine were not among the people I respected the most. They didn't know
what literature was, or the literary or artistic impulse. So it didn't last. But
things like that don't last in America. They come and go. And the magazine
business itself is in a condition of flux, getting harder and harder economically—increased printing costs, a damaging policy on the part of the federal
government on postal rates, and all the rest. Now, in 1980, the magazine
business is in a squeeze, as seen by the decline of the general interest magazine and the upsurge of the specialized magazine such as those aimed toward
doctors who fly their own planes and drive blue Mercedeses and like to ski
in Aspen.

Jones: Did you want to leave Texas?

Morris: I was ready to leave. I believe I have in my concluding pages of
North Toward Home a description of my contrasting feelings on Texas and
Mississippi. My feelings for Mississippi were always much more abiding. I
learned a lot there in Texas, I got educated there and still have many good
friends there. It just doesn't have the dark shadows for me that Mississippi
does.

Jones: Where were you when John Kennedy was killed?

Morris: I was out to lunch in New York. I was alone. It was a Friday, and
I returned to the office. Most of the older editors would take off Friday afternoon and go home early. I think I was the only male in the office. All the
secretaries started sobbing. One of them said Kennedy and Johnson had both
been killed. But I got this phone call before they started crying, and it was
from this law professor at Columbia who'd written an article for *Harper's*. It
was going to press. It had some kind of time element on it. It was about
Kennedy's appointees to the federal bench. This man called me from Columbia University law school and said, "Have you heard the news? Kennedy and
Johnson have both been killed in Dallas." I said, "My God!" And he said,
"Well, I hate to tell you this, but I was only calling to see if this was going
to have any effect on my article." Evan Thomas, who was a prominent editor
at Harper and Row—we shared the same floor with the top editors of the
publishing company—came in and said, "We're President Kennedy's publisher and we're going to close down the house today."

Jones: In *North Toward Home,* in your New York section, you write about
going to parties given for literary celebrities, and you talk about how alienated you felt at those parties. I wanted to ask you how you came in touch

with people you saw at those parties, like Norman Mailer, whose "The Prisoner of Sex" [*Harper's,* March 1971] you ran.

Morris: We also did Norman's book-length piece that won the Pulitzer Prize, which we called "The Steps of the Pentagon" [*Harper's,* March 1968]. In this book he changed the title to *The Armies of the Night* [1968] from the Matthew Arnold poem "Dover Beach." New York City probably seems intimidating to people who've not lived there, but it's really a small world. In the literary and publishing world everybody gets to know everybody else. And I got to know Mailer, eventually quite well. We were friends, and I think we still are. We worked closely together on some of his best work, maybe his very best. You'd run into people at parties. There's an interesting story about how Mailer did this longest magazine article in history: "The Steps of the Pentagon." I remember it was the morning after Houghton Mifflin had given me the big publication party for *North Toward Home,* which would've been in October of '67, in one of those fancy hotels on upper Madison Avenue. They had hundreds of people there, the whole of New York's literary and journalistic establishment, including many of my dear friends: Bill and Rose Styron and Larry King, Dave Halberstam, that group. The next morning I got to my office hung over, and Cass Canfield, who ran Harper and Row, called me on the phone and said, "Norman Mailer's been arrested in Virginia. I hear he's going to do a 10,000-word magazine article on it," this being, of course, during the height of the Vietnam war. So I got on the phone. I couldn't get Mailer, whom I knew, but I got his agent. We talked on the phone all day without even talking to Mailer, and we settled the deal. I think it was 20,000 words for $10,000. And as such things often happen in that strange and intoxicating city, I had to go to the Algonquin Hotel and meet somebody for drinks after work—I think it was the old fellow who wrote the column for the *Commercial Appeal* in Memphis, who had a few bourbons and told me I'd sold out the South—and I was walking up Eighth Avenue toward the subway stop at about six in the afternoon, and who did I run into but Mailer. I said, "Dammit, Norman, we've settled this deal." He said, "I know. I'm gonna write you the finest 20,000 words you've ever had. I'm going to Provincetown tomorrow and start on it, and I'll have it to you one month from today." Well, one month to the day I flew up there in a little plane, and he had 90,000 words. I called up my managing editor Bob Kotlowitz, because we were facing a deadline. And I said, "Bob, we've got 90,000 pretty good words up here." Kotlowitz said, "Great. How many should we run, do you think?" I said, "I think we ought to run them all." He said, "Oh, you do? In three or four installments?" I said, "No, I think we should shoot our wad, run it all at once," and there was this silence on the phone. Longest magazine article in history. But also as a matter of course you'd get to know many of the best writers, such as William Styron, who became one of my dearest friends. I'd actually wanted to meet him, and I knew the only way to meet Bill, whom I'd admired so much through his first novel, *Lie Down In Darkness* [1951], was to get him to write for the magazine. So that's how we met. He was working on *The Confessions of Nat Turner* [1967].

Jones: Yes, and he wrote "This Quiet Dust" for you.

Morris: Yes, that's what it was. I put out a special issue of *Harper's* in April of 1965. God, it was a wonderful issue.

Jones: *The South Today.*

Morris: *The South Today: 100 Years After Appomattox.* I wrote Bill in Connecticut and asked him to write a 5,000-word piece on what it was like being a southerner in the North, you know, all the ironies of that. He said he'd be glad to. The day of the deadline this manuscript came in, and it wasn't 5,000 words, it was 15,000, and it wasn't about.a southerner living in the North, it was about his obsession with slavery and the Nat Turner rebellion. We put the title on it, "This Quiet Dust," from a memorable little poem by Emily Dickinson.

Jones: About going to the old house where Nat committed his first murder?

Morris: Finding the old house. I've subsequently been there. My son David is fast becoming a great photographer. And a writer, too, though he doesn't know it yet. He will, bless him. Several years ago David and I and an old peanut farmer named Dean Waggenback, who has a farm right on the North Carolina-Virginia line, which is Nat Turner country, went around with a local historian who showed us everything, all these old houses. David got some memorable pictures of the Whitehead house, where Nat committed his only murder—killed Miss Margaret Whitehead, the belle of the county, with a fencepost. You've got to go up there sometime. Those houses are falling in. They're not close enough to any city where rich people would come out and renovate them and live in them on weekends. They're lying there in decay—the Whitehead house and all the others where this incredible rebellion took place. David got a whole group of distinctive photographs of the houses and the countryside, the brooding peanut country. Good old David was fifteen then. He developed them and mounted them, and we gave them to Bill Styron on his birthday.

Jones: That's something that the house is still there. He wrote that article in '65.

Morris: Yes. And we were there about five years ago, and it was still there. Our peanut farmer friend Dean Waggenback wanted to buy it. He could've bought it for $15,000 with a little land. We were going to do some repairs and engineer a trick on Styron. We were going to have Styron and his wife Rose down and have a little party at the Whitehead house. Actually on that trip my son and my peanut farmer friend and I visited all the battlefields, including, of course, Appomattox, which is a touching place.

Jones: I loved what you wrote in *James Jones: A Friendship* about your visit to Antietam.

Morris: Oh yes. That was Jim Jones and his boy and my boy and me. At that time I was on a stint with the *Washington Star* as a guest columnist. That was in '76, our bicentennial year. I wrote a syndicated column for them three times a week. I don't know why I did that, because I was really out of practice on deadlines. But I'm glad I did it if for no other reason than that trip the four of us took through the Civil War country. Jim Jones died about a year after that.

Jones: I wanted to ask you about the idea behind *The South Today: 100 Years After Appomattox.* Was it your project?

Morris: Yes, I guess so. It's such a hallowed anniversary, and I figured something could be said of some note on the occasion. It was a very fine magazine issue. You know, magazine issues don't have long lives, they're like cotton candy: they taste good but don't last too long. That's why magazine editors are as a breed singularly curious people. The ones who don't write themselves tend to be a little jumpy. So do book editors who don't write, because they have to exist through someone else's work. But in capturing a moment a magazine can be important to the consciousness of a society. This one particular issue, this *Harper's* issue of April, 1965, was as fine an issue as any American magazine in this century.

Jones: How did you get Walker Percy to contribute?

Morris: I didn't know Walker at the time. I was a great admirer of his, of his first novel *The Moviegoer,* which I read shortly after it came out in 1961. Then when I was running *Harper's,* I think maybe it was before I became

editor, we ran a sizeable portion of his book, *The Last Gentleman* [1966].
Before that I persuaded Walker to do a piece on "Mississippi: The Fallen
Paradise" [*Harper's,* April 1965]. Later on I got Walker to do a wonderful
piece on New Orleans ["New Orleans Mon Amour," *Harper's,* September
1968]. And he did some other things for us. I had a feeling at *Harper's* that
you had to approach the best writers between books when most writers are
in the mood to do something they can see in print in two or three months.
And it worked. It worked with some of the best writers of our day: Styron,
Percy, Mailer, Ellison, and I got the playwright Arthur Miller to contribute,
and you can go right on down the list, the most courageous and splendid
writers of our day in America. I met Walker—went to visit him in Covington,
Louisiana—and then he came up to New York once or twice. We had a hangout. At this time I was living on Long Island. I'd left the city. When people
would come to town—Jim and Gloria Jones from Europe, or the Styrons
from Connecticut, and others—we'd always stay at the Blackstone Hotel on
Fifty-eighth Street between Park and Madison. It was inexpensive, and they
knew us and were good to us, knew we were all crazy writers. And they had
a good bar called the Dogwood Room, which we changed to the Dogpatch.
Walker came up to be a judge on the National Book Awards. He doesn't like
New York City at all. He's like me. I have reservations about Manhattan
Island myself. I've even got reservations about Memphis. Hell, Tupelo's too
big. Walker came up, and I remember bringing him over to the Dogpatch
Room. He hadn't met Styron or Jim Jones or these people. We took over the
whole bar, and my friend Bobby Van, a restaurateur from Bridgehampton,
started playing the piano. We all ended up at P. J. Clarke's and closed down
the place.

Jones: About what year was this?

Morris: Early '70s: '72, '73.

Jones: Well, *The South Today* came out in hardback. You were also able
to get C. Vann Woodward to contribute.

Morris: Vann Woodward, Louis Rubin, Jonathan Daniels, and did we have
Ralph Ellison in there?

Jones: No.

Morris: Well, I subsequently got to know Ralph Ellison quite well. Ellison
and I came to Jackson once. We gave a joint lecture at Millsaps.

Jones: What year was that?

Morris: I think this would have been '69 or '70. We brought the young son of the president of Random House down who was a student at Brown University and was thinking about doing an exchange program at Tougaloo. This Yankee kid, his eyes were opened when he came to Mississippi.

Jones: Ellison had a tough time at Tougaloo in '68 when he was shouted down by the militants for his commitment to being an artist first and then a black.

Morris: Was that in '68?

Jones: '68.

Morris: Well, that was not the same visit. We came down together later. Ellison always fought for the artistic imagination. *Invisible Man* [1952] is one of the towering novels of American literature.

Jones: Let me ask you this: during the time when you were with the *Observer* and then beginning with *Harper's,* the civil rights movement was ripping the Mississippi of your boyhood apart at the seams and changing the lives of everyone who was here during those years. How did that affect you or your art?

Morris: You're talking about the early '60s?

Jones: Yes.

Morris: The height of it?

Jones: Right. All the violence of '63, '64, '65.

Morris: Well, you see, I witnessed that from afar on the television screen in New York City.

Jones: How did it make you feel?

Morris: It affected me profoundly, as I suppose it would any civilized southerner or American. I was torn up by it, literally torn up piece by piece. But, of course, I was not here during the middle of it. Witnessing from afar those events on one's home ground was a devastating experience for me. I later got to know many of the people involved. I was in Austin, Texas, when the James Meredith event hit this campus.

Jones: One hundred yards away.

Morris: Right up the road. I almost came over. It's been eighteen years, and, of course, the changes that have taken place all around us here on this campus are interesting to observe. I often wonder what William Faulkner would think going over to the Old Miss Coliseum and seeing 60 percent of the Old Miss basketball team black. He would've gone to watch, too.

Jones: Yes. That's really part of what I was asking. As a Mississippi writer who grew up before this happened, how the changes in the very fiber of the state of Mississippi brought on by the movement changed the way you approached your art that is so deeply rooted in place.

Morris: Yes. Well, let me make another point first. I always had a strong feeling that grew in me more and more in the late '60s that the important thing for the Deep South, and especially Mississippi, that was both symbolic and substantial, was the massive integration of the public schools. When that came in 1970 I wrote a little book about it called *Yazoo*. I had to come back to see that. I was in charge of a national magazine at the time, and I had to be far away from the office to do it. I wish I'd have had another four or five months on that book. I couldn't take the time; I was running a magazine. Once that happened, even given all the shortcomings of it, and the private academies and the failures and everything, it ushered in a whole new period. It took a lot of pressure off of people, including white people, in the Deep South. Mississippi is not the tense place it was, you know, the wrought-up, tense place obsessed with one issue: race, which it was. This has all taken place in the last ten or twelve years. Not to say that this is a paradise, but, hell, nothing under the Lord's sun is paradise.

Jones: Do you think the civil rights movement will have an effect on Mississippi's tradition of spawning many great writers, the home of Faulkner and Miss Welty and the whole list? Do you think the unquestionableness of the race question for so many years is what perhaps created that climate?

Morris: No, it's part of a much larger fabric, and the larger fabric is that of a basically communal society with a storytelling tradition, with blacks living among us so close giving it its flamboyance and color, so to speak, and its guilt, and its substance. The more sizeable question in future years for Mississippi and Mississippi writers and southern writers is, can this kind of heritage continue to elicit good writing. I don't want to see the suburbs of Memphis get down here as far as Yoknapatawpha County. I don't want to see the New South in Holly Springs. I have mixed feelings about the New South. You can get off at the Atlanta airport, that whole modern cosmos, and you *still* know you're in the South. Yet I feel in my soul that southern writing will endure.

Jones: You know, I'm just beginning to read the kind of book you've probably read a hundred times, that's trying to explain the great outpouring of southern writing from '25 to '55. Some people say it's the race question in Mississippi and the Deep South, and the fact that it was intractable. Other people say it's a question of coming to grips with history, setting history, the difficult history of the South, to rest. Others say it's the problem of the southern family romance. I don't know.

Morris: Well, which came first, John, the chicken or the egg, to use the terrible cliché. It's all a part of it. I remember the first question I got on my final examinations at Oxford University, which lasted about six hours a day for two weeks; it just so happened that my first essay question covered that period from 1850 to 1861 in American history, which haunted me for a year. They'd give you twenty questions on each of many papers, and you were required to answer, I think, four essay questions, so you had a choice. You had to dress up in an awful stiff white shirt with a tie and a blue suit and a gown and mortarboard, and they wouldn't let you smoke in this big Victorian examination hall in Oxford. I was chewing bubble gum, and these Englishmen around me accused me of making them do poorly because of my bubble gum. I even brought in some chewing tobacco to the examination hall at Oxford University; first time I'd chewed tobacco since my baseball-playing days back in the Mississippi Delta. It was even "Brown Mule," which I'd bought at the PX of an American air base. I brought a little paper cup and was writing these history questions and spitting. These Englishmen didn't like that either. But the first question was: "Was the American Civil War fought over the black man?" And I looked at that question and said, "Oh, Goddammit." And then I never even finished it. I wrote the whole three hours on that single question. I think I got the equivalent of an A+ on it, even though I only wrote on this one question. So what's the answer? The blacks by their very presence, the whole history of the institution of slavery, made the South different. One of the impulses to the truly distinguished southern fiction over the years has derived from *differentness;* the fact that the South was both a part of the broader American civilization, and removed from it. And it still is removed from it, even though up here on Sorority Row last month in November of 1980 all you saw were Reagan stickers. The South still is somewhat removed from it. And the Ole Miss coeds, whom I call "goldfish," are certainly different. You know why I call them "goldfish"?

Jones: Why?

Morris: If you've ever watched goldfish in a bowl, they love for you to look at them, they dart around a lot, they don't think too much, and they don't like to be still for too very long, and then when you put your hand down in the bowl to touch one of them they swim away furiously. Oh, well—just an observation.

Jones: That's it. I did a really interesting interview with Evans Harrington up here about the changes that have come about since Meredith, and he said the Ole Miss coed today is no different from the Ole Miss coed of 1961; it's just that being polite to blacks is part of her repertoire now, whereas she'd always been polite to rednecks.

Morris: Evans and I've talked about that, and I think there's truth to it. They're polite now the way they used to be to the Snopeses. It's fascinating, the ironies you see here. I'm really intrigued with Old Miss. I love the place. A state university is supposed to be a reflection of the state that nurtures it. The greatness of Ole Miss lies in places other than the classroom. The ironies that you observe here! I was sitting one afternoon in the bleachers of the baseball field. Sometimes I'd go over there last spring in the sunshine and grade my papers and watch my friend Jake Gibbs, the Ole Miss coach, and his squad work out. There were these four black Ole Miss basketball players whom I recognized from the games—the season was over and they were going to the gym to jog or something—being led by Sean Tuohy, the white, playmaking guard from New Orleans. "Now boys, now come on, let's go. Come on!" There was an interesting moment at the Ole Miss-Mississippi State football game. Were you there in the rain?

Jones: Yes, in the end zone.

Morris: Yes, a couple of weeks ago. There was a moment that was actually more important than the game. A black male cheerleader, the first Ole Miss black male cheerleader, who's a freshman now—they unveil their freshman cheerleaders the last game of the season—holding up the white coed cheerleader. I hear he got some shouts, too. He works for my friend William Lewis who owns Neilson's, and the kid told William that he got some taunts, people yelled at him and the white girl.

Jones: Have you ever read the poem by a college professor, "To Aphrodite On Your Leaving"?

Morris: No. Is it about the Ole Miss coeds?

Jones: It's about coeds in general.

Morris: Did you ever read Terry Southern's classic piece in *Esquire* about the Old Miss baton twirling clinic ["Twirling at Ole Miss," *Esquire*, February 1963]?

Jones: No.

Morris: Look that up sometime.

Jones: To return to what we were talking about earlier. Here you were in New York City running a magazine that I'm sure was running you crazy; how did you ever find time to sit down and write up *North Toward Home?*

Morris: I took a leave of absence for several months. I remember I had to go to the bank and borrow money because I wasn't getting paid by *Harper's.* I had a certain amount of it already written. This would've been in 1966. There was a wonderful editor with Houghton Mifflin in Boston, Dorothy de Santillana. We started corresponding back when I was with the *Texas Observer.* She wanted me to do a book. They had and still have the most distinguished prize for first books, called the Houghton Mifflin Literary Fellowship.

Jones: Which *North Toward Home* won.

Morris: That's right. They've given it to some good people: Robert Penn Warren, Philip Roth, Bill Brammer, a lot of people.

Jones: Ellen Douglas, who's teaching here this semester, won one.

Morris: I think Elizabeth Spencer got one also. Dorothy wanted me to apply for that. I got it on the basis of an outline. But I remember I wrote the bulk of *North Toward Home* in an apartment we had on West End Avenue and Ninety-fourth Street. I wrote a good part of it on a big table in the kitchen. I think I wrote the first draft of the Mississippi part in about three weeks. I later had to go back and do a lot of work on it, of course. I do remember that my leave of absence ended, and Jack Fischer and others wanted me to come back to work, and I hadn't written my New York section. So I'd do that on weekends and at night. We bought an old farmhouse north of New York around Brewster. I'd go out there and work on it.

Jones: And ride the commuter train.

Morris: I did that one summer with an Ole Miss man named Bob Childres, whom I'd known at the other Oxford, now also dead. Everybody seems to be dead these days. Childres and I were close friends, and our wives were close, so we bought a farmhouse up where they had a place sixty miles north of Manhattan. Bob Childres and I commuted all summer, the summer of '66, I think. By the end of the summer we were wrecks. We'd try to meet for the 4:29 Express for Brewster in Grand Central Station. We'd always meet in the bar car. The last day of that hot terrible summer—it was two hours each

way—we sat down and ordered two big gin and tonics, and as I recall Childres had to wear a bowler hat. He was practicing law at Thomas E. Dewey's.
We didn't say anything for about five minutes and the train pulled out, and
finally Childres turned around and said, "Goddammit, Morris, what are two
old Mississippi boys doing up here commuting, being commuters?" But
North Toward Home—it struck a strange chord somewhere, and not just in
the South. I got literally thousands of letters from all over the country. I think
one of the reasons I got so many was that I was accessible when the book
came out; you know, I was at *Harper's* and had a mailing address. I don't
know what it was.

Jones: Everyone I know has read it.

Morris: Well, I've had that experience too; everybody's read the thing. Of
course, I guess that's what writing's for.

Jones: Where did the impulse come from to sit down and write up your
memoirs at thirty?

Morris: I don't know. I had a lot to say. I had stories I wanted to tell.
That's where the impulse comes from: your memory. Writing is memory, the
burden of memory. It's a big burden. You exorcise the demons.

Jones: Was there any autobiography that you read during that period that
gave you special inspiration, such as *Lanterns on the Levee?*

Morris: Of course I read *Lanterns on the Levee* [1941]. I'll tell you one
that really did impress me: it was an early book by Mark Twain called *Roughing It* [1872].

Jones: Yes, about his experiences gold mining and such.

Morris: Yes, going out to the West. The first half of that book is one of
the best memoirs in American literature. It falls apart in the end for some
reason. But that book summoned me, as if Mark Twain were whispering
something private to me, just between the two of us, saying: "Hey, kid, do
it." Autobiographical writing is a sturdy strain in American letters. *The Autobiography of Lincoln Steffens* [1931], I remember I loved that. *Lanterns on
the Levee* is a fascinating book. *A Moveable Feast* [1964] by Hemingway.

Jones: Cruel book.

Morris: It was a cruel book, a posthumous book. A lot of posthumous
books are cruel.

Jones: Tell me how sitting down and writing nonfiction differs from writing fiction.

Morris: It's easier. Fiction has to have a flow to it over a long period of time. Nonfiction is quite different, of course, and easier. The patterns are more systematic.

Jones: You were saying that there were parts of *North Toward Home* that you would change today if you could.

Morris: Well, anything you look back on that you've written years ago, your natural impulse is to improve the language. I guess you get better as you get older, I don't know. You certainly accumulate more experience, which should have wisdom inherent in it, and writing is an expression of everything you know. But in putting out some of these nonfiction pieces of mine that Larry Wells is publishing next spring. I've come across things that I'd forgotten I'd ever written. That's a funny feeling. I had to go back and reread some parts of *North Toward Home* and *Yazoo*, and even my memoir of Jim Jones, that I'd forgotten I'd written. Especially parts of *North Toward Home*. I think my first feeling was: "Hey, this is pretty good." But not having read any of it since you wrote it is an exceedingly strange feeling. Of course you have a temptation to change your hard-earned words, but you have to go with what you were at a given moment, what you were thinking about, what you were obsessed with, who you really were. You can't tamper with yourself. You have to grow with your own work.

Pete's getting on this tape, barking at the kids out on Faculty Row. This may mystify some ascetic scholar of the year 2075. He's the best dog in the world. He'd come to my classes at Ole Miss last spring. One day I thought I was being quite intelligent on something that had to do with American fiction, and Pete, my dog and brother, was up on the top row of the lecture hall lying down next to my friend Dean Faulkner Wells, and in the middle of the sentence I was coming out with I heard this gasping yawn that reverberated through the lecture hall, and I thought, "Oh, my God, I'm just putting them to sleep." It was my dog Pete yawning. He'd heard it all before. When my friend Pete dies, I die.

Jones: Did your experience at *Harper's* sour you on journalism?

Morris: No, it didn't sour me. I was unhappy for a while. I missed the perquisites of high station. I missed my two secretaries, one Jewish, one black, and the "appurtenances of power," in quotes, like Manhattan expense accounts. But it didn't sour me on journalism or magazines. It buttressed certain things I'd always felt: never put too much trust in rich people, especially rich Yankee Wasps.

Jones: You've had first-hand experience with real repression of a type that few people in this country experience. At the *Daily Texan* you were censured as an undergraduate editor. At *Harper's* you were in conflict with the people who represented the money behind the magazine, and you resigned over the mention of censorship. I was wondering how that affected your sensibilities.

Morris: I ain't bitter, just reflective. Any time you get close to the heart of things, to the source of human things, you're going to run into this trouble, especially when you have a reckless regard for the things that you have to hold up. As my friend James Dickey would say, sometimes a man has to be reckless in behalf of the qualities he cares for passionately. And say, what the hell? This is a democratic society where the First Amendment works most of the time. I guess the ideal situation at an institution like *Harper's* in those years was to have owned the mimeograph machine yourself. But it takes money to own the mimeograph machine. Of course money controls; on a national scale, the young editor must find the right money. It's hard. It's draining to deal with rich owners, especially when you don't talk the same language about your own civilization. Putting those years at *Harper's* in their context, I do think we said something about the America of that day, the exacerbated mood of the country during the Vietnam years, and I do think we tried to stand for something civilized. We had a good magazine, maybe the best of our generation. But, as I say, these things come and go.

Jones: Where did you get the idea for *Yazoo?*

Morris: I saw a little piece in the *New York Times*. This federal court order had come out of New Orleans in December '69, and it caught my eye, buried on a back page. This was, of course, sixteen years after Brown vs. Board of Education of 1954. The South had fought this through the thickets of the law for sixteen years, but the federal court order out of New Orleans was it. I wanted to be down at home to see and to observe the consequences. I'm glad I did. It was a fascinating moment. It was sad, and funny, as most important moments are.

Jones: You certainly froze it in time.

Morris: I think the book was fair enough. Historians are going to have to use it. I just wish I'd had maybe four more months, which I simply couldn't take due to the circumstances of my profession at the time. But I'm pleased with it. It's in a way a continuation of *North Toward Home.*

Jones: Was it in *North Toward Home* or *Yazoo* when you talk about going to the Citizens' Council meeting?

Morris: That was in the first book. That would've been in the summer of 1955. They had an organizing meeting of the Citizens' Council in Yazoo City then.

Jones: After seeing that kind of recalcitrance, did you think by 1970 that desegregation could come about peacefully?
Morris: No. Quite the contrary, I saw violence in the future. What did Big Hodding Carter call the Citizens' Council? The Ku Klux Klan with a clipped moustache. It was the establishment. Eventually the courts had to win out.

Jones: I've been doing a project on the civil rights movement in Mississippi, and I've always been amazed how over just five years from the violence and bloodshed of 1964 there could've been a turnabout in Mississippi. I would've thought the old segregationists would have to die out before it could be done peacefully. But it is remarkable that in five years, an incredibly short period of time in terms of history, this could have happened.
Morris: It really is. I think it had something to do with having no more choices. Once the inevitable arrived, the Deep South by and large responded very well. It responded from its finer instincts—as Abraham Lincoln said in his inaugural, "the better angels of our nature." It's one of the most interesting things to watch, the ramifications of the things you see, like Sean Tuohy and the black basketball players, and the black cheerleader. Cleve Donald was the second black to attend Ole Miss after Meredith, and he's been my neighbor across the street over here on Faculty Row. He's on a leave of absence in Washington now. Cleve and I have had some pretty good talks drinking beer here or at his house.

Jones: He's an interesting man.
Morris: Yes, I like Cleve. I miss him.

Jones: He was deeply involved with Medgar Evers down in Jackson.
Morris: Yes, that's right. I hope he's doing a book on Medgar Evers. He's done a fine essay on Evers. The University Press of Mississippi has done a book called *Mississippi Heroes* [1980], which Dean Faulkner Wells edited and asked me to do a little introduction to. That essay is included.

Jones: You know in your book *Yazoo* you talk about Melvin Leventhal and meeting him, an NAACP attorney, and his wife Alice Walker in Jackson. Mel Leventhal wrote a criticism of *Yazoo* where he said you were only interested in desegregation in terms of the white community.

Morris: That was a congressional hearing, wasn't it?

Jones: I don't know.

Morris: I think it was. Maybe Mel Leventhal had to say that. Hell, he was protecting his political flanks. Don't blame him. The book itself may last longer than Mel Leventhal. I believe he did say that my main interest was the white community. Well, I'm white, and I suppose that bias was inevitable. I'll stand by the book. I think I was basically right in that book. *Yazoo* is two throws away from being a classic, even if I say it myself. I'm always surprised that there's been so little good nonfiction on this subject. Surprisingly little—Marshall Frady's done some good things on this. I made some presumptions at the time that I'm not too sure about now. I think I underestimated the efficacy and the durability of the white private academies. That was probably the biggest flaw in that book. That and the durability of great poverty on any kind of civilizing change.

Jones: I think everybody was saying at the time that no one could afford to send their three or four kids to private schools from grades one through twelve, not in Mississippi.

Morris: Yes, I thought so.

Jones: But I've always been amazed at how accurate you've been in your presumptions and predictions, not only in *Yazoo*. I saw an interview done with you in June of '73, fully a year before Richard Nixon's resignation, where you said impeachment is a nineteenth-century procedure and that there's no way our system could stand it, but that the president would effectively be rendered of his power to the point where he'd have to resign.

Morris: Did I say that?

Jones: Yes. You predicted the outcome of Watergate precisely, fully a year before it ended with Nixon's resignation.

Morris: Where was I when I said that?

Jones: On the ETV *A Conversation With* series with Howard Lett, when you were talking about *The Last of the Southern Girls*.

Morris: Oh, that's right. I remember that, down in Jackson.

Jones: You did. And you were one of the first people I ever read that said that Mississippi would be the land where racial reconciliation, in whatever form it was going to take, would occur.

Morris: Yes, I think I was the first person who said that, and some people criticized it then.

Jones: I think it's true.

Morris: I do too. There's a long way to go, though. Of course, the person who really understood this so well in his generation was Faulkner. There's no more revealing a story—it's one of my favorite short stories—"Delta Autumn." You know, the story about Uncle Ike McCaslin's last hunt, and the mulatto woman who comes with the baby to the hunting camp. There's a resonance in that story. Mr. Bill knew what he was talking about. And of course the northern liberals gave him hell. There's a word called *prescience.*

Jones: It's in Percy's book, *The Last Gentleman,* on every other page: "the prescient engineer."

Morris: Yes, some people don't like prescience.

Jones: Do you still believe in desegregation?

Morris: I'll tell you what I do believe in strongly is *access,* having access to the institutions, the public institutions. Desegregation may not be working terribly well in Mississippi right now, or on the Ole Miss campus. You know the two institutions in Oxford where desegregation is working the best? The athletic department at Ole Miss and the bar at the Holiday Inn. Have you ever been in the bar of the Holiday Inn with Clyde Goosby, the black bartender?

Jones: Yes, I went there in college.

Morris: The schools in a democratic society had to be desegregated, had to be open to blacks. Even if there are places that are 90 percent black, and there are schools out in Yazoo County that are 90 percent black.

Jones: Hell, in Jackson.

Morris: In Jackson and various places, the public institutions are open to them. That's coming a long way. And it happened ten years ago. The northern liberals laughed at William Faulkner in the mid-1950s in an interview he had with *Reporter* magazine, and he later claimed he was drunk when he gave the interview ["A Talk with William Faulkner," *Reporter*, March 22, 1956]. They asked him what he thought was the future of race relations in the South, desegregation and all that, and he replied that it's not going to be so much a matter down here of whether the whites want it, it's going to be a matter of whether the blacks want it. And, of course, the northern liberals laughed at him and called him an old Mississippi fool. He was right. Maybe the blacks don't want it, but at least given the great sweep of history, let's give them the choice. If they don't want it, fine. Mississippi is about the only state in America that cares about all this anyway. Even the old conservatives are somewhat bemused. Why not? It's an interesting society. Even the old racists are fascinating. All this crazy stuff is an expression of why Mississippi is the most interesting state in the Union. This is a funny time here, and very touching. Let's keep our eyes open and not forget how to laugh and cry, maybe at the same time. At least we care. Who gives a damn but crazy old Mississippi? Who cares in Wilkes-Barre?

Jones: Mr. Faulkner said, "The whites have already lost their heads. It's now up to the blacks whether they'll keep theirs."
Morris: He knew what he was talking about, Mr. Bill.

Jones: Are you very distressed at the attacks on busing and school desegregation with the new conservative tide? In *Yazoo* you manifested a strong belief in the possibilities of desegregation in Mississippi. Do you still believe in those possibilities?
Morris: Yes, I do, I suppose. As I say, I think a lot of it will depend on the black attitude. You know, it's still so early. I hear stories all the time about the friendship between white and black kids here at Oxford High School: white and black kids playing sports together, going to parties. This is bound, over the long stretch, to have an effect on the next generation and the generation after that. It's up to them, what they want here. After all, we're talking about civilization, which is the hardest, most precarious thing in the world, people trying to be kind to each other, reasonably tolerable. And this is a biracial society, by God, or the closest America has to one. Good for it! Human beings tend, of course, by our nature to be so much the creatures of our own time, of our own generation. That's also part of being human. We're creatures of our own moment. I've always been a student of history, and I don't believe in the inevitability of anything. I don't have too many set theories about history, except that history goes on. It does that. It goes on and on.

Jones: Let me ask you this: you had always been a man of social convictions and worked with social concerns in your days with the *Observer* and *Harper's*. Was it hard to put that all aside when you sat down to write *The Last of the Southern Girls?*
Morris: Not really. I guess it's a matter of one's role. I had this notion when I went to work for *Harper's* that a man could be both an editor and a writer. I think I got this idea from the nineteenth century. I thought I could be like William Dean Howells, you know, who was editor of both the *Atlantic* and *Harper's*, and a writer. I was wrong. In the nineteenth century, among

other things, they didn't have telephones. You can become the victim of telephones. That's why I hate talking on the phone. Sometimes I put it in the
refrigerator. It's because of my days on *Harper's*. I'd go out to the men's
room and come back and there'd be eight messages, none of which mattered;
but it didn't take me very long to be disabused of that idea of the dual role.
You can't be both a magazine editor and a writer. The functions of the two,
far from supplementing each other, are mutually antagonistic for me. It was
good for me to get out, to be on my own and not be the editor anymore. It's
a young man's profession, being an editor.

Jones: Really?

Morris: I've seen too many people get old in that profession, or too ideological, or too spoiled by one's self-importance. An editor ain't really all that
important, when you get right down to it. You really are an expression of
other people. You live through other people's work. And if you're a writer,
no one's going to help you. You're on your own with no one to help you.
This has both its rewards and its hazards. It's lonesome. You get scared to
death sometimes. Especially when you're between books and the money's
not coming in and you're paying $15,000 a year tuition, or $12,000 up at
Amherst, Massachusetts, and your agent hasn't sold your latest magazine
piece quite yet. You've got to keep your dog in Alpo. Right, Pete? But the
rewards are the rewards of being your own person. I'd rather sleep til noon
than commute on a train every day. So I guess looking back on it I was
probably ready to leave. I missed it for a while. The question of the social
role, being political and everything, I've never really dwelt on that too much.
I don't miss that activist role at all. At *Harper's* we weren't directly political,
of course. As for writing, I believe in it, and I've some good books in me
before I hang my saddle on the wall.

Jones: Certainly. May I ask you just a few more questions?
Morris: Sure.

Jones: Would you have fought for the South in the Civil War?
Morris: I've thought about that. I guess I would've. So would Foote and
Whitehead and Hannah and Percy—and in fact all the present-day Percys of
Mississippi. Shelby's already served twenty years of labor on his *Civil War*
[*The Civil War: A Narrative*, 1958, 1963, 1974]. He knows the passion and
blood. Hell, so does Walker. So does Eudora. That war is the thread which
runs through us as a civilization. You've got to understand that war, all of it,

to understand America—the greatness and sadness of America. Our tragedy and promise and redemption. I'd have opposed that war, just as Shelby and Walker and Eudora would've. But when it happened, we'd have been with the South. How could we not? Shelby would've got it at Shiloh, which is fitting, Barry at Corinth, Whitehead at Iuka, Walker at Spotsylvania. With luck I'd have lasted till Petersburg. Eudora, our nurse in the hospitals, would've survived us and written some words about it—sad words, but some ironic and funny ones too, great words—remembrance, which she does anyway. We'd have been fighting over a lot more than slavery. As Faulkner said, the love of the land mattered most, all that. Sure, I'd have fought and died, though with some considerable reluctance. Wouldn't you? Time has dealt with us here.

Jones: Will you go on writing?

Morris: I don't know what else to do. I hate wearing a shirt and tie. They make my neck itch. I really do like to sleep till noon. I loathe committee meetings. I like taking a leak outdoors. I can't tolerate office hours. I can't suffer the organized fools. I like sitting down on an afternoon and dwelling upon the things I care about, or remember with feeling, and then trying to give a little sense to them. Moments of passion remembered in times of tranquility, Henry James said.

Jones: So words give you strength?

Morris: Well, again I don't have an alternative. I have no alternative to words. I guess they're better than sex. They last, though sex and words are good together.

Jones: If your great-grandson and great-granddaughter came into these state archives in Jackson, Mississippi, many years from now to read these words transcribed from this tape, is there anything you'd add for their eyes?

Morris: I'd certainly like my great-grandson or -daughter to read them. I'd want my great-grandson or great-granddaughter to know that I love and care for them deep in my heart, even though I'll never know them. I'd want them to know they're on my mind. I'd want them to feel that human life, at its best, is a cycle of love. I'd want them to care passionately for the presence of the past—you know, the little moments and the big historic ones. I'd like them to go to the cemeteries in Yazoo City and Raymond. I'd like them to care about their fellow human beings, maybe in an Old Testament sense— that we're all in it together, and all in for a tough time. They'll learn soon

enough that to live is to suffer, that there are places in our hearts in which
suffering must enter. I'd like them to care passionately, however, for the fine
moments of life—all of them—and to savor life's immemorial delights, and
to not let much guilt and shame get them down.

Jones: And what would you tell them about death?

Morris: Oh, to hell with death. I'd say, "My children, continue the Missis-
sippi-American line. Care for Western civilization." Death's not all it's made
out to be. Death is overrated. The poet Marvell said, "Had we both world
enough and time." We don't get either, the world or the time, but if we care,
we'll leave our reminder: we were here, and we were part of it.

Like Other Mississippi Exiles, Writer Willie Morris Comes Home

Elizabeth Mullener / 1981

From the *New Orleans Times-Picayune*, 15 March 1981, sec. 3, 10.
Permission granted by The Times-Picayune Publishing Corporation.
All rights reserved. Reprinted with permission.

In 1967, after the conclusion of a dramatic visit back to his family in the South, Willie Morris wrote that as his plane took off and headed for New York, he was going "north toward home." Today, he is living in Oxford, Mississippi, and serving as guru-in-residence at Ole Miss.

"Sometimes I have to smile at myself," he says, acknowledging the contradiction. "You know, Truman Capote told me once that all southerners go home sooner or later . . . even if it's in a box. Well, I didn't want to wait that long. I'm glad I had the wisdom to come back before it was too late. It's been a real homecoming for me. I love this old place. And they haven't thrown me out yet.

"Anyway, I think home is where the heart is. The real question is: where is the heart?"

Willie Morris's heart seems to be wherever his typewriter is. "I couldn't live without writing," he says. "I'd have no reason for living. I can't do anything else. I can't put on a coat and tie. Hell, I don't even like to wear clean socks!"

Morris is a genial, gracious fellow with a round, open face and an amiable manner. His ideas are well formulated and eloquently expressed. He has a hearty laugh and a ready sense of humor. He loves his dog Pete, he loves his Moosehead beer, and he loves to tell stories. Willie Morris is wonderful company.

He has been writing since he was a kid concocting baseball reports for the local radio station in Yazoo City, Mississippi, where he spent his youth. He grew up to go on to more sophisticated endeavors. After college at the University of Texas, he went to Oxford, England, ("We call it the *other* Oxford," he says with a wink) as a Rhodes Scholar. He returned to Texas for an adventurous stint as a newspaper editor, and then he went on to New York and a job with *Harper's* magazine.

91

Morris was a wunderkind in the fast-paced, super-chic world of New York publishing. At the age of thirty-two, in 1967, he was made editor in chief at *Harper's*. That same year, he published his first book, *North Toward Home*, an autobiographical account of his years in Mississippi, Texas, and New York. "That book struck a chord," he says, "and not just among southerners. I got thousands of letters when it came out. I still get letters. I don't know why, but people said it really got to them."

Morris stayed at *Harper's* until 1971, leading the nation's oldest magazine into a golden era of sorts. Under his tutelage, *Harper's* published pieces by many of the most prominent writers on the American scene, from Walker Percy and William Styron to Gore Vidal, George Plimpton, and Truman Capote.

"We put out a good magazine," he says modestly. "We had a good time, too. It was exciting. And hectic. You had to have your juices flowing to keep up with the pace.

"I'd go to the bathroom, and by the time I'd get back, there would be twenty-eight phone calls to answer. None of them really mattered, either. These days I don't even answer my telephone. Answering the telephone brings no good: it's either a waste of time or an imposition. As a matter of fact, I keep my phone in the refrigerator. Or sometimes the Deepfreeze. I've tried the oven, but it melts.

"When I first went to work at *Harper's*," Morris goes on, "I had this notion that a person could be an editor and a writer at the same time. It didn't take me long to be disabused of that one. The functions are mutually antagonistic. If you're an editor, you exist second-hand through your authors. If you're a writer, you can't do that: you have to live through your own writing. To have a real commitment to running a magazine is kind of at the expense of one's own private work."

Morris's own private work has consisted of four books since *North Toward Home*: *Yazoo* is the story of the integration crisis in his hometown; *Good Old Boy* is a book of homespun tales for children; *James Jones: A Friendship* is a tribute to his fellow author and late friend; and *The Last of the Southern Girls* is a novel about an Arkansas belle in Washington.

"I think my best stuff is yet to come," says Morris. "I really feel that strongly." Some of what's to come includes two novels contracted for with Doubleday. "One is set in a little town in Mississippi during the Korean War where they're bringing back the dead. I think it will be called *Taps*. The other is set in Oxford, England.

"I've also got a collection of essays coming out from Yoknapatawpha Press called *Terrains of the Heart and Other Essays on Home*. It's always good when you can rescue from oblivion things you've done for magazines. My son is a photographer, a wonderful photographer, and he's done the jacket cover. It's old Pete and me at twilight walking around on the fifty-yard line of the deserted Ole Miss football stadium. You see the interplay of the shadows and the dark. It's beautiful," Morris says proudly.

One of the most memorable pieces *Harper's* published during Willie Morris's reign was Norman Mailer's "The Armies of the Night," a book-length article on the Vietnam War, which won a Pulitzer Prize. [*Editor's note*: Mailer's article, "The Steps of the Pentagon," *Harper's*, March 1968, was published later that year in book form under the title *The Armies of the Night*.] But it was another Mailer piece—"The Prisoner of Sex"—that proved to be Morris's Waterloo [*Harper's*, March 1971].

"It all started," he explains, "when I called Norman one day for lunch. He said, 'Look, Willie, I'm working on something right now and I don't want to have lunch with you because I know you're going to have another one of your ideas. And I really don't want another idea because I want to get this project finished.'

"But a few days later," Morris continues, "there we were at a midtown Manhattan restaurant and after two or three bloody marys, Norman said, 'All right, Willie, you have this idea and I know you have this idea and I know what your idea is.' So I said, 'Well, what's my idea?' So he proceeded to tell me what my idea was. And I said, 'Yeah, that's my idea. Go ahead and do it.'

"Well, Norman always works down to the wire on deadlines. So as usual, I went out to Provincetown, where he was, and took one of my editors along. I read over the manuscript and I said, 'Norman, this is really great. But it's probably going to cost us our jobs.'"

Morris was right. Shortly after the publication of "The Prisoner of Sex," which was a controversial piece on the complexities of the women's revolution, he left *Harper's* magazine and, as he puts it, "everybody left with me."

He's a little vague—and very tongue-in-cheek—as to exactly where the lines of battle were drawn, but the enemy was clearly the magazine's publishers.

Why, in the end, did he leave the magazine? "I didn't like the people who owned the mimeograph machine." What was the problem with Norman Mailer's piece? "They didn't like it too much." What did they object to? "Things like the subject matter and the words."

Later, in a more serious vein, he explains that, "I felt they (the magazine's owners) were losing interest. I didn't see any long-range commitment on their part to making *Harper's* a truly distinguished journal, harking back to its old days. I don't think they knew what a great magazine it was."

Oxford, Mississippi, is a far cry from the glamorous Manhattan literary scene. But Morris seems to be adjusting just fine. "I missed it at first," he says. "I missed the perquisites of power. I missed having three secretaries and giving speeches at the Waldorf-Astoria and having lunch with Lauren Bacall. But I don't miss it anymore. Power is like cotton candy: it tastes good but it don't last.

"The only thing I miss now is people, a few specific people. We had quite a community out on eastern Long Island. It wasn't a writer's colony, thank goodness. But it was quite a group—people like Irwin Shaw, Truman Capote, John Knowles, Kurt Vonnegut, Joseph Heller.

"But in Mississippi, there is for me a kind of oneness with myself as a writer that I could never feel up there. It wasn't that I was out of place so much. But I wasn't in my own culture. For a while there, Mississippi—undoubtedly more than any state in the union—had a genuine set of exiles. Almost in the European sense. But a lot of people are coming back now. A lot of people."

Willie Morris is one of them. And he doesn't seem to regret it for a moment.

"What I love about Oxford," he says enthusiastically, "is the juxtaposition of campus and town. The ironies of this juxtaposition are wonderful. It's the blend of the old country culture with the milieu of a state university. It intrigues me. You've got a town of about ten thousand and a university of about ten thousand and the fact that they're right next to each other gives the place a kind of bittersweet nuance that I like.

"Then also in this town you have the pervasive spirit of Mr. Bill Faulkner. As a Mississippi writer, I don't think I could have lived in Faulkner's hometown twenty years ago—the place he spent a lifetime writing about. The shadow effect would have been too much. But now I get a strange sustenance from his spiritual presence. It's a kind of emotional support for me. I'm glad the old bastard lived here."

The only thing Willie Morris likes better than telling a favorite story is telling it again. "Back last winter," he starts, with a wonderful sense of bravura and style, "I was sitting around with some of William Faulkner's relatives. And one of them said to me, 'Willie, this is really a very interesting town, a fascinating town.' And I looked her in the eye and I said, 'I agree. I think it's so interesting that somebody ought to write a book about it!'" And with that, Willie Morris bursts into an irrepressible, wholehearted laugh at his own witticism all over again.

"I feel free in Oxford, and relaxed," he goes on. "More than I ever could in Yazoo City. Yazoo is the town I grew up in and I know every tree and every corner and every yard and every back road. And every small spot obsesses me with memory. Here I don't have that burden of memory.

"Also, the hill country up here is different from the Delta. The Delta's much wilder. It's mad and crazy and wonderful. I love it to the depths of my heart and I'll always write about it, I guess, in one form or another. But I just feel more free here. I don't feel I have to answer to my own past.

"I would say that Mississippi—of all the fifty states—is the most distinctive. Everybody *knows* that Mississippi is different from California and Ohio and New York. But Mississippi is even different from Louisiana and Tennessee and Arkansas. And that is not a myth. It's true, by God," says Morris, pounding the table. "Mississippi is *unique.*"

Mississippi is not only different from the rest of the states, according to Morris; it's different from the way it used to be as well. One of the most profound ways in which it's different is in terms of racial integration.

"I think it takes a native Mississippian to see the extent of the changes that have really taken place here," he says. "Integration has changed the face of the South. It's taken away so many of those self-destructive pressures. It's no longer the single sensitive issue it was.

"We won't be fully aware of the ramifications for another generation, I don't think. You know, it's only been ten years. Ten years! That's a very short time in the affairs of the human race.

"This is a very exciting period. Integration has produced ironies. Everywhere you go, you see them—ironies that can break your heart. You know, I like sports. Always have. I think a writer can learn a lot about a society from its bread and circuses.

"So the other night I was at a basketball game and things were hot. And I was with a friend who said, 'Do you see what I see?' And I looked across the gym and there were about fifteen little black Cub Scouts helping the Ole Miss cheerleaders cheer. And you know what they were doing? Waving Confederate flags! Now that was much more important than the basketball game.

"On Courthouse Square here, you see little black and white kids holding hands. When you get up to the seniors in high school, they still have separate dances, the blacks and whites. But what will it be like in a few years for those little kids who have gone through twelve years in integrated schools? It's all up for grabs.

"The racial situation was an albatross here for many years. But once Mississippi had to integrate, they did it and they did it pretty damn well. A hell of a lot better than Boston or New York.

"The North is much more racist than Mississippi. In every way. They've never had any experience in sharing a common land with their black contemporaries in large numbers.

"Northerners are amateur bigots. And if there's one thing I can't stand, it's an amateur."

An Interview with Willie Morris

Studs Terkel / 1983

Studs Terkel interview with Willie Morris recorded in first broadcast by WFMT, Chicago, Illinois. Audio cassette tape from the Willie Morris Collection, Department of Archives and Special Collections, J. D. Williams Library, University of Mississippi. Published by permission of Studs Terkel.

Terkel: You always wonder what is it that transforms a person or a town or a society from what some might say a beknighted condition to something highly enlightened or highly exciting. What is it that does it? He may be a young football player named Marcus Dupree. Now many of you may have heard of him—perhaps you have not. But he is a celebrated figure in college football, no doubt pro football. Marcus Dupree came from Philadelphia, Mississippi: a bespectacled, 17-year-old football player weighing about 230 pounds.

And Willie Morris is one of the most celebrated of southern writers. I merely say southern to identify him; he's an American writer. His *North Toward Home* is a beautiful memoir. You might say it's a story of not one man growing up, but of a country at a certain moment. Willie Morris has now written a book published by Doubleday called *The Courting of Marcus Dupree* and it's about transformation. Maybe it's about redemption and maybe it's about celebrity, but we'll talk about that in a moment. It's a re-markable work and in fact, Walker Percy has said it deals with the very theme of transformation. But it also has its ironic overtones, and Willie Morris always is good at irony and understanding South and North, and he's my guest today.

Morris [reads]: "On this hot September night, Number 22 walked through the door of the gymnasium with his fifty or so teammates. He stood there beyond the end zone and waited with them to run onto the field. They were a small-town Mississippi football team.

"The stadium behind the old brick high school was crowded with four thousand people. There was a pale quarter-moon on the horizon. A train whistle from the Illinois Central echoed across from Independence Quarters, and crickets chirped from a nearby hollow. The grass was moist from yester-day's rains.

"He was big. He was carrying his helmet, which he put on now over a copious Afro haircut kept in place by a red hairnet. He was seventeen years old and he was wearing glasses.

"There was more behind his entrance on this night than football itself."

Terkel: Of course, that's Willie Morris reading the opening of his book *The Courting of Marcus Dupree*. I think that no one could have written this book but a southerner such as yourself, Willie, because you're from Mississippi.

Morris: Born and raised. My people founded Mississippi as warriors and statesmen. I wouldn't have written this book if Marcus Dupree had been from Indianapolis or even from Kosciusko, Mississippi. I was drawn to the tortured locale which produced him.

Terkel: We better go into that, because this is the exquisite (if there's such a word fitting it) irony. Marcus Dupree, a young seventeen-year-old, black football player—a star—is being courted by recruiters to the various big colleges of the country. The town he is from is Philadelphia, Mississippi. Now for listeners that may or may not ring a bell.

Morris: Philadelphia, Mississippi, and Neshoba County, at the height of the civil rights struggle, were symbols of the recalcitrance and brutality which greeted the Freedom Summer of 1964 and the whole civil rights movement itself. Martin Luther King came in to register the blacks to vote. He called it the worst town he had ever seen and said it was one of the two places where he had feared for his life. They murdered the three civil rights workers there in 1964: Michael Schwerner, Andrew Goodman, and James Chaney. The town was in the grip of the Ku Klux Klan, one of the most tightly disciplined Klan units of that day in America.

Terkel: We're talking about 1964, nineteen years ago, so when you were doing the book some seventeen or eighteen years had passed. So in those eighteen years there's a crazy irony that the town, white and black, is proud of the seventeen-year-old kid who can run and carry a ball.

Morris: Marcus Dupree was born one month before the murders of the three workers. He went into the first grade the very year that the public schools all through the lower South massively integrated and was in the first integrated high school graduating class, as what happened through much of the South in which the white and black youngsters had gone through all twelve grades together. He was a member of the black Baptist church, just around the corner from his little house in Independence Quarters in Philadelphia, Mississippi, that had opened its doors to the civil rights people. In front of it now is a memorial to Schwerner, Goodman, and Chaney. So the ironies have accumulated for me as I spent more and more time in Philadelphia, Mississippi, and being a native of the state I could not elude those ironies, which enveloped me just as much as drama envelops young Marcus Dupree. I had no choice but to write this book.

Terkel: The book is multidimensional, but specifically there are two dimensions to it. The chapters almost alternate, and there is the almost comical importance to the courting of Marcus Dupree by the college recruiters. Of course they are key figures in your book, but the other chapters deal with what happened *back then.*

Morris: I tried deliberately to intersperse the past with the present, which I think is perhaps more vital in the Deep South than in most other parts of America (though I may be wrong). There is the whole business of the burden of the past, the burden of fame and celebrity, as you say, of a young black who is gradually (I wouldn't want to exaggerate this too much) bringing the white and black communities together in this town. It bespeaks of the almost ritualistic importance of football in that area, of winning, and it bespeaks of fame, as I say, of a young black who lost his privacy at the very age when most of us are beginning to understand what privacy is. And the young substitute—little number eighteen who is Marcus Dupree's friend, helping him with his tear-away jerseys and his shoulder pads and bringing him water during the games—is the son of Cecil Price, the Deputy Sheriff who was convicted in the murder trial. How ironic can you get?

Terkel: Stop right there! I have that marked in about ten different places. Irony. Cecil Price, Jr. is a sidekick and devoted admirer of Marcus Dupree. Cecil Price's father was the Deputy Sheriff to Sheriff Lawrence Rainey. These are the two figures we connect with the murders of Chaney, Goodman, and Schwerner, and Price served time in jail "for conspiracy to deprive civil rights." What a euphemism!

Morris: And it must be one of the biggest euphemisms, because I would think the largest deprivation of one's civil rights would occur if you killed somebody!

Terkel: We have to come now to football. The ritual of football and winning is almost synthesized in this one kid. It's ironic as it becomes the means of transforming a town from a medieval moment racially to something in the twentieth century.

Morris: We have a wonderful old black football coach in Mississippi by the name of Marino Casem, who has coached football for years at Alcorn State University, a predominantly black school around Natchez. We called Coach Casem the black godfather of Mississippi and he once observed, "In the East, college football is a cultural attraction. On the west coast, it is a tourist attraction. In the Midwest, it is cannibalism. But in the South, it is religion."

I detected an act of religiosity in a very real sense in the courting of young Marcus Dupree and everything which that implied. These recruiters from all the major football powers coming into that little town, along with the bevy of reporters. And again, another irony to this story is the white people in town. Their only other experience with outsiders like this was in the 1960s, and they came in then for a very different purpose. Now they were coming in to report something rather wholesome. Their young black hero has become a national figure at the age of sixteen. That's quite different from reporters and outsiders coming in to report murders and nocturnal burials and earthen dams. [*Editor's note*: The murderers of the three young civil rights workers buried the bodies beneath an earthen dam a few miles outside of Philadelphia, Mississippi.]

Terkel: To what extent has Marcus Dupree affected the black communities and others? He is a celebrity and being a celebrity, white or black, puts someone on a whole different level, so he's had an effect quite obviously. Of course, you have some ironic comments made by older ex-football players who are black.

Morris: Black men who came along a little too early. In my opinion the key was the massive integration of the public schools in the South in 1970. That opened up a whole new ball game. And the superlative black athletes (who came along before the predominantly white universities in the South were courting the black athletes) had rather limited alternatives to go to a black school in the state, as they came along a little too early. I saw a number of those once great black athletes there in the town, who now just kind of drift around, taking pills. I saw one of them one day just hitting a road sign with his fists. But young Marcus Dupree came along at just the right time, where he did become a genuine folk hero at such an early age, certainly a hero to the blacks there. He's returned to Mississippi now and plays for

University of Southern Mississippi, and I really think this is going to have a
good effect on our bewitched and crazy state.

Terkel: By the way, for those in your bewitched and crazy state, it's incredible. He returned because he was homesick. For those of you who thought
he went to Oklahoma, one of the key universities recruiting Dupree, he came
back because he was homesick.

Morris: He was homesick! I was talking to some people while I was traveling around the country, and I found this insatiable interest all over America
in this young black man, Marcus Dupree. He is now a household word; he's
probably the most famous teenager in America now, with the exception of
Brooke Shields. He went out to Oklahoma and he came home because he
was homesick. I find something profoundly touching in this. I didn't return
to my native Mississippi until I was forty-five years old. Marcus Dupree had
the sense to do it when he was nineteen.

Terkel: But here's a black kid—seventeen, eighteen, or nineteen—
returning to his home in Mississippi. He was born just a couple of months
after the killings of the three civil rights workers. Is there a historical continu-
ity there? Do his contemporaries (white or black) have any knowledge of that
period, or has it been wiped out?

Morris: They have a knowledge of that period, but I don't think they have
any strong feelings about it. This is what I found out living in that town of
Philadelphia, Mississippi, for a long time. That period seems so remote for
them because they have been going to school together—the whites and the
blacks—for a number of years now. One of the national television networks
ran a documentary based on Don Whitehead's 1970 book, *Attack on Terror:
The FBI Against the Ku Klux Klan in Mississippi*. That documentary came
out when Marcus Dupree and his white and black contemporaries were probably in the sixth or seventh grade, and they didn't grasp it, they didn't com-
prehend it. That brutality was not part of their experience.

I'm not suggesting that this town is now the symbol of brotherly love—far
from it— just as I'm not about to imply that even in its worst moments in the
1960s it was a symbol of absolute human evil. There are a lot of paradoxes
here. It's a very poor town. Mississippi is the poorest state in the union.
We're fiftieth per capita income and we'll never even catch up with Arkansas
in forty-ninth. The poverty is oppressive and it exacerbates every issue. In
the old black section of Philadelphia, Independence Quarters, some of the
scenes there of poverty will break your heart. But the young white and black

children growing up together really fascinated me. I became obsessed with them and with the whole feeling of the older white community and their memories of the 1960s, and with the very phenomenon of a Marcus Dupree and what older white people thought of him and how they viewed him.

Terkel: I was thinking as you were talking that we had to come back to Willie Morris himself—you—because your writing, your impressions, even just your phrases are deeply moving. The very phrases—even the descriptions—that go back to a southern boyhood: empty towns drowsing in the summer sun, bare-faced kids shooting baskets, unpainted houses, loblolly pines. The only time I heard the word "loblolly" was from an old black man on a train to the 1963 march in Washington, and he spoke of loblolly.

Morris: The loblolly pines which line those roads heading south in Mississippi to Neshoba County actually make dark tunnels along those highways. They go into anguished shapes in the middle of storms and they can be very frightening.

Terkel: Let's turn to why you were drawn to Philadelphia. It is all about your home state, the phenomenon with this boy, and it's this crazy aspect of the recruiting; we have to talk about that. And also this woman who was your informant, the liberal white woman, Florence Mars.

Morris: Florence Mars. Her courage comes in strange packages. She was forty years old during The Troubles (they always called that period "The Troubles") and here she was one of the handful of human beings in the town who stood up to the Ku Klux Klan. The Klan controlled the police and a lot of the city government. In fact, it interested me that almost the only people in the town who stood up to the Klan were women. A few of them were the wives of Catholics who knew their husbands were not secretly members of the Klan because of the Klan's traditional stance against the Pope, of course, but that was about it. The newspaper collapsed utterly.

Terkel: The *Neshoba Democrat.*

Morris: Which was Turner Catledge's old paper, who later became editor of the *New York Times.* But it was almost a classic example, as Hodding Carter said, of responsible moderate leadership retreating and having no leadership and no spokesman, no one to rally around to remind them of what civilization is and what civility is. Of course, over the years in Marcus Dupree's lifetime the effect of the federal presence cannot be denied. Lyndon Johnson's two watershed pieces of legislation, the Civil Rights Act and the

Voting Rights Act of 1964–65, have had just a monumental effect on the Deep South. But something more subtle has happened over the years: a softening of anguish, a feeling that we hit the bottom of the barrel with these three murders in 1964, and that the better people of the South and of Mississippi must, as Abraham Lincoln said in his second inaugural address, "Try to respond to the better angels of our nature."

Terkel: Of course, there was always someone like Florence Mars standing up, though she was in the minority.

Morris: A small woman who wrote a fine book about the murders called *Witness in Philadelphia* [1977].

Terkel: It's always these middle-class women who go to the courtroom when a black man is on trial. They'd sit up in the front row, and sometimes they'd affect that judge; he'd get a little scared of them. They'd sit there to see that the defendant, the black, was not abused. There was this group in a number of those southern states. You and I both know a woman named Virginia Durr of Montgomery, Alabama.

Morris: Yes, and Virginia Durr is just one of the greatest examples of this group. They've always been present in moments of crisis, and you can imagine what an intimidating presence Virginia Durr would be in a courtroom like that!

Terkel: You'd want to call on someone like her or Florence Mars. Now we come to a phenomenon we have to discuss and that's football recruiting. It's not a new phenomenon, but it's overwhelming today because of the commercial aspects of it.

Morris: I think the influx of the big television money has had a great deal to do with making winning in college football so important. I've been informed that a team that's on national television now (let's say next Saturday on the national game of the week) will get 1.2 million dollars for this appearance. So these college recruiters descending on this little hamlet in the red clay hills in Mississippi are really involved in a big business.

Terkel: Now we come to it, don't we? They're there to recruit a certain kid who carries a ball well, who can help that team win and be number one. If that team is number one, it is millions, multi-millions. It's a little crazy, isn't it?

Morris: There is no rationality to it at all.

Terkel: *The Courting of Marcus Dupree* is obviously more than the courting of a young black kid who is seventeen and big and carries a football well.
It's really a study of a certain aspect of our society right now. Now you have
to describe who a recruiter is, what his life is like, and the techniques in
recruiting.

Morris: I became very familiar with the recruiters. I had an informant
before I went in there whom I called Temple Drake, who probably knew as
much about college football recruiting as anyone.

Terkel: He is your Deep Throat.

Morris: Right, he's my Deep Throat, and I said I would protect his identity
on pain of being incarcerated in the Mississippi state penal farm in Parchman.
And Parchman is not a very pleasant place, as you know, and that gives you
some understanding of how deep my commitment is to protecting his identity. The college football recruiters are assistant coaches on the big teams,
and they also will coach the defensive ends or the running backs or whatever.
They are on the road constantly, going after these superlative high school
football players—black and white, of course. They are away from their families and they forget their children's birthdays or what grade their children are
in, and they live lonesome lives in motel rooms and rundown hotel rooms.
They go into dry areas and the bourbon runs out and they call up the front
desk of the motel and ask, "Will you send up two cold beers?" The woman
will say, "What are you honey, a dreamer?"

They're constantly in touch with their home offices. (I'd hate to see their
telephone bills!) But you see, they are usually men in their late twenties,
thirties, early forties, and they work all the time. They are after these athletes,
and their careers could rise or fall on whether they sign or do not sign a
Marcus Dupree. They go into the homes of the athletes and they woo the
mothers and the grandmothers (especially those of the black athletes in the
South, many of whom do come from broken homes as in the case with Marcus Dupree). It all boils down to getting the young football player's signature
on that document.

Terkel: Now describe the scene and the homes. You have a scene here
that's heartbreaking, as one of the recruiters describes this home and the
abject poverty.

Morris: Yes, there is a whole folklore about college football recruiters
who go into the impoverished black houses of the South. Here's one tale
among many which I picked up from various coaches. The recruiter went

into a little black shack just before Christmas, and it's almost barren of furniture and he said there wasn't even a television set in there. He said the house was cold and there was cardboard in the windows instead of window panes. There were a lot of little children and they hadn't eaten, and he asked the recruit, the one he was after, "When was the last time you ate?" He said, "Yesterday at noon. I had a bologna sandwich." And the little children hadn't eaten—they had a bologna sandwich the day before—and he could hear their stomachs growling. He took them all out and bought them about thirty dollars worth of hamburgers. He said, "This was against the NCAA rules, but there are a lot more important things in life than sticking to the rules."

Terkel: Now that kid from that home is offered what? How does this work?

Morris: A high school athlete receives a scholarship to a college, which pays for his room, board, and tuition, and these days that amounts to about six or seven thousand dollars a year for four years. (And presumably they get a college education, although many of them do not go on to get degrees; they just play.) The recruiters are not supposed to give any gifts and no payoffs, but that's a whole other consideration. What they used to do, my informants told me, was to pay off in cash, in twenty-dollar bills in a suitcase, and get the family to bury the suitcase in the back yard under the chinaberry tree and spend it twenty dollars at a time. One kid was paid off with a brand new twelve gauge Remington shotgun stuffed with one-hundred-dollar bills. But those blatant gifts have become more difficult because the governing body of college sports is more rigorous now. The payoffs are much more subtle involving long-term payments and credit and all of that.

Terkel: There is a great deal of hypocrisy involved here, of course.

Morris: Yes, in my descriptions of the recruiting I try not to sound righteous or moralistic or to cast any direct value judgments. I just let the descriptions of the whole ritual of football recruiting speak for themselves.

Terkel: You quote Red Smith on the importance of disguising the names of the student athletes. We talk about some blatant cases, but it would be unforgivable to hold a kid up to public ridicule because he can grab and hold on to a flying football. He is only a victim; the culprits are the college and the system. Now this applies to both white as well as black super-athletes: just how much education do they get?

Morris: That's a good question. They have special courses for athletes in so many of the major college football powers. One of the strangest ones I came across was an elementary geology course at one midwestern university that all the athletes take—a very easy course, which they call "Rocks for Jocks." And they take courses in jumping and in dance just to keep them in class and to make just the grade point average they need to play.

I cite the statistics of those athletes, particularly in college football and basketball, who have actually gone and got a degree. In the Southwest Conference schools (that's Texas and the University of Arkansas) the figures are about 17 percent who've gone to get a degree. Louisiana State University in Baton Rouge: 16 percent. There is something wrong there. The athletes are just being used as meat on the hoofs, so to speak. When Marcus Dupree disappeared recently from the University of Oklahoma (he actually was home; he went back to Mississippi), it was discovered that he was so homesick and unhappy out there at the University of Oklahoma that he hadn't been going to class. And one of the academic counselors to the athletes at Oklahoma told the press, "Well, Marcus has not been going to class, but that would not have prevented us from letting him play ball on Saturdays, and we didn't want to keep him from playing ball on Saturdays."

Terkel: It makes you wonder what a college is. It's obviously for getting dough because we come back to the fact that this is about money. This is really about money.

Morris: An examination of college football would make a Marxist out of a States' Rights Democrat.

Terkel: You've chosen a town, Philadelphia, Mississippi, because of the ironies involving the history of the town. If one were to choose the most horrendous moment (there were many, but just one) during the civil rights movement, it would be the killing of the three civil rights workers and their burial by the officials of the town. And here is the town where Marcus Dupree is from.

Morris: Yes, I think I'd agree with you that that moment might have been the bleakest in that whole period of American history. Of course, those bombings of the church in Alabama, where the little black girls were killed, were monstrous. But I constantly raise the question to myself and to so many of my confidants there in that town and in that county: what has happened? What has really happened here to usher in a period where this young black can mean so much to both the black and white communities in this complicated and tragic town and county? What happened?

I drove up one day with my dog Pete and I found the spot where the three murders had actually taken place—on Rock Cut Road, with its red earth and gullies. I went up there at sunset and had a palpable sense of these killings taking place in those red gullies, and I thought of those two Jewish boys from New York coming from very educated, civilized families, both very young, and of the young illiterate black who was murdered with them. Surely Marcus Dupree had to be a catharsis in the recent history of the South. The South and Mississippi could not stoop any lower.

Terkel: At the same time there is a comical aspect to the whole phenomenon. It's football that brought it about, and it's the money behind football and how it transcends almost everything.

Morris: Yes, it's almost farcical. I think there are a lot more evil things in America than the excesses of college football, but by the same token, I think this whole process—the emphasis on winning and the comical routines of the recruiters going in to snare their game—is a reflection of much of the extremes.

Terkel: You also have these contests between the recruiters—this competition.

Morris: Oh, they follow each other in cars at night. They steal each other's motel messages. They will get together for coffee in a place like the downtown hotel in Philadelphia, Mississippi, at 8:00 A.M., where they have a real camaraderie. Then that afternoon one of their number is missing, and they will get in their cars to go try to find him because they think he'll have the recruit hidden away somewhere.

Terkel: It's really dog-eat-dog, because it's their livelihood, isn't it?

Morris: It's their very life and all of this (the backstabbing, the following each other at night, the constant phone calls back to the home office) leads to the seemingly innocent pageantry of those golden afternoons in the college football stadiums.

Terkel: Of course, then there's winning; we come to that. I suppose that affects our whole country too: winning no matter what.

Morris: Yes, it's just an emphasis that pervades every aspect of American society. You have to win. But I can't conceive a southern writer writing a memoir about his success called *Making It*. He might be lead to write a book with the title *Losing It*.

Terkel: We have to come to you now, with your memory of southern boyhood and your *North Toward Home*. You and Marcus Dupree came from different backgrounds but had the same turf, that same home turf. It had to have an effect on you.

Morris: I'm really glad you brought this up because as the author, I kind of think this is the web of my book. As you so well know, writing itself—just the act of it—draws on the subconscious, which is the greatest ally of the writer in his moments of solitude. And the more I got into this tale the more I began to perceive that it really wasn't a book about football, although football is the thread that runs through it. It's a book about two Mississippians: a seventeen-year-old black and a middle-aged white. The seventeen-year-old black's odyssey into the great outside world almost coincided with the middle-aged white's return to his soil after a long exile. The two of us sprang from a radically different heritage, yet from a mutual one—a profoundly mutual one as well.

Terkel: As you say that, I think again and again of the experiences I've had of talking to southern whites and southern blacks in Chicago. Both came up here to make a living. The poor southern white (whether from the Appalachian country or from the Deep South) and the black from the Deep South both came to Chicago. You find that in Detroit and in Cleveland as well. And in both cases, when they meet (and I've been there when they've met), they would ask each other, "Where are you from?" If they are from the same area, they get excited and they start talking about *home*. Home is not where they are now; it's where they both came from.

Morris: That's so true. I would see that time and again when I was living in New York City: the mutuality of the southern blacks living in the great cities of the North and the Midwest with their white contemporaries. This is something that runs through Faulkner. I've always felt that this sense of community and a sense of a common past, despite so much of the anguish and pain of that past, would be one of the great salvations of the South. And sometimes I think the South is really America writ large, so it's the salvation of America also.

Terkel: Who but Willie Morris could capture so many paradoxes? And the word here is paradox, and also metaphor, because the story of Marcus Dupree is really a metaphorical tale of this teenager Marcus Dupree. C. Vann Woodward, distinguished southern historian, and Walker Percy, southern writer, also speak of the transformation due to of all things—football.

Morris: This crazy fraternity in ritual football.

Terkel: You said "ritual." So we come to that again, don't we?

Morris: Yes, ritual, religiosity. Sometimes I think football in the South is more important than the church altar. But they're all wrapped up together, see? It all involves redemption.

Terkel: Redemption?

Morris: Yes. And in Marcus's case it's a strange blend of redemption, celebrity, and courting, and all this is so deeply involved with the past.

Terkel: It's funny—you used five different phrases there. Past, present, celebrity, redemption, sports. Celebrity I think is the key aspect of it here. To what extent has the celebrity of Marcus Dupree (whose own life has been changed) affected other blacks in that area?

Morris: Marcus Dupree has had quite a galvanizing effect on the other blacks there his age. I've been watching them and there was a lot of envy, of course, because of his remarkable achievements and his virtuosity on the athletic field—inevitable envy among other young blacks from other schools and his own school. The Marcus Duprees of this world inevitably have a magic about them and carry a burden—a burden of fame, of national exposure in this television era—that is an uncommonly heavy burden. I think it's just one of those prices that has to be paid for talent. Great talent exacts a very high cost.

Terkel: Now we come to the boy himself, the young guy Marcus Dupree. At one point he's on a plane, the plane has a telephone, and he's calling his high school coach on the ground. To a kid out of a shack, that has to be. . . .

Morris: He's on a Lear jet with two former University of Oklahoma All-American football players, being taken to Oklahoma by an oil millionaire. I was there that day he left Philadelphia, and he had on a blue windbreaker with the name "Dupree" on the back. About an hour-and-a-half later the phone in his high school football coach's office rang. And Joe Wood—country boy, white man, of course—answered the phone and said, "Who is this?" "This is Marcus," came the reply. And the high school coach asked, "Marcus, where are you?" Marcus said, "They told me I could telephone you on this radio. And they also told me that I am forty-one thousand feet over the state of Oklahoma, but it seems to me like I'm halfway to the moon."

Terkel: I'm thinking about that whole crazy change in circumstances. You mentioned the coach, Joe Wood. The role of the high school coach is almost a high priest's role, isn't it?

Morris: Yes, it's an important role. He can help bring an adolescent to glory, and if the athlete is any good, eventually riches. He has enormous influence over these adolescent boys, and it's a big responsibility. A bad high school coach can really damage a kid because he does exert a power over these adolescents. In the case of Marcus Dupree's high school coach, he was a wholesome influence, a very fine man of character.

Terkel: Temple Drake. We come back to Temple Drake, the name you gave to your key informant, your Deep Throat. This also has a comic note because if his name were revealed he could really get in trouble, couldn't he?

Morris: Yes, because he told me some interesting things that people who are writing don't usually get. But I think he'll be all right, for nobody knows who he is.

Terkel: So we come to changes in the town too. Not because of Marcus Dupree, but because of the very nature of the civil rights movement itself. There are the changes that took place with the local newspaper.

Morris: With my newspaper background I have always believed in the importance of a great and courageous newspaper (and it's so hard in small towns because the people you write about or criticize are the people you see every day). I'm convinced that in this classic case—the collapse of the civilized element in a town like Philadelphia, Mississippi, during The Troubles—it was the abdication of the local paper which led to the disasters that followed. A new editor came in three or four years later who was a civilized and educated man, so it's different, but I think the press in the South is also getting better. The papers in Jackson, Mississippi, which once were probably the most race-baiting in America, bar none, are now perhaps the most enlightened pair of newspapers in the South.

Terkel: The *Clarion-Ledger*?
Morris: And the *Daily News*. They used to be just atrocious, but the importance of the newspaper in a troubled climate was and is to me absolutely crucial.

Terkel: The book is *The Courting of Marcus Dupree* by my guest, Willie Morris. Some of you perhaps have read his other works and know he is an excellent writer. As you can probably tell, the book itself is a metaphor. It's exciting reading, it's funny, it's very moving.

But it comes back to you and Marcus Dupree, and it ends with the fact that both of you are two young guys who came back home. They say that Dupree couldn't get along in Oklahoma. He was basically homesick, and you are back in Mississippi.

Morris: I think that's the key to the book and I'm so happy you perceived this: the similarities between this young black and myself and the way that we responded to our different generations on our common ground is really what I was trying to write about.

Terkel: Perhaps you can read the last part, because there is the death of your dog, and that too is part of the metaphor.

Morris: In the last paragraphs of this book I'm burying my dog Pete, who was really my brother—bless my dog and my brother. Pete was this great black Labrador who was with me through all of my journeys down in Neshoba County. We buried Pete up in the town cemetery in Oxford (the mayor got him up there very close to the Faulkner plot) and this is just the last two paragraphs of my book.

[Reads]: "I thought of our inseparable days on the earth. He and I had come together at the right time, just perhaps as young Marcus and I had; and he, too, had been at Marcus's courting. There was immortality in Pete's gentleness, as there was in the way Marcus ran.

"Something of me was gone with Pete, so much of my deluded youth and vanity, my loves and fears as a writing man, my American comings and goings. Marcus's boyhood in Neshoba, and everything Neshoba meant to me, his destiny on the Oklahoma plains, were an inextricable part of my strange, bittersweet return. Laying Pete there in the Mississippi ground evoked for me the blue immemorial mists of Fitzgerald, for I see now that this has been, after all, a tale about the South. It was Pete who came home with me."

Terkel: Willie Morris reading the very last passage from his book *The Courting of Marcus Dupree*, published by Doubleday. Thank you very much.

Morris: You are one of my heroes and I'm glad to meet you and to be here.

The Good Old Boy's Taste in Books

Michael J. Bandler / 1983

From the *Chicago Tribune Book World*, 20 November 1983, 35–36.
Reprinted by permission of Michael J. Bandler.

Willie Morris, once the wunderkind of American magazine journalism when he was named editor of *Harper's* magazine at the age of thirty-two, is a native Mississippian and Rhodes Scholar whose trenchant memoir, *North Toward Home*, exemplifies the mood and spirit of a rural boyhood. That book, and subsequent writings on politics, society, and literature, established him as a prominent southern literary voice. At forty-eight, he is writer-in-residence at the University of Mississippi in Oxford, and author of *The Courting of Marcus Dupree*. Recently, he discussed the evolution of his reading taste and other matters with Michael J. Bandler, contributing editor and book columnist of *American Way* magazine.

Bandler: What are you reading now?

Morris: I've gotten into the curious habit of reading several books at the same time. I'm reading the first volume of Bill Manchester's biography of Churchill—*The Last Lion* [1983]—and a wonderful book on the battle of Antietam, *Landscape Turned Red* [1983], by Stephen W. Sears. I'm also in the middle of a murder mystery set in the college football world—*Replay: Murder* [1983], by John Logue. And I just finished a very good book, *Let the Trumpet Sound* [1982], a biography of Martin Luther King, Jr., by Stephen Oates.

Q: When you were growing up in the South, were there any books that gave you perspectives on the North?

A: I grew up in the period before television. We were creatures of radio. It's only in retrospect that I've been able to see how isolated we were. I think I got most of my perceptions of the North from the radio. But I had a wonderful English teacher, Omie Parker. She was married to the town barber, and she was utterly devoted to literature. So I was reading the English classics, mainly, through school. Then I started going to the library and dipping into books. (We didn't have books at home—my daddy was a great reader of *True Detective* and Erle Stanley Gardner mysteries.) I went off on a sort of Thomas

Wolfe tear. I remember having read an interview in a movie magazine with someone like Hedy Lamarr or Dorothy Lamour, who talked about Wolfe as being the great poet-novelist of the South. So I went to the desk in the library and told the lady I wanted to check out *Look Homeward, Angel* [1929]. I must have been fifteen. She said, "Oh, I just don't want you to check out that book—it's dirty." But then she let me, and I started living my life out of the pages of Thomas Wolfe—those wonderful sequences of going off to the East, and to New York City. Wolfe's feelings of the small-town provincial southern boy in New York affected me deeply. So in a sense, I made it to the North long before I lived there—through Wolfe.

Q: Can you remember your first reading experience?

A: As with so many southern children, it was the Bible. I loved it. Parts of it scared me to death. Other parts of it mystified me. It's obviously one of the great books of literature, and it was my first real contact, I suppose, with the possibilities of the written word. Then I used to go down to the library and get in a corner and read things like the magazines *Open Road for Boys*, *Boys' Life*, and the sports novels of John R. Tunis, like *Highpockets* [1948] and *The Kid From Tomkinsville* [1945]. When I was in the eighth or ninth grade I started reading a Mississippi writer named James Street, who wrote historical novels with a lot of sex in them. We'd pass those books around— books like *By Valour and Arms* [1944] and *Oh, Promised Land* [1940]. Of course we got Erskine Caldwell's *God's Little Acre* [1933], which we'd read under the desk. But then my high school English teacher got me onto Charles Dickens and William Thackeray, and I just loved all of it. Much later, when I was at the University of Texas, I visited the apartment of a married couple who were in graduate school. They were kind of the intellectuals of that era at the university, and their walls were lined with books. I'd never seen anything like that before in a private dwelling, and I was overcome. I kept looking at the books out of the corner of my eye. The people made me comfortable, gave me a beer and asked me what I wanted to be. I just blurted out that I wanted to be a writer. And I'd never said that before.

Q: Having come to the fore with your memoirs, to whom do you look as exemplars in autobiography?

A: I originally started writing by trying a novel, and it just wasn't working, so I started fooling around with the autobiographical form, and I liked it. I read a book in that period that not many people have read--*Roughing It* [1872], by Mark Twain, one of his early books. The first three-quarters of it is vintage Twain, and then it falls apart at the end for some reason. But still, I was enormously taken with the form of the book. Then I read *The Autobiography of Lincoln Steffens* [1931]. I'll tell you another one that affected me— *Lanterns on the Levee* [1941], by William Alexander Percy, a memoir of a turn-of-the-century southern white aristocrat.

Q: Who provides the best insights into the South today?

A: William Faulkner. Like so many great artists, he was a prophet of the human soul. I'm also a great admirer of William Styron, who happens to be one of my closest friends. C. Vann Woodward's writings always have meant a lot to me, and Walker Percy's fiction has captured the contemporary South more effectively than any other southern writer's works. Barry Hannah, who lives right here in Oxford, has a very distinctive voice. I've always been a great admirer of Marshall Frady, who's from Georgia. I always felt he was going to write great fiction, and he may someday. And if you think about Texas writers, there's no one who knows Texas better than Ronnie Dugger.

Q: What was your first exposure to a black writer?

A: I started reading Richard Wright at the University of Texas because he was a fellow Mississippian. People from Mississippi are curious: even when they don't like each other, they're loyal. And I was very interested in Wright, because when he was a kid he spent some time in Yazoo City. His father was a tenant farmer or sharecropper there. Then I read him again when I was in Oxford, England. From there I went to Paris for the first time, and I knew he was living there, so I called up Art Buchwald and asked him if he had Wright's number. Of course he did, and he gave it to me. I called Wright, and told him I was an American student in England and had read his books and would love to buy him a drink. He seemed very aloof, cold. So I told him I was from Yazoo City and immediately the tenor of his voice changed; he got kind of warm and invited me over. We went out that night and got drunk, and subsequently corresponded. That was my first contact with a black writer. Besides that, I don't think there's a more splendid contemporary American novel than Ralph Ellison's *Invisible Man* [1952]. And I really loved some of James Baldwin's early essays and his autobiography [*Notes of a Native Son*, 1955].

Q: What's the most disappointing book you ever read?

A: I was a great admirer of John Steinbeck. When I was living on Long Island, everybody was talking about a novel he'd written called *The Winter* *of Our Discontent* [1961]. Boy, that let me down something terrible. It must have been one of those novels that a writer has to write. But I was monumentally disappointed. I was disappointed in a different way by Ernest Hemingway's *A Moveable Feast* [1964]—a beautifully written but mean-spirited book.

Q: What do you read to escape?

A: Oh, a little bit of everything. I've probably read the Georges Simenon mysteries—all of them—three or four times. You can go back to them years later because you've kind of forgotten what happened. I read a lot on the Civil War. I'm always dipping into Shelby Foote's three volumes [*The Civil War: A Narrative*, 1958, 1963, 1974]. And I've got this book on Antietam. Also, I'm rereading an absolutely engrossing book that not too many people know, called *I Rode With Stonewall* [1940], by Henry Kyd Douglas, who was a young man on Jackson's staff. The book wasn't published until 1940—it had been in an attic somewhere.

Willie Morris Is Home Again at Ole Miss

Mary Lynn Kotz / 1984

From the *St. Petersburg (Florida) Times*, 22 July 1984, sec. D, 8. Copyright *St. Petersburg Times* 1984. Reprinted by permission of Mary Lynn Kotz.

Oxford, Miss.—It's not exactly Elaine's, but the Warehouse is a proper pub, and Willie Morris and his friends hang out here. Willie, who used to hold court at Elaine's during his days as editor of *Harper's*, is known now as the Literary Lion of Oxford. Now and then, some of the old crowd from Elaine's even come down to join him in his den—after they have spoken to his classes in contemporary American literature or magazine writing at the university.

This is the Oxford where novelist William Faulkner mined his Nobel Prize-winning treasures. Morris, the *enfant terrible* of the New York literary scene during the sixties, who wrote in *North Toward Home* that his intellectual home was in New York, has come back to his native Mississippi, on the trail of Faulkner's muse.

"I agreed to come for one semester as writer-in-residence at Ole Miss," says Morris. "I had no idea that I'd be here for four years. But I fell in love with Oxford. It's a good ol' working country town, enhanced by the palpable sophistication of the university. (It's of a size to manage! The town has about ten thousand, Ole Miss another ten thousand.) I'm staying on next year, as journalist-in-residence, because it's a pleasant place to live and a good place to work. I love it for the same reasons Faulkner did.

"After all, it is home," he adds, sipping on a Moosehead beer at the Warehouse.

Just off the Courthouse Square, where a marble-white Confederate soldier still faces due South, the Warehouse was just that while Faulkner was alive. Now the rough-planked building houses boutiques, two restaurants, a bookstore, a photo studio, and a bar where Ole Miss sorority sisters in running shoes and shorts (and hair spray and mascara) and good ol' boys-in-training swarm around Morris, their mentor and friend, shouting above the beer and hard-rock din of a college hangout.

Willie Morris presides over a table, just as he once did in New York. William Styron has joined him here, and John Knowles, and James Dickey—who brought a whole suitcase full of poems and stories that he called his "magic box"—and Winston Groom and George Plimpton, among others. They come down, some for free, to talk about their writing.

The writers really come to Oxford because of their friendship with Willie and their fascination with Faulkner, and they sit around with the students after classes at the Warehouse or the (cotton) Gin, another restored relic of a building that also now is a watering hole for the Rebels, as the students still are called.

Willie's students are ecstatic about the course. Harriet Riley, of Meridian, Mississippi, a journalism major, told me, "My brother went to graduate school in English at Berkeley. He couldn't believe I'd actually met those writers. 'Styron?' he said. 'You've got to be kidding!'"

Morris admits that the reading list for the graduate-level course is rather eclectic. The students plowed through eighteen books a semester ("I thought that was a lot when I began," said Riley. "Now there are about fifty more I want to read,") on a list that—in addition to Faulkner, Fitzgerald, and Hemingway—included John Knowles, *A Separate Peace* [1959]; James Jones, *The Pistol* [1958]; James Dickey, *Deliverance* [1970]; Winston Groom, *Better Times Than These* [1978]; William Styron, *Lie Down in Darkness* [1951], *Sophie's Choice* [1979], and *The Long March* [1956]; Walker Percy, *The Moviegoer* [1961]; Irwin Shaw, *The Young Lions* [1948]; Robert Penn Warren, *All The King's Men* [1946]; Truman Capote, *Breakfast at Tiffany's* [1958]; Mark Harris, *Bang the Drum Slowly* [1956]; Eudora Welty, *The Ponder Heart* [1954]; Budd Schulberg, *What Makes Sammy Run* [1941].

"I wanted them to experience the variety and diversity of U.S. writing," he said. "Also, I structured the list around people who could come down here, and people I knew well. The purpose of the course was to teach them things about the mind of the working American novelist."

In addition to the authors themselves, Rose Burgunder Styron, the poet, came to talk about the tribulations of living with a novelist: when Styron is entrenched in work, it seems he doesn't see anyone or anything outside his mind. He stumbles about the house, running into furniture, walls—he's concentrating that hard.

Michael Burke, President of Madison Square Garden, came to talk about his friendship with Hemingway. Another guest speaker was Motee Daniels, Faulkner's bootlegger. And Dean Faulkner Wells, whose father, killed in a plane crash before she was born, was Faulkner's younger brother, came to talk about "Pappy"—her uncle, the novelist.

(One day in 1957, she burst into his workroom, usually a sacrosanct place. "Pappy, Pappy, I've got the greatest news," she said. "An Ole Miss girl has just been crowned Miss America."

"Well, Missey," Faulkner replies. "At last somebody has put Mississippi on the map!")

Faulkner—his spirit, his vision, and painful understanding of the albatross of racial hatred around the neck of the South—permeates Willie's classes. The writers who come to Oxford to join Willie in enlightening the students come to Faulkner's shrine as well.

Willie takes them and the students for seminars on the grounds of Faulkner's serene antebellum estate, Rowan Oak, where they sit beneath the ancient cedars and magnolia trees and beside the May-blooming roses in the formal gardens Faulkner designed himself.

"I'll never forget John Knowles, wandering around Rowan Oak," said Cindy Till, a petite blond broadcasting major from Jackson, Mississippi. "Just Knowles and Willie and Pete, Willie's dog. It was like they were on hallowed ground."

Cindy, in that wide-eyed cherubic way of Mississippi college girls, went on and on about Knowles: "He told us when he won the William Faulkner award for writing A *Separate Peace*, he was thrilled to death that he'd get to meet Mr. Faulkner himself. But he'd heard that Mr. Faulkner was so aloof, he wondered what in the world he would say. Well, Mr. Faulkner just handed Mr. Knowles his award and said, 'Here Y'are, Suh!'"

"Willie loves Faulkner," reported John Morgan, another student, rotund like Willie and a frequent drinking buddy at the Warehouse. "He has taught us how to see the South as Faulkner saw the South. He has taught us how southern people relate to stuff, and he has taught us how to see ourselves as southern people."

Willie would happily spend the whole year talking about his idol, but he allows that the students think that Styron, not Faulkner, is the greatest American novelist of the twentieth century.

Styron—whom Willie calls "Stingo"—has been to Ole Miss twice to talk to Willie's classes. He told them about the autobiographical strains in *Sophie's Choice*—he did know a Sophie in a boarding house in Brooklyn. And how he'd drop little greeting cards among his prose for his friends. (A reference to Yazoo City, Mississippi, for example, was for Willie.) He told them about what he intended in the novel, how he approached his subject, and he left them spellbound and inspired.

And then, of course, there are the stories from Morris himself. He is not a teacher, he insisted, he is a storyteller.

"Willie makes the books you read so much more alive," said Julie Critchlow, from Union City, Tennessee. "We read Truman Capote's *Breakfast at Tiffany's*, for example. Well, Willie told us about Truman: Truman drives a real big car, and he is little bitty, and he just barely peers over the steering wheel. One day Willie was standing on the street corner when here Truman comes driving along in that big car, and he stops and opens the door and says, 'Come on, Willie, let's gossip.' And Willie gets in and they drive around and around for about forty-five minutes just gossiping away."

Willie told them about the time he and Robert Penn Warren were inducted as fellows into Stillman College at Yale, speaking to about fifty students who were interested in writing. One asked, "Why do such seemingly civilized men come from such a barbaric region as the South?" and Warren answered, "I'm sick and tired of hearing that question from Yankees. I suppose my answer has to do with inoculation against hookworm!"

Willie Morris has had the range of experience to make the course meaningful to the students, with or without the visiting authors.

A native of Yazoo City, Mississippi, far to the south of Oxford, he gained his degree in English at the University of Texas in 1956. Following a four-year stint at the Other Oxford as a Rhodes Scholar studying history, he edited the *Texas Observer* from 1960–1962, went to New York to work for *Harper's* as associate editor, then served there as editor from 1967–1971. In addition to *North Toward Home* in 1967, he wrote *Yazoo* in 1971; one novel, *The Last of the Southern Girls*; and a children's book, *Good Old Boy*. He put together James Jones's notes and tapes to finish *Whistle* [1978], on which Jones was working when he died, and wrote *James Jones: A Friendship*, in 1978. Recovering from the loss of his friend, he came South partly to recapture his own literary soul.

Morris moved to Oxford from Bridgehampton, Long Island, where his neighbors and friends—the late Irwin Shaw, Truman Capote, Kurt Vonnegut, Wilfred Sheed, Craig Claiborne, Knowles and Plimpton, Joseph Heller, A. J. Liebling, and the late Jean Stafford—were mostly the writers who now figure largely in his literature course.

He lives now on Faculty Row, a street of identical white bungalows shaded by lush live oak trees, in a house to which many of his Bridgehampton neighbors find their way after lecturing to the Mississippi students. He lives alone now. His beloved companion, Pete, a black Labrador retriever whom he called his "brother," died last year. (Pete went to class, of course.)

Above the mantel in his sparsely furnished living room there is a photograph of Pete with Willie and his son, David, at the edge of a woods, goin' huntin'. David, a graduate of Hampshire College in Massachusetts, now a photographer for a south Mississippi newspaper [*Scott County Times*, Forest, Mississippi], occasionally comes up to Ole Miss for a visit.

On the mantel also is a photograph of Eudora Welty, looking out her window in Jackson; on the wall, a large portrait of Faulkner. On a battered oak table in the dining room sits a very large old Smith-Corona typewriter and a thesaurus. The novel Willie is writing, to be published by Doubleday, is set in a little Mississippi town during the Korean War. Its title is *Taps*.

"I was in high school in Yazoo City when they really started sending the bodies back. Another boy and I always played 'Taps' at the military funerals," he says.

Willie writes in the early morning hours, after the students or visitors have left his house, and on days when he doesn't have classes (he puts his telephone in the oven so he won't hear it ring), and during the summer. At those times he feels Faulkner's muse somewhere thereabouts.

As writer-in-residence at the university, Willie Morris has found writing in his own small residence (with telephone in oven) most productive. During these Ole Miss years he wrote *The Courting of Marcus Dupree* (Doubleday, 1983), primarily about football's most promising and impetuous young star, which he calls "the story of a middle-aged white man and a teen-aged black football player who get together in a town where three civil rights workers were murdered in 1964." The book is really about social change in Mississippi and how sports has become a metaphor for that change.

This spring Morris, for writing *Dupree*, won the thirty-fifth annual Christopher Award for "artistic excellence in books, films, or television specials that affirm the highest values of the human spirit."

Early this year, bookstores also began distributing *Always Stand in Against the Curve* and other stories from Morris's past, written at Ole Miss and published by Yoknapatawpha Press, as was *Terrains of the Heart and Other Essays on Home* in 1981.

Yoknapatawpha, located in Oxford and owned by Dean Faulkner Wells and her husband Larry, has also reprinted in paperback Morris's *Good Old Boy:*

A Delta Boyhood and *North Toward Home*, which continue to be sold out as soon as they are distributed.

The Wellses are reprinting *North Toward Home*, which moved a generation of expatriates (and educated a generation of northerners) in a hardcover edition this fall.

In between his work on *Taps* and his teaching, Willie is playing with another novel, this a satire on the new/old breed of southern sorority sisters, called *Goldfish*. His observations of their behavior on the campus and in the Warehouse are that most of these "Southern American Princesses," like shimmering goldfish, are ornamental—flipping their tails enticingly, but always swimming away too fast before the good old boys can catch them.

In the Warehouse, Willie holds forth after class, swapping stories with the students, memorizing sensations and quotes for his own future writing, but mainly giving of himself to them in a way they are unused to receiving from one of their parents' or professors' generation. In his old navy windbreaker, the padding of his middle years below the still-smooth round face lends Willie the appearance of an amiable bear. Or a friendly lion.

He laughs, jokes, teases them ("Come on out from behind that cigarette machine, Chris. You can't hide from me. You know you're s'posed to be home reading *The Moviegoer*). He treats them as if they were his peers, not the other way around.

There is no question but what he is loved here, as sincerely and as deeply as twenty-year-old college students first discovering literature are capable of loving. ("I'm just crazy about him," confides Morgan.) Willie knows their pain and their joys because they confide in him, and he shares his with them.

After he tells some back-slapping yarn or razzes some student unmercifully, all expression can suddenly vanish from Willie's face, and some distant suffering clouds his blue eyes.

"Being with them both exhilarates and saddens me," he says. "I am thrilled by their exuberance and energy and intelligence—the best students here are as good as the best students anywhere and they don't have the blasé attitudes you have in the East. But it saddens me to look at them, because they are so young. They don't know the terrible s—- ahead—you know, the blows life has in store for them."

Willie has had his share of losses: both his parents and some of his closest friends have died; his former wife Celia is now married to former Representative Bob Eckhardt of Texas; his friendship with Barbara Howar, inspiration for *The Last of the Southern Girls*, is over; he lost his job as editor of *Har-*

per's, which he held dear; and he has sustained other, more private of the blows life deals out.

He shares with his students the stories about James Jones, for example, whose death in 1977 still grieves Willie. What Willie gives the students is what he gave James Jones and other old friends who go out of their way to see him in Oxford, as well as the old *Harper's* crowd—Larry L. King, Marshall Frady, David Halberstam, et al., who come in to speak to his class in the journalism department—is a quality of caring.

Says Dean Faulkner Wells: "Willie has inspired me, and helped me every day, and given me the courage to try to write, and then has critiqued what I have written. Willie? He's my brother."

Wells and her husband, Larry, both former English teachers, operate the Yoknapatawpha Press, an ambitious young publishing company named for Faulkner's mythical Mississippi county. The press, whose goal is to publish quality southern writing, is located in the office on Oxford's Courthouse Square that was occupied by the lawyer Gavin Stevens during the filming of *Intruder in the Dust* [1948]. Willie spends time there, helping proofread galleys for the Wellses' *The Great American Writers' Cookbook* [1981] and for his own books, which they publish, pack, and mail. Willie has inspired both of them to go to work on their own novels.

After speaking to Willie's literature class, Dean Wells enrolled in it the next semester.

"He cares passionately about those students," she says, "just as he cares about literature."

The literature course became as popular as Willie himself, as has his writing course in the journalism department. Last year his students published a magazine [*Ole Miss Magazine*] and to his surprise, the native son who was so troubled about his state during the sixties has found a new affinity for the Mississippi of the eighties.

"The state has changed in twenty years," Willie says, "enough to make it bearable. Race is no longer obsessive—the albatross around the necks of both whites and blacks.

"There's been a liberation of sorts. These are historic times for the Deep South—especially for Mississippi."

Coming back after years of exile, Willie sees a revolution: "Who would have imagined, fifteen years ago, that you'd ever go to a Southern Conference basketball game and watch ten black players on the court at one time? Or a bunch of black Cub Scouts helping the cheerleaders in the stands? Or white coeds embracing a victorious Elston Turner, a black All-American forward?"

Willie shakes his head in wonder, and a kind of pride at visible change since federal troops were called in to quell rioting at the enrollment of James Meredith in this Deep South university in 1962. A black cheerleader at Ole Miss caused a national flurry last year when he refused to unfurl a Rebel flag at a football game, for example.

Blacks have captured academic roles there as well as in sports. Now a public relations specialist for IBM, Rose Jackson of Clarksdale, Mississippi, capped scholarship and leadership titles in her double majors of education and journalism, was one of *Glamour* magazine's "Ten Top College Women," and came hair's-breadth close to winning the top popularity contest, "Miss Ole Miss," her senior year.

Aggressive and talented black journalism students are working in newspapers and television stations all over the South and have interned on *Money* magazine in New York, *Better Homes and Gardens* in Des Moines, and the *Washington Post.*

However, Willie does not paint an all-rosy picture of the South to his students.

"He makes us realize that Mammy Callie's daughter still goes to the ice house to get water," said student John Morgan, who grew up in Oxford. "And you can go out a couple of miles into beat two and find people not even living in the twentieth century."

"Mammy Callie" was the Faulkner family's black servant, the model for his Dilsey, "who endured," who worked for the writer's family until she died at the age of one hundred—and then lay in honor in Rowan Oak.

Willie says, "I have a recurring image of running into Mr. Bill in front of Shine Morgan's Drug Store. 'Well, Morris,' he says, 'Let's go sit on the front porch, have a little whiskey, and talk about what's been hap'nin' in Mississippi since I left.'"

Willie Morris, who is now Home again, could tell him.

A Son of the South: Author Willie Morris Speaks Out from the Land He Chronicled in the '60s on Life There in the '80s

Dick Polman / 1988

From *The Philadelphia Inquirer*, 9 March 1988, sec. D, 1, 4. Reprinted with permission from *The Philadelphia Inquirer*, 9 March 1988.

McComb, Miss.—To find Willie Morris these days, you've got to ask around. He doesn't like strangers much, and even his friends are never sure whether he's home in Oxford or down here, at the other end of Mississippi, holed-up in a lakeside cabin without a phone. He's been in a troubled mood anyway, because the southern novel that has rattled around in his head for most of this decade is still up there and not down on paper. So you've got to know someone who knows Willie in order to see Willie.

To find Willie (down here, nobody uses his surname), you have to head down to pine-tree country, near the town of McComb in southern Mississippi, a raucous place where the truck-stop vending machines offer up Porn O' Plenty picture packets for four bits. A nature spot where one of the greatest living southern writers does his drinking, ruminating about the racist past, watching old days end and new days begin from the barroom of the Dixie Springs Cafe.

He's been home now for eight years, as the University of Mississippi's writer-in-residence, having burned himself out (by his own admission) during a decade lived in the Manhattan limelight, where he edited *Harper's* magazine in its halcyon days and confessed to his love-hate view of Mississippi on the pages of his 1967 memoir, *North Toward Home*—an act that made him controversial in a state still wrestling with the demons that had held it back so long.

But these days, Willie is feeling more kindly about his home, where one ancestor served as the first territorial governor and others fought for the Confederacy. Just the other night at the cafe, not long before the Super Tuesday presidential primaries, he was greatly bemused by the changes that homogenization has wrought on the ways and mores of the Old South.

"Seems like there's Republicans everywhere now," he said. He was drinking Jack Daniel's on the rocks from a tall plastic cup. "My grandmother, who was my most favorite person of all time, was one of seventeen children, and her father ran a printing press in Jackson during the Civil War. Well, one of the Union generals sent some soldiers into town during the battle of Vicksburg and threw his printing press down a well.

"So for years after, all I'd hear my grandmother say was that 'the only thing protecting Republicans in the state of Mississippi were the game laws.' But now you've got Republicans everywhere, running the country clubs."

He was chain-smoking Viceroys. He ordered a steak, then another Jack Daniel's. His friends worry about him. They ask each other, "Is he eating right?" The truth is that Willie, with his Babe Ruth face and his bad case of writer's block, has been known to sleep only when sated by food and drink.

Yet, on this night, his phrases grew mellifluous as more of the liquid passed his lips. He was sitting with a few close friends, and one of them mentioned the new suburban sprawl around Jackson, the capital city, and how these harbingers of a new industrial age seemed to be breeding Republicans in this former stronghold of segregation and one-party politics.

"I was born in 1934," Willie said, "and I remember Jackson as a sleepy ole town when I visited it. So neighborly. You'd walk by someone's house and they'd be out front saying, 'You want some ice tea?' My great-aunt always had kidney problems when I was walking with her, and she'd knock on every eighth door and she'd ask whoever answered, 'Can ah pleeeze use yo' *facilities?*'

"Then after the war," he grumbled, "that's when the people from the small towns started coming to Jackson. They'd become creatures of TV and they wanted drama and histrionics in their lives, and they weren't gonna find it in Yazoo (his hometown). Am I right, guys?"

Brad Chism nodded. He's a good old boy who likes to hunt and fish; he's also a Rhodes Scholar who met Willie when Willie, a Rhodes Scholar himself, was on the screening committee. "Rednecks love some of the stuff on cable TV," Chism said. "Some of 'em, with an eighth-grade education, wouldn't dream of missing *Crossfire* (a political show). Rednecks love a good fight, and that's a whole lot better to them than watching pit bulls go at it."

"TV's not gonna last down here," Willie said. "People are gonna go back to writing on walls of caves, which is what southerners have always done anyway. Southerners are writers, kind of old-fashioned. They're talkers. *Love* to talk. Sometimes just like to hear the sound of their own voices."

Willie was candid about race long before most Mississippians, and in a sense, he paid the price. Books like *North Toward Home* and *Yazoo* (a report on the desegregation of schools in his hometown, Yazoo City) still rankle in the minds of many down here. Folks complain about Willie going off to *Harper's* in New York, to that bastion of Yankee culture, and selling out his old neighbors. ("Oh Willie boy," huffed Veazy King, a sixty-eight-year-old farmer who knew the Morris family. "He dredged things up that should've been dead years ago.")

But Willie had no hard feelings the other night. He drained his Jack Daniel's and ordered a bottle of red Bolla wine. "May I say something?" he asked. "We've had a lot of race problems in Mississippi, and we've got a long way to go, but we're much more integrated than Pennsylvania. Although that's not saying a lot. But I've got a *generation* on y'all. I'm *older* than y'all. We made many mistakes. But this is a different society now."

His moon face took on a mournful expression. "It's no paradise, though. You drive through the Delta (the swampland along the Mississippi River that is home to thousands of poor black people) with its poverty, and it's another world. It *scares* Yankees. I love to see Yankees scared by the Delta. I've been scared by it a long time. The land itself, the brooding land, the horizons, the dead cotton.

"I remember being in New York, feeling guilty about leaving it behind. Robert Moses (a noted civil rights worker) came up to my office one day and we went to a bar to talk. He'd just emerged from solitary confinement in a Mississippi jail. We drank beer. *I* did, anyway. I don't know if a saint drinks beer. Anyway, it was one of those accidental meetings you get in the cultural capital. He unfolded this tale of bad things happening, and I felt guilty about missing the tough times."

Brad Chism interrupted. "There are no clear-cut moral choices now, Willie," he said. Chism, who was running the presidential campaign in Mississippi of United States Senator Albert Gore, Jr. (D-Tenn.), had been trying for weeks to find a way to lure black votes away from Jesse Jackson without implying that Jackson was a less credible candidate because of his color. He had not found a way. "My generation lacks patience," he said. "I'll be damned if I have to be forced to pay for the transgressions of my grandparents. I never lynched *anybody*."

Willie sighed. "If you love Mississippi," he said, "then it'll always touch your heart, because everything is complicated. We all love Mississippi, but sometimes it doesn't love us back."

"When I was twenty-one, the White Citizens' Council held a meeting in my hometown to try and get blacks to take their names off a petition calling for integrated schools. They mapped out the whole thing—how the banks would cancel blacks' credit and how landlords would throw them out. This was my hometown! All the leading citizens were there, including my father, God bless him. All the neighbors I grew up with. There are nuances that'd just break your heart."

Willie soon ordered another bottle of wine. His companions peeked at the clock. "But may I pose this question?" he said. "In how many other states, in how many other restaurants, do we have people sitting around and talking these things out with sincerity and intensity? Look, at Ole Miss we just got our first black Rhodes Scholar from the Deep South. And there were blacks at a dinner party in McComb last week, one of the few times I've seen it here.

"Don't you see? These little things *mean* something. It's up to you young people to reap the harvest from all this tragedy and move forward with intelligence, grace, insight, and humor."

Even as Mississippi begins to absorb the influx of Ramada Inns and Pizza Huts and to wrestle with the subtle race issues that are common in the North, Willie still thinks traces of the Old South will survive, and he harkens back to a magazine piece he wrote a year ago: "It is the old, inherent, devil-may-care instinct that remains in the most abundance. . . . The reckless gambler's instinct that fought and lost that war, a black mother working sixteen hours a day to educate her children, a genteel matron borrowing from the banker to send her daughter to a university sorority so she'll marry well. It is gambling with heart, it is a glass menagerie, it is something that won't let go" ["The South and Welcome to It: Does It Still Exist?" *Southern Magazine*, October 1986].

The bar was closing. A friend was waiting to drive Willie to the cabin, where his quintessential southern novel lay in fragments. "I had a difficult scene to write today, and it wasn't coming at all," he mumbled. "So I put out some bird feed and watched the cardinals swoop down for it. Did that for hours. The *hell* with writing a book. *Beautiful* cardinals. All I want to do is finish my goddamn book. Is that too much to ask? I don't even have a dog."

So with a wave and a handshake, he vanished into the pine-scented night— back to his bed, to the burden of memory, to the terrors of the empty page.

An Interview with Willie Morris

Charlie Rose / 1993

From *The Charlie Rose Show*, New York, New York. Published by permission of Rose Communications.

Rose: In 1967, at the age of thirty-two, he became the youngest editor in chief in the history of the country's oldest magazine, *Harper's*. While at the helm he provided a forum for Norman Mailer and David Halberstam and Truman Capote and Joan Didion and William Styron and many others. A southerner by birth, Willie Morris's first book in 1967, an autobiography entitled *North Toward Home*, was a classic. Now twenty-six years later he has given us its sequel, *New York Days*, about those heady and turbulent times in the literary community of the 1960s, and I'm pleased to have him here. Welcome.

Morris: Good to be here, Charlie. I like your show.

Rose: Thank you. Let me first just talk a little bit about *North Toward Home*. What was the magic? You wrote that, you young Rhodes Scholar, you smart kid from the South who comes to New York, and you not only become editor of *Harper's* magazine—this magazine that meant so much in the history of the country and in the history of magazines—but you also published *North Toward Home*, and *it* resonated. What was it about that first memoir?

Morris: I think that *North Toward Home* probably struck some strange, almost mystic chord in America, especially among small-town people and not exclusively southerners either. I've gotten *thousands* of letters on that book over the years. It was really my young man's book. *New York Days*, I hope, is my book of maturity, but I think *North Toward Home* captured some kind of spirit of adventure, of being a young American and moving around the country a lot and moving around the world in that particular period. It kind of caught the fancy of small-town Americans in the South, Midwest, and everywhere else.

Rose: So Yazoo was everybody's small town, and every young man or woman who leaves it goes somewhere to find fame and fortune?

Morris: I think so, because as you know, growing up in a small town in America you knew everybody. So in *North Toward Home* I tried to capture

128

this seething cosmos with truck drivers, baseball players, our high school English teachers, basketball coaches, Baptist preachers. I tried to do this same thing later in *New York Days*—the diverse range of people that I knew in New York City in the sixties.

Rose: But the difference is all those people you knew in New York City in the sixties were celebrated; they were *famous*.

Morris: Well, I have some reprobates in this book, some charlatans, but, yes, they were. But I was trying to use the same principle as I did in *North Toward Home*, which was to capture the spectrum of human beings that I knew and the effect they had on my life as a young American.

Rose: Why did it take you *twenty-six years*? Now these are not the only two books you've written: *North Toward Home*; *Yazoo*; *Good Old Boy*; *The Last of the Southern Girls*; *James Jones: A Friendship*; *Terrains of the Heart*; *The Courting of Marcus Dupree*; *Always Stand in Against the Curve*; *Homecomings*; *Good Old Boy and the Witch of Yazoo*; *Faulkner's Mississippi*; *After All, It's Only a Game*; and now *New York Days*. But twenty-six years to write what looks like will be a trilogy, your own autobiography.

Morris: I'm glad I waited twenty-six years. I needed that passing of time to deal with my own sense of memory. I think *New York Days* in many ways is about memory and time and its passing. I also had to have settled back happily into my native soil of the Deep South to have been able to write it. A number of people have been after me to write this book over the last quarter of a century, but there was something in the very nature of the passing of time that allowed me to deal with my southern perspective on our cultural capital in that turbulent period of the 1960s.

Rose: Was it simply because time had to pass to make it less painful for you to write it? Because in the end, this is a story of a young man who comes to New York and he is at the center of the excitement of this city in one of the most interesting times in the country, the sixties. You had giant political conflict going on and you were at the center of that and you brought together writers. And yet you lost what was your connection to the city (which was the editorship of the magazine), but in the end you got along well and you go back to Mississippi. Was it so painful you needed time to come to grips with it?

Morris: It wasn't so much pain, although there was a certain tinge of pain involved. It was how to deal with old memories and emotions in an honest and responsible way, because I knew when I set out to do *New York Days*, as a sequel to *North Toward Home*, that it was going to be a lot more than about the writing world of New York in the sixties. It was going to be about America and time passing, and I tried to deal with all this with a generosity of spirit that I think if I had tried to write this book earlier, I might not have had.

Rose: Tell me what the story is as you see it.

Morris: This is a story of New York City in the sixties and the sense of community which we had: the interlocking worlds of literature, publishing, journalism, the arts, entertainment, politics, even sports. Everyone seemed to know everyone else. Everything seemed to happen *first* in New York City in the sixties. And a provincial's coming to the great city. This is one of the sturdy chords in American literature—the provincial coming to New York and being immersed in its drama, its power, its glamour (and in my case the great old magazine in America) and trying to capture the intense pressures of the sixties and what was happening to the country. The divides across class and racial and generational lines. Everything exacerbated by Vietnam, the violence and all the rest. Trying to get one's magazine to reflect the realities of our day.

Rose: Do you think that *Harper's* magazine, during the time that you were editor, was one of the great shining moments in the history of that kind of magazine of opinion in America?

Morris: I think we certainly tried, and I think again it was part and parcel of the 1960s themselves. When I consulted with my friends and collaborators of that day when I was beginning to write *New York Days*, we all agreed without exception that the sixties amounted to the most intense period in our lives, personally and professionally.

Rose: Because of Vietnam, because of civil rights, because of . . . .

Morris: Everything. Countries seemed to be falling apart, and at the same time things ironically seemed to be coming together. But it was the *energy* that we had (of course, we were young). It was almost kinetic, and we just vibrated with energy and we cared for our nation.

Rose: Do you think it's different than the *New Yorker* is today, or other magazines like the *New Republic* in Washington, in terms of young reporters and young writers?

Morris: I like what Tina Brown is doing on the *New Yorker*. I think she appreciates fine writing and I think she has an understanding of the country, and I wish her well.

Rose: How about Andrew Sullivan at the *New Republic*?

Morris: *New Republic* [nods head]. There are fine things in *GQ*, and I like things in *Esquire* and the *Atlantic Monthly*. There's *always* fine writing out there, Charlie.

Rose: But is it different than what it was, or was *Harper's* in that time different because of the writers you assembled, because of the times to which you have already spoken, or because of something else?

Morris: I think it was different then because we had a sort of driving goal to represent the best in the country, to try to shape our civilization (a very tough time) without trying to be self-righteous. But we were propelled to do that. I'm truly glad that we tried, because I've gone back over those musty bound volumes of the sixties and they're like a cherished diary for me. Every article, every story elicits a memory that brings back youth and vitality.

Rose: And you look back at that with what? More than a cherished memory?

Morris: Oh, I look back on it with a profound sense of fulfillment and gratification. It is one's youth which always vanishes. And it is enveloped by something that obsesses me as a writer, which is old mortality itself. Perhaps one was fighting (as writing itself, I think, does for me) against old mortality, and we were also having a good time.

Rose: Your friend, William Styron, was just here Friday night a week ago and he talks a lot about death, immortality, and also about race.

Morris: Those are the things that obsess me too.

Rose: Let me talk about some criticisms of the book. Too much, they say, of a length, and too much of the parties, and too much of Willie Morris, celebrated editor, in awe of all these famous people that he had a chance to be cheek by jowl with.

Morris: Well, I think I've dealt with my own experiences honestly. I mean, that was my *life* then.

Rose: But were you too enamored of that?

Morris: Well, it was an honest emotion. It was an absolutely honest emotion, and I felt a writer *has* to be honest. And when I came up here and the word got out in the New York gossip columns that I was to be the editor of

America's oldest magazine, almost overnight it seemed I became a New York. But I was always returning to the South in those years; the South always has been a magnet for me. But as for the people who populate my book, I worked very, very hard to use the diversity of the human beings in my narrative as part of a deeper fabric of a young man's travels, of his adventures through life. I think I was being very honest there.

Rose: I agree with you. You were being honest, and you do show it, but some people say, "I wish I saw that, and he's clearly honest to say he was enamored of it all." Because it is extraordinary, this most powerful of cities with all the spectrum of wealth and talent and celebration of all that's good, but at the same time some of the deepest conflicts that men and women can have. And immediately because of this publication you were put in the center of it. You went to the finest homes, the finest parties, the finest of everything. You saw it! And at thirty-two years old that's got to be . . . .

Morris: Well, it happened to me and I felt it was my responsibility, Charlie, to describe that.

Rose: How hard was it to give this all up and go away to Long Island and then to Mississippi?

Morris: I had withdrawal symptoms at first when I moved out to eastern Long Island. I'd be less than candid if I didn't say I missed some of the perks, the power, and the glamour. The telephone stopped ringing.

Rose: You say here that when you were the editor in chief of *Harper's* at that time, *anybody* would take your call. *Everybody* would take your call.

Morris: That's true. And there I was, all of a sudden in the middle of a Long Island winter, and I pretty much concluded that I was going to devote the rest of my life to my own writing. I had a lot of good offers, of course, but I'm really glad I edited *Harper's*. I've been very much a writer at heart since I was a teenager. My whole experience as an editor, I think, has helped me as a writer and vice versa, and so I have dedicated myself to my own work, and I think a writer's own private work must constantly evolve. I'm glad I made that decision. I am very proud of *New York Days*; it was a difficult book to write. I gave my whole heart to this book and I just want the responsible reader to make his or her own judgment on it—not to mention the final enduring arbiter of posterity, which always is the last judgment.

Rose: So mortality—immortality or mortality—is in a sense a driving force here that Willie wants to say [taps book with fingers], "What it was through my eyes."

Morris: What it was really like in America, in New York City, at that time so that future generations will have some sense of what we lived through.

Rose: But how do you explain the fact that Lewis Lapham saw it differently? [Explains] The later editor of *Harper's* magazine, the man who didn't resign when you left.

Morris: Well, Lewis had to protect his own turf. I will respectfully suggest that my turf is rather more firm. Also, he takes to account in his reply to Elizabeth Hardwick's review of *New York Days*, the longest book review in the history of the *New York Times Book Review*—["'I Had Had My Pinnacle,'" *New York Times Book Review*, September 5, 1993].

Rose: [Interrupts] Wait. The review of your book was the longest book review in the history of the *New York Times Book Review*?

Morris: That's what I'm told.

Rose: So then they allow him to write a letter saying . . . .

Morris: A two-page letter ["Advertisements for Themselves: A Letter from Lewis Lapham," *New York Times Book Review*, October 24, 1993]. But I stand to be corrected if I'm wrong about the review, but that's what I've been told. I read the review of *New York Days* down there in Mississippi and it was just wonderful.

Rose: How was it? Tell me how it was.

Morris: Well, it made me feel good! Because Elizabeth Hardwick wrote it. Elizabeth Hardwick, one of the truly great writers and literary critics for many years, a towering reputation in American letters. And if Mr. Lapham is asking us to choose between himself and Elizabeth Hardwick . . . Lewis, you're making it *mighty* hard for us. [See also Willie Morris, "The Battle Over *New York Days*," *New York Times Book Review*, December 19, 1993.]

Rose: Here is what some say, though. You have made too much of a villain out of the Cowles family. There are two tracks and you draw on the one track this extraordinary story of the excitement of the times—I mean William Styron and Norman Mailer and David Halberstam, and who else?

Morris: Larry L. King, Marshall Frady, Arthur Miller.

Rose: You sent these writers out on their own journey to report back through the pages of *Harper's* magazine what was happening in America and how they saw it. That was clearly an exciting time and you were at the center of that as this brilliant young editor. On the other hand, and at the same time, they say you villainized and made a scapegoat out of the Cowles family, the publisher of *Harper's*.

Morris: I did not want to villainize the Cowleses. I think I dealt with them with generosity—I certainly tried to—but as the editor I was presented with certain alternatives that I simply couldn't live with. And I felt, "Let them get someone else to do it; I certainly couldn't live with it." All this took place twenty-three years ago, and your viewers might ask, "Editorial controversy in the middle of New York City in the 1960s and early 1970s—what does that mean?" There are resonances for that *always* in the world of journalism and literature.

Rose: And the resonance is what? What does it say to us?

Morris: To get the best writing you can. To stand for something in your own civilization. It's always hard to do, and I really wish the young people involved in the magazine profession now (in New York City and elsewhere and in newspapers) the very best. It's a tough profession, it's very demanding, it's innervating, and I may be old fashioned, but I think it demands a lot of resourcefulness and a great deal of principle.

Rose: But do you find that they might say to you, "You had it lucky, Morris, because the great conflicts were there in your time—civil rights and Vietnam—whereas we don't have as clear and decisive and divisive political conflict"?

Morris: That's a very good point, which I don't think I can answer. I look back on the sixties, and I do not share, Charlie, with many of my contemporaries a totally negative view of the sixties. There were some salubrious things happening then: a growing awareness for the fragility of the planet, the women's movement, more personal freedom, and now the baby boomers' southern branch are running the country. Maybe something good of the 1960s may be returning to the 1990s. I look forward to knowing.

Rose: Who's the best writer of your generation?

Morris: There are so many. Of course, my friend, William Styron, whom I admire so much for his fiction. He has captured so much of the realities of the South and of America. I'm a great admirer of Norman Mailer, who did wonderful stuff for us. There were some fine, fine words being written in the 1960s. I love Eudora Welty, who's a little bit older. She's part of my generation in spirit and in heart, and many other writers.

Rose: I'm out of time, but are there any great regrets? Are you sorry you gave it up?

Morris: I have no regrets. I'm glad I returned to my native ground to live, but what I mainly miss about New York City is the memory of the spirit of that time, and I miss my friends who still live here, my many friends.

Rose: This is a hymn to the city of New York, and to Manhattan, and to the energy and the passion, and all of the extraordinary talent that lies here— and other places too, but certainly a collection of it on this small island. I would suggest and guess (and I may have read this somewhere, so I can't take credit for creativity) that the autobiography continues with *South Toward Home*?

Morris: That's what I'm going do. I'm going to round out my memoir-trilogy with *South Toward Home*.

Rose: Great to have you.

Morris: Thanks, Charlie. Good to be here. Good show.

Rose: Willie Morris, *New York Days*. Back in a moment.

Praying for Baseball

Wayne Pond / 1995

Wayne Pond, Director of Public Programs at the National Humanities Center in Research Triangle Park, North Carolina, interviewed Willie Morris and Barry Moser on *Soundings*, a radio program distributed to some 450 stations in the United States. The interview was aired on the *Soundings* series during the week of July 16, 1995. Published by permission of the National Humanities Center.

Pond: Writer Willie Morris and illustrator Barry Moser. They're here to talk about their new book, *A Prayer for the Opening of the Little League Season*. Welcome to *Soundings*, a magazine of ideas and insights from the National Humanities Center.

The strike of 1994–95 put baseball and its fans through the wringer, but regardless of how you see the players and the owners, for most Little Leaguers the innocence and wonder of the game remain undamaged. In a new book for kids of all ages, writer Willie Morris and illustrator Barry Moser have created an invocation for the baseball children of the earth, for their families, friends, and neighbors. In short, for all who recall, enjoy, or anticipate the pleasures of a Little League evening. Reading *A Prayer for the Opening of the Little League Season*, here's Willie Morris and Barry Moser. [Morris and Moser alternately read the book's stanzas.]

Pond: Willie Morris and Barry Moser, welcome to the National Humanities Center and congratulations on this wonderful book you've done here for the Little League season. Tell me how this book came about. Mr. Morris, let me begin with you.

Morris: We have a very close mutual friend in Jackson, Mississippi, named John Evans, who owns one of the great bookstores in America, Lemuria. He's a big Little League coach, and for years he had been after me to write a prayer for the opening of the Little League season and to throw out the ball at the first game. I kept putting it off for years, and finally my wife and I were coming home from dinner one night in Jackson, and I said, "I'm going to get Johnny Evans off my back and I'm going to write that prayer." I wrote the first draft (and stayed up all night doing it) and polished it a lot.

136

Then I had the good fortune to hook up with, in my opinion, the greatest
illustrator in the United States, Barry Moser. He got into it when Johnny
Evans read it to you [talking to Moser] on the telephone, right?

Moser: Right. He called me on the phone one night and said, "You have
to hear this." So he read it to me and told me that he had had it printed as a
broadside, and I said, "Johnny, you have to send me one of those broad-
sides." So he did and I was even more impressed with it when I read it. The
broadside happened to be lying on a table in my studio when a friend of mine
who was also my agent, Jeff Dwyer, came by and he saw it. He has long been
an admirer of Willie's and so he read the thing and he said, "Gosh, Mose,
you know, this would make a good book!" And it hadn't dawned on me that
it might be a book because it was more like a poem, but we broke it up into
various stanzas and presented it to Rubin Pfeffer at Harcourt Brace & Company. He, being a Little League coach himself, thought it was a pretty good
idea.

Pond: I want you all to tell me how your respective imaginations worked.
Willie Morris, not to put too fine a spin on this, but when you wrote *A Prayer
for the Opening of the Little League Season*, was this a big spiritual experience, or was this really the sort of "writerly craft" at work? Then I want to
hear Mr. Moser talk about putting pictures and vividness to these words that
you came up with.

Morris: Wayne, I think it was both of those aspects. It was a writing craft,
but also my long-standing, spiritual involvement with baseball. I was a baseball player myself in Mississippi years ago, and my father taught me the
game. I grew up before the Little League phenomenon, but in writing this I
drew on my experiences with baseball and my knowledge of the game, and
once I got into the spirit of it I truly enjoyed doing it.

Pond: Do you believe we should use words like "metaphysical" and "religious" when we speak of baseball?

Morris: Well, I think it's deeply rooted in the psyche of America. When
Barry and I were collaborating on this book and he was starting in on his
wonderful illustrations, we had this whole mess with baseball. We're not
talking about the eternal verities of the game now; we're talking about federal
injunctions, salary caps, luxury taxes, and free agencies. So there is an irony
there, but I think baseball will endure and I believe that our book catches
that.

Pond: Now we are at a distinct disadvantage, Barry Moser. We are on the radio. We are not on television. We can't look at these wonderful pictures that you have created. Tell me what was it that cooked in your mind and imagination to bring them up?

Moser: First of all, they had to be accurate. One of the things that sometimes is a liability for me is when I get involved in making illustrations of things that I know nothing about.

Pond: So you're not a baseball fan to begin with?

Moser: No, not really, and I'm not a baseball fan on account of when I was in the seventh grade I went out for the baseball team at my school, and I ended up the season having *never* connected with the ball—a batting average of zero.

Pond: Don't we all have experiences like that sometimes?

Morris: Oh, of course we do. In fact, we have a stanza in here that was Barry's idea to add to my draft, about the little kids who languish on the bench or who never get a hit.

Pond: Well, give us a sense, Mr. Moser, of the range of images that you present in this.

Moser: The first image is the one that's on the jacket. It is a photograph of John Evans's team in North Jackson, Mississippi, the Lemuria Bookstore team. The arrangement of the figures which I composed out at the ball field with these kids is sort of a play—a very abstract sort of play—on Albrecht Dürer's *Praying Hands*. It's a beautiful drawing, but a very corny image.

Pond: Well, now wait. We're resorting to the classics here. I mean, we're looking at biology and anatomy and all of these sort of . . .

Moser: It's just the composition. It rises from the two sides into a peak, which is reminiscent of the *Praying Hands*, or reminiscent if you will of an arched window in a church. There are a few changes made; these are the sorts of things that I have to deal with. Johnny's team was all boys and there were no black kids on the team, so I altered that. There is a girl very dominantly shown in the picture.

Pond: Now are you surrendering to political correctness or do you really believe in these things?

Moser: From my point of view (I'm the father of three daughters and the grandfather of four . . . well, three . . . it might be four today; I'm not sure—I haven't called home yet), I'm very interested in and have been very interested in women's issues, having raised my three daughters and have a hand in raising my three . . . four granddaughters.

Morris: Also, Barry and I have been traveling around the country extensively on this book and we find that a lot of girls are playing Little League baseball.

Moser: Absolutely, and now there are the Denver Silver Bullets. And if anything has peaked my interest in baseball it is the advent of a women's professional baseball team.

Pond: When I looked at *A Prayer for the Opening of the Little League Season* I don't mind telling you it brought tears to my eyes, and I thought to myself, "My goodness, you all are evoking this incredible sense of innocence and wonder." Let me ask you to step back from the book itself, gentlemen. Take the measure of the society that we live in, and at one end you have a book such as the one you have done here, and at the other end you have got the terrible circumstances of American culture with all of our problems: education, one thing and another— you can tick off this long litany. Is this a sort of last gasp here of American innocence?

Morris: I certainly hope not, and I don't think it is. However, I think the problems of organized baseball in the United States today are a reflection of the broader society, as indeed baseball has been historically. A marvelous Ken Burns Public Broadcasting System documentary captured something of that essence [*Baseball*, 1994]. But I think what's happening in organized baseball today is a reflection of a general greed in American life. (I think the owners are more greedy than the players, but not by much.) But at the same time, in contrast, you have these rituals and cadences and rhythms of the game itself, which spring from the pastures of America.

Pond: Who was the author who wrote a book called *Take Time for Paradise*? [A. Bartlett Giamatti, *Take Time for Paradise: Americans and Their Games*, 1989.] In other words, when we get out there it is sort of our little moment of the celestial kingdom. Whether it's little kids (or if we suspend our disbelief and watch the grownups do it) it still has this wonderful clarity; it's a kind of parenthesis in our lives.

Morris: It's these historical cadences of the country. It's interesting—just when this book came out I was in a bookstore and I saw a man thumbing through our *Prayer for the Opening of the Little League Season*, and he was crying. Big tears were coming down his face and I was a little worried. (I had first aid in the Boy Scouts and I feel some responsibility to the Boy Scout Oath.) I went over to him and asked him if he was okay. He said, "I'm an umpire and I've just been reading your stanza in yours and Mr. Moser's book about umpires. This is the first time I have ever seen any sympathy expressed for umpires." The little stanza goes: "Absolve the umpires from the consequences of their flaws, bequeath them transcendent vision, and sanctify them above all for the close calls at the plate, for they, more than any of Thy creatures, are afflicted with tribulations." So this fellow was still crying. I didn't know umpires cry.

Pond: See, here is strong evidence for the fact that baseball is a sort of theological exercise, that we're into large words like "sin" and "redemption" and "salvation."

Morris: I think that on its more pristine level, it is very theological.

Pond: Mr. Moser, I want you to talk about the illustrations that you provided for *A Prayer for the Opening of the Little League Season*. Put baseball into the spectrum of American iconography. How does it figure in our art and the kind of work that you do?

Moser: It's a very strange thing that it has become something of a mainstream for me now, even belying the fact that I am not really a baseball fan. The first book was one that I did with David Godine a number of years ago, the centennial edition of *Casey at the Bat*, for which Donald Hall did an introduction [Ernest Lawrence Thayer, *Casey at the Bat*, 1988]. Then last year I had a book come out with Richard Wilbur called *A Game of Catch* [1994], and then Willie's and my book this season, and a year from now there is going to be another book that I did with Donald Hall, called *When Willard Met Babe Ruth* [1996]. So I began simply because I'm somewhat methodical and fastidious about my research on these things, as I hate being caught in a mistake. It is so embarrassing.

Pond: Well, you used the word *accurate*; you wanted to be accurate.

Moser: Yes, absolutely. And when you don't know something and the only thing that I have to rely on are my eyes, my observation, that observation has to be keen; it has to be right on the money. So I have been observing a lot of things and the more I observe about baseball, particularly about its history and the photographic iconography that exists (I've made my trip to Cooperstown, New York, to do my research and all that sort of thing), the more I've become fascinated. I've really become fascinated with it.

I don't know that if I were not making images for books, how much base-ball would influence my iconography. As an easel painter, my imagery might be very different from my work as an illustrator. The two things are not the same thing, because when I am making illustrations (and this is something a lot of people have a very hard time understanding) I don't particularly see my paintings as being the objects of art, if you will. It's the book; it's the whole book. Each one of these paintings is a piece of an entity. And then the typography. I spend more time working on the typography in a book like this than I do making the pictures.

Pond: Now, did you all talk back and forth a good bit or was it sort of "each man to his own and then we'll let an editor put this book together?" How did that work, Mr. Morris?

Morris: We did talk some and Barry has an interesting story. The book needed some additions for the sake of a thirty-two-page signature, so one of the things I added by telephone (Barry lives in Massachusetts and I live in Mississippi) is the part about the kids who sit on the bench all the time. Here is the stanza: "Comfort the smallest of the ballplayers, who have never gotten a hit, and those who strike out time and time again or languish on the benches day after livelong day, for their moment, too, is destined to be." And Barry has a classic watercolor of the little boy who is always striking out, but two years hence might be hitting the curve ball.

Pond: I have to hand it to you for the way you have put the words and the pictures together here. The book is kind of nostalgic and yet it is very imme-diate in the present. It's a great consolation to look at the way you have brought these words and pictures together.

Moser: Thank you. I think another interesting thing about it is the trim size. It's a very small book. I had to actually do some arguing with my editor about that, because the format of the book is the first thing I have to deal with. And the standard thirty-two-page picture book for children is eight-and-one-half by eleven inches.

Pond: Now I can't let you get away sounding quite so positive. I remember interviewing a novelist, a man named Steven Yount, who had written a book called *Wandering Star* [1994]. It's about the end of the world in High Plains, Texas, in 1910, but there is a wonderful baseball episode in this thing. And what that book reminds us of is that baseball really has a kind of mixed past. There was a time when it was not respectable; it was an excuse for bullies and loudmouths to go out and beat up on people. How do we think about baseball?

Morris: That's absolutely true. Bullies still populate the baseball scene, and I think in contemporary major league baseball a lot of players are not setting good examples for the kids. I'm not talking about off-the-field matters, but on the field. They become such showboats. This is not a good example, but I guess some people feel that a childhood is an adult pastime. I disagree. I happen to be perhaps the United States's oldest living sixth grader. I'm obsessed with childhood and I've written a lot about it, and if I may say so I think Barry Moser's beautiful watercolors catch so much of the mood of childhood itself. I think this book is not just about baseball. It's about childhood, about growing up, and the patterns of growing up. And baseball does test you at an early age. You boot a grounder, and you're not going to have anywhere to hide.

Pond: Absolutely. Were you aware of yourselves, as author and illustrator, fitting into this larger pattern of . . . shall we call it the little boys' book or the little persons' book? I mean, on a grand scale we could talk about things like Huck Finn and that sort of . . .

Morris: Huck Finn couldn't hit the curve ball though. He was okay on the knuckler. Barry and I have never really collaborated on a book before; we will in the future. The first time we met was in the Governor's mansion, in Jackson, Mississippi, at a party for Eudora Welty. Barry is an old friend of my wife, who is a book editor, so we got into this thing. How do you [talking to Moser] feel about this as a childhood-type book? You don't see it as a child's book, do you?

Moser: No, I really don't. In fact, I don't want to get pedantic here but we do have in our country a serious discrimination against children. There are very few writers in our country who will write, or who can write, or indeed who will write for adults *and* children. And you can basically name them on your fingers and have a few fingers left over. Willie Morris, of course. Donald Hall has done it, Eudora Welty has done it, Alice Walker has done it, and so forth.

Pond: Let me stop you. Whom is this book for, then? Is it for the whole spectrum of our population? Whom did you have in mind when you wrote the words [talking to Morris], and Mr. Moser, when you did the pictures?

Morris: I say everyone.

Moser: That would be my answer too.

Morris: Everyone. Children of all ages, as Ringling Brothers and Barnum & Bailey used to proclaim. I don't see this as a juvenile, quote, juvenile book, but I see it as a book for everyone. Don't you, Barry?

Moser: I do, absolutely. When I did the pictures for Dante [Dante Alighieri, *The Divine Comedy of Dante Alighieri*, 1980; *Inferno*, 1980], and illustrations for other classics, I did not maintain any different degree of craftsmanship, nor sincerity, nor maturity, nor intellectual acumen.

Pond: You don't condescend to the subject, in other words.

Moser: Absolutely not, and that's the great mistake when people *do* write for children, in that they *will* condescend to them. And children have enormous (I'm not sure whether I can say this on the air so I'll put it another way) detectors for feculence.

Pond: Well, this is a G-rated radio show so we'll let the listeners translate that for themselves. Gentlemen, I want to thank you for coming by the National Humanities Center. Willie Morris and Barry Moser. The book is *A Prayer for the Opening of the Little League Season*. It is a wonderful bringing-together of words and pictures. I thank you for your time on *Soundings*, and I certainly wish you well in your work.

Moser: Thanks.

Morris: Thanks so much.

Pond: This is *Soundings*, a magazine of ideas and insights from the National Humanities Center. I'm Wayne Pond. My guests this week were writer Willie Morris and illustrator Barry Moser.

An Interview with Willie Morris

Charlie Rose / 1995

From *The Charlie Rose Show*, New York, New York. Published by permission of Rose Communications.

Rose: He played football, he loved baseball, he fell for a girl named Rivers, and he broke up church services in Yazoo City, Mississippi. His name was Skip, and when he and Willie Morris were young, they were constant companions. *My Dog Skip* is Willie Morris's boyhood memoir of growing up in the South during World War II. His journey has taken him from Yazoo to Oxford and a Rhodes Scholarship to his New York days as editor of *Harper's* magazine in the sixties, and back again to his Mississippi home. And I am very pleased to have him back on this show. Welcome.

Morris: Good to be here again, Charlie.

Rose: Thank you. Did you ever think that during all those times—because Skip was such a central part of your recollections of your boyhood—that someday you'd put Skip in a book?

Morris: Skip, Charlie, was not my dog. He was my brother and I still miss him. When I recently walked into the Yazoo City Historical Museum and saw that Skip's tombstone was on display, I realized what a chord that our inseparable days together had been in that vanished era of World War II and beyond. We were, in every sense, brothers.

Rose: What was it? Tell me what was it that made you want to say this. Was it a recollection? I mean, here you have written about your New York experiences. You've written about going back to Yazoo City.

Morris: Yes, a lot of controversial books.

Rose: That's right, and here is a book about your childhood and growing up with your best friend, a dog.

Morris: I think as one—shall I say—grows more mature, and you are in a rush, you're brought back to your childhood and boyhood days. I think this is a common experience for human beings, and by the very nature of writing a memoir about yourself in relation to your beloved dog of your boyhood, you will revisit those childhood experiences.

It was the World War II era, in a small American town in the South, and

Skip and I would wander all around together. Once he broke up our baseball game while I was playing center field, and he kept my friend and me up in an elm tree for two hours because we'd thrown a stick for him and then hid in the tree. He found us and kept us up there so long we missed a Cub Scout meeting.

But I think people are kind of interested in couples—Caesar and Cleopatra or Nicholas and Alexandra. And what more enduring combination through the ages than a boy and his dog? Or, I will say, a girl and her dog.

Rose: Yes, Rivers Applewhite. What a name for a young girl. She was your first love?

Morris: Yes, and Skip's too. On Skip's fourth birthday, Rivers gave a birthday party for him in her back yard and invited all the neighborhood dogs. She made a cake of baloney, which was his favorite food, and dog food. On top she spelled out with salted peanuts, "Happy Birthday, Old Skip." That cake was gone in about forty-five seconds.

Rose: This is what Winston Groom, who wrote *Forrest Gump* [1986], said. [Reads]: "Willie Morris takes us back to a Huck Finn America, a time when boys and dogs spent endless days in irreverent play and serious joy. Morris's years with Skip tell us about canine love and courage, friendship and loyalty. With true artistry and exquisite writing, Morris portrays an America rich in the tradition of decency and good humor."

Morris: And you know that Winston has a dog, a sheepdog named Forrest Gump, who slept in a bed with me once in their house down in Mobile.

Rose: Was it more difficult to write this, or just a breeze to write?

Morris: Well, it wasn't a breeze, but I will say that this is the only book I've ever written that I enjoyed writing. It was sort of a warm catharsis for me.

Rose: Because there was no pain.

Morris: No pain, except, you know, the inevitable pain of the passing of time, because back then Skip and I didn't know that we were going to grow old. An interesting thing is happening, Charlie. I've been traveling around and signing this book to a lot of dogs. The first time, in Oxford, Mississippi, this woman came up and said, "Sign this to Cindy." I said, "Well, are you Cindy?" And she said, "No, Cindy is my cocker spaniel." And another guy said, "Sign this to King Solomon." And I said, "Are you King Solomon?" "No, King Solomon is my black Lab."

Rose: What does it do for you to revisit your childhood like this, to really have to think about it and think about a quieter, different time when you are long since distant from that time?

Morris: It seizes me in my very soul, the passage of the years. I grew up before television, and Skip and I would sit out on quiet, hot summer nights on the front porches—also before air conditioning—with the old people and listen to their stories. They were really trying to give us a way to see, although we would not have known it at the time. A fire truck would come by about eight o'clock on a hot summer night. Skip and I would jump in my father's old green DeSoto and follow the fire truck. We were a small town then, and we were so isolated.

Of course we had radio. It was the World War II era, and Skip hated to hear Hitler on the radio. It would make his ears rotate like miniature windmills to hear Hitler's rhetoric on the shortwave. I've never known a dog so down on Hitler, but he loved FDR's *Fireside Chats*.

Rose: Do you have a dog today?

Morris: No. I took my dog, Pete—a Yankee dog who was the mayor of Bridgehampton, New York—to Mississippi when I moved back years ago. Skip was the dog of my boyhood, but Pete of my middle age. He learned how to bark with a southern accent and eat collard greens. When he died it split my heart. We buried him close to the old William Faulkner plot in the Oxford, Mississippi, cemetery. People kept asking me, "Will you ever get another dog?" I said, "I'll get another wife first." Which I did.

Rose: You as a writer are looking back at an earlier time in your life. This is when you were a boy and you had an extraordinary opportunity. You won a Rhodes Scholarship. You got a first-rate education. You became a center of the conversation of this city and with all the power that magazine publishing has. You saw that power taken away, though you still continue to write. What would you do differently? I mean, when you sort of size up those experiences that you have had, what would you do differently, if anything?

Morris: I've often thought that if I had it to do over again, I would just have stuck with my own writing, rather than that fabulous experience I had running the oldest magazine in America, *Harper's*, in the turbulent sixties. It's a hard question, but I have pondered it. I might have just stayed home and devoted myself to books and writing, although I would take nothing in the world for spending those years in this fabulous, complicated city.

Rose: Do you think you were as good as you could have been?

Morris: I don't think anyone ever thinks that. I certainly don't, but, you know, I've made a shot at it. I have, and there's still a lot more books I want to do. I'm proud of *My Dog Skip*. I will say that quite genuinely. It's right towards the end when I cried—the only time I ever cried when I was writing a book. My wife, JoAnne, saw me cry.

Rose: What were you writing when you cried?

Morris: I was writing the end. But I also cried a little when I was writing the first two pages, when I first saw him as a puppy. But this was the only time I ever shed a few tears when I was writing. They were good tears. But I usually don't cry much.

Rose: I want you to read something from this, but I just want to read one thing myself. [Reads]: "And that Skip himself had somehow grown old. He was eleven when I graduated from college, and feeble, with arthritis in his legs. Sometimes he still had the devilish look of eye, but he did not retrieve sticks anymore, and preferred lying in the shade of the trees, or under the steps to the back door, and he did not want to ride in the car, and he never woke me up in the mornings; it was I who had to wake *him* up."

Morris: Let me see that book, Charlie. [Reads]: "The first time I saw him, my father had picked him up at the depot and brought him home in a portable kennel. I led him into the house and gave him some puppy food in a dish. That night he jumped into my bed and stared at me, as if he were looking me over. Then, perhaps because he missed his mother in Missouri, he went to sleep in my arms. I was an only child, and he now was an only dog."

Rose: *My Dog Skip*. This was for Duke and Magic and Max. Willie Morris has been here. It's a pleasure to see you, as always.

Morris: Always good to see you, Charlie.

Rose: Thanks.

An Interview with Willie Morris

Michael Feldman / 1996

From the *Whad'Ya Know?* Show, Public Radio International, Madison, Wisconsin. Recorded in Jackson, Mississippi, before a studio audience. Published by permission of Michael Feldman.

Feldman: You think this applause is for me; it is not for me. Ladies and gentlemen, it is for Willie Morris, joining us right now. I was going to introduce you and everything, Willie, but you kind of upstaged me there.

Morris: Michael, welcome to the great and sovereign state of Mississippi. You bring great cheer from our distinguished sister state of Wisconsin, and I say, "Go, Wisconsin Badgers!"

Feldman: Yes, you do. Or as we like to call it up there, "Ole Wis."

Morris: I've heard about your legendary audiences, Michael. I look around this big auditorium in Jackson, Mississippi, totally packed, and it looks to me as if you have the most distinguished assemblage of people together under one roof since Elvis dined alone on catfish. *Southern* catfish.

Feldman: Willie, it's great to have you here. *My Dog Skip* is the new book from Willie Morris, and that's out right now.

Morris: Just about out in paperback. Michael, before we begin, I've always loved live radio. I was a disc jockey at the age of sixteen in Yazoo City, Mississippi.

Feldman: I didn't know that. Is that right?

Morris: And here our call letters: "This is radio station WAZF, 1230 on your dial, in downtown Yazoo City, Mississippi, Gateway to the Delta, with studios high atop the Taylor Roberts Feed and Seed Store."

Feldman: And what was the format like on that stage?

Morris: It was very loose. I had a show called *Darkness on the Delta*, and I have a little scene in *My Dog Skip* about how he would come into the radio station with me, and he would help me with my call-ins.

Feldman: Did he drive you down there himself?

Morris: He drove me down himself. Skip was the most remarkable dog. He could drive a car—with a little help. He played football. He and I were in love with the same girl, Rivers Applewhite, and Skip held for years the world record for fox terriers in the 100-meter dash: 4.7 seconds.

Feldman: Now what was the secret with the football? It's hard for a dog to carry a football—ordinarily.

Morris: Skip was a single wing formation tailback. Back then my great idols were the Tennessee Volunteers, the Ole Miss Rebels, and the Mississippi State Bulldogs. But Michael, we had to tear a little part of the leather strip on the football so he could carry it in his mouth. I was the blocking back in the single wing, and Skip followed me wherever I went. We would have these football games in my front lawn in Yazoo City, and we would stop traffic. Skip would score touchdowns right and left, and one old man once shouted, "Look at that ol' dog playing football. Can he catch a pass?"

Feldman: And could he? You didn't work that out, did you? It's hard for a terrier to receive, right? As a receiver they're limited.

Morris: Skip was not in our pass patterns; he was basically a running back. He was also a pretty good Methodist.

Feldman: How did you know?

Morris: My mother was the organist in the church, and Skip would come in, and once he disrupted the service while Mrs. Stella Birdsong—who had the highest, worst high-C quaver, with the tenacity of a steel riveter—was singing. This was long before air conditioning, Michael, that great desecrater of conversation (that and may I say television? But live radio is good). Skip came down the aisle one day with these other dogs, and when Mrs. Stella Birdsong hit that high C he started moaning, left, and we could hear him from six blocks away.

Skip always knew where I was and could get into any place where I was. He was an extraordinary dog and had the most uncanny sense of ESPN—I mean ESP! He knew where I was at any given moment. We grew up together, and it was in the very process of writing this book that I of course got to relive those childhood and boyhood scenes, which were in a small southern town in the World War II era. It afforded me a chance to revisit those fantastic memories.

Feldman: And this was in Yazoo City?

Morris: In Yazoo City, Mississippi. You know what "Yazoo" means, don't you?

Feldman: No, I don't.

Morris: "Yazoo" is an old Indian word that means "death" or "waters of the dead." So when we were playing sports in the Delta Valley Conference, people from, say, Belzoni or Indianola or Itta Bena always called us . . . "Death City." But we always whipped 'em!

Feldman: But that's the kind of reputation you *want* for a team, right? You don't want to be known as the "Fighting Okra." That doesn't inspire fear.

Morris: Not even the "Thundering Herd," or maybe the "Badgers."

Feldman: So to this day you go back to Yazoo City on a regular basis. Do you have relatives up there?

Morris: I live right here in the capital city, Jackson, with my lovely wife JoAnne, who is the executive editor of the University Press of Mississippi, which in my opinion, per capita, may be the finest university press in America. And JoAnne is from downtown Indianola.

Feldman: Now when you say Indianola I notice there is something in your voice. What is it about Indianola that—

Morris: Well, they're Yankees. They're further north.

Feldman: All right. I thought something was there.

Morris: Indianola is the hometown of Craig Claiborne, the great writer for the *New York Times*, and B. B. King, of course. My wife, JoAnne, entered the University of Mississippi with James Meredith in 1962, which I always call the Last Battle of the Civil War. And JoAnne is a Chi Omega intellectual. Now that is *not* an oxymoron.

Feldman: What about them Fighting Okra, though? Are you familiar with the Fighting Okra? You're a big sports fan in general, aren't you?

Morris: Yes. What is the nickname of Marshall University?

Feldman: I don't know.

Morris: The Thundering Herd. The Fighting Okra are Delta State University.

Feldman: Did you play all sports yourself?

Morris: All sports. I played all sports.

Feldman: Were you a good baseball player?

Morris: I was a good baseball player. I was struck out four times in the

Southern Finals when I was sixteen in the stadium at Louisiana State University at Baton Rouge by a little left-hander named Seth Morehead. He is now a car salesman over there, but made it to the major leagues with the Chicago Cubs and the Old Milwaukee Braves. He struck me out *four times* in one game, but it was the first game we ever played at night.

Feldman: Oh, so you didn't adjust to that?

Morris: We had never played at night, so we really couldn't see that curve ball.

Feldman: Did they have lights?

Morris: They had lights in the Baton Rouge Stadium, but they were rather weak and sometimes you could not tell the baseballs from the bugs.

Feldman: Do you get back to New York much these days?

Morris: I go back a lot. I lived in New York for twenty years. One of my regrets is that my dog Skip never went to New York. I think if Skip had gone to New York he would have been mayor. He would have beaten Ed Koch. But I mainly miss my friends up there.

Feldman: But you had a dog in New York, didn't you?

Morris: Oh, I had a black Labrador. Pete was the mayor of Bridgehampton, Long Island. I brought him down here. Michael, it was one of the most histrionic moments in the tawdry history of my life when I persuaded my Yankee dog, Pete, who was the mayor of Bridgehampton, to finally jump in the car with me and come to Mississippi. My son, David Rae, and I came down, and Pete fell in love with the South. He started eating collard greens. His favorite song was "You Ain't Nothin' but a Black Lab Hound Dog."

Feldman: Do you get tired of being asked to explain the South, or what the southern voice is, or what's different about the South?

Morris: Well, now, what is the South? Where are we now? Is this the South?

Feldman: To me this is the South. South Milwaukee to me is the South.

Morris: I have an explanation about why Mississippi and the South have produced so many great writers. Men, women, blacks, whites, and such marvelous blues musicians. And such *great* athletes—white and black—like Jerry Rice from Mississippi Valley State University, Walter Payton, Brett Favre, Steve McNair, Charlie Conerly. I've been asked all over America, Michael, why Mississippi is so distinctive. You know, we have our failings, but we're coming along all right. But as to why Mississippi is so artistic and athletic I always say there is something in the quality of two things: memory . . . and the sour mash bourbon.

Feldman: I would think one would affect the other. But people talk here. Do they still sit around and talk?

Morris: This may be the only state in the union remaining where people finish other people's sentences. I first met Eudora Welty, who is one of my heroines, at the age of eight in the Jitney Jungle [a grocery store chain] in Jackson, Mississippi. She was a friend of my Great-Aunt Maggie Harper, who never married because she was born during the Civil War period and there were no men to marry; they had all been knocked off by guys from Wisconsin.

Feldman: We were still in the Ukraine so don't look at me.

Morris: Okay, that's good lineage! But anyway, I met Eudora Welty during World War II and Jackson, Mississippi, was marvelous. It was a big army base and the Dutch airmen were here. Maggie introduced me to her and I shook her hand (Eudora later said I had on a sailor's cap and I was barefooted). But as we were leaving the Jitney Jungle, my Great-Aunt Maggie— who was about eighty-five at the time and was wearing an old, flowing black dress—whispered in my ear, "Eudora Welty, she writes them stories her *own* self."

Feldman: What if Faulkner had been born in Hibbing, Minnesota? Would that have changed the course of southern literature?

Morris: No, his name would have been Garrison Keillor. He would have written *The Sound and the Snow*. That's a good question. I'm not being facetious.

Feldman: Oh, go ahead. I do it all the time.

Morris: I think great artistic vision exists anywhere. If Faulkner had been born in Hibbing, Minnesota, he'd have written great stories. They would have been *different* stories, but they would have been great stories with a marvelous universality and with the chords of his Nobel Prize speech: the old enduring heart and the human heart in conflict with itself. If Mr. Bill Faulkner, rather than being in Mississippi, had grown up in Minnesota, his marvelous tales of human beings would have been just as great, but they would have been set in cold weather. He wouldn't have had any mosquitos to speak of.

Feldman: But would the characters have been there?

Morris: They would have been there. They would have been different characters but there is a universality I think to the human genius of a William Faulkner, or a Eudora Welty, or any number of our great writers, from Ellen Douglas right on down the list. Richard Wright, his characters would have been different characters. But they would at the same time have meant a great deal to people in Minnesota, as his characters mean now to people in Mississippi. It's a matter of feeling and degree, I think.

Feldman: And does that still exist in the South? That matter of feeling is kind of a southern trait, the matter of being talkative, the matter of taking literature seriously and reading it for the insights it brings. Does that still exist? Do we still have a breeding ground for writers?

Morris: Very much so, Michael, despite the shopping malls and suburbia and the subdivisions with outside walks. We don't sit on the front porches anymore and tell stories and hear the old people tell stories. Now we are inside because of air conditioning and because of that great silencer of conversation, television. I love live radio! But yes, indeed, the southern tradition of storytelling in the King James Version of the Bible and old people telling young people stories (in which they really gave us a way to see, although we didn't know it at the time), is still very much true, I think. I hope I'm not being too sanguine. People often ask me, "Are you a southern writer?" I consider myself to be an American writer who lives in the South. I love the South. I think we've had our problems, but we've come a long way and we will *always* forever tell stories, especially when people from Madison, Wisconsin, come in.

Feldman: Tell me one of those stories, Willie. Do we have time for a short story? [Aside].

Morris: Okay, I'll give you a story about *My Dog Skip* because it's coming out in paperback next week. Skip hated Adolf Hitler. My story about my dog Skip is set in World War II, and Skip would listen to Hitler on the radio. This is just as World War II was about to break out, and I never knew a dog so down on Hitler. He would hear the Führer's shrill, fiery speeches, and ol' Skip's ears would move like miniature windmills, and he would start howling at the Führer. Skip did not hate Mussolini as much as he hated Hitler.

Feldman: There you go! Willie, thank you for coming.

Morris: Thank you, Michael.

Feldman: Willie Morris, ladies and gentlemen.

A Conversation with Willie Morris
Jack Bales / 1997

The University of Mississippi's Department of Archives and Special Collections acquired Willie Morris's papers in 1995. Two years later Jack Bales pored over most of the seventeen thousand documents during a summer research trip to Mississippi. During his stay, while visiting Morris and his wife, JoAnne Prichard, in Jackson, the author took him on what he calls his "sixty-four thousand dollar tour" of Yazoo City.

"My town," Morris has frequently acknowledged, "is the place which shaped me into the creature I am now." Thus, it is not surprising that while driving along virtually every street and road in Yazoo City he reflected on the formative years of his youth, pointing out buildings, streets, and numerous other sites both personal as well as historical.

Morris has transferred many of these boyhood landmarks to the pages of *North Toward Home*, *Good Old Boy*, *My Dog Skip*, and other books, and on a sunny, unseasonably mild June day he was a patient guide in the midst of persistent questioning and furious note taking. "Now in *North Toward Home*, Willie, you say that on Saturdays you went to the Kiddie Matinee at the Dixie Theater. Are movies still shown there?" "Is the building where you had your radio show still standing?" "Where is the cemetery and the grave of the Witch of Yazoo?"

With their journey through the past completed, the two returned to Jackson. That afternoon Bales formally interviewed Willie Morris, setting up a tape recorder in the dining room while one of the family cats, Spit McGee, hovered quizzically nearby.

Bales: Willie, your latest book is *My Dog Skip*, published in 1995. You have mentioned that this is the only book you enjoyed writing, and after reading it, I got the impression that it bears the imprint of a satisfied, serene, and confident man who has returned to his roots and is clearly at peace with himself and his surroundings. Is this an accurate assessment?

Morris: Yes, I think reasonably so. A happy marriage helps, of course. JoAnne is also a wonderful editor who assists me a great deal, and it was she and my agent, Theron Raines, who really got me to do *My Dog Skip*. Theron saw a possible Hollywood movie in it. I was ready to write it because my previous book, *New York Days*, was a very difficult task. It involved a lot of hard work, was quite emotionally draining, and took me about two-and-a-half years to finish. It brought back exhilarating memories, *New York Days* did, but also painful memories. But I'm very glad I did it. I had been postponing *New York Days* for quite a long time, and with *My Dog Skip* I wanted

154

a change of pace and to write something rather affectionate with warm memories. What better project is there than to write about the beloved dog and brother of one's boyhood?

Bales: You paint a portrait in *My Dog Skip* of life being rather carefree with cane pole fishing, Nehi soda, and the old-time grocery store. Was life really that idyllic?

Morris: No, it was not all that idyllic. I think I wrote a more complete portrait of Yazoo City during that period in the Mississippi section of *North Toward Home*. But it was also a period in one's life where it *seemed* idyllic, and that was the point for me and is the narrative flow of *My Dog Skip*. It was the war-time period in an isolated, deep-southern town and I recount the adventures and pranks that my dog and I played. I have received just hundreds of letters from people around the country on this book. It has touched a chord somewhere and it is even being published abroad.

As I said, I have received just *such* a response to it, and in various book signings around the country, from California to New York City, I have found that I was signing books to people's dogs, both living and dead. The only difficulty was in Square Books in Oxford, Mississippi. The owner, Richard Howorth, offered to discount some of these books to people who brought their dogs, and it worked out pretty well for a while but then a big dog fight broke out.

At a big book signing I had in New York City the organizers also invited people to bring their dogs. JoAnne and I were judges in look-alike contests—which dog looked more like an American writer than the others. We picked out one big dog that looked like Kurt Vonnegut, and another dog that looked a little like Eudora Welty.

Bales: Your attitude toward the South in general, and Mississippi in particular, has changed over the years. What specifically have you observed from when you were a boy until about now?

Morris: Mississippi is a very funny, complicated place. Of course, it has changed since my boyhood time, and for the better. It could not have been any worse than in the fifties and sixties. It was for black people essentially a police state and that obviously has improved. Blacks vote now. They could not vote back then. They could not go into the restaurants and could not go to swimming pools. There were gravel and unpaved roads in middle-class black districts. Now Mississippi has more elected black officials than any other state. Jackson, Mississippi, last week just elected its first black mayor in history.

So on the surfaces, there has been a sea change since the forties, fifties, and sixties, but race is still the central thread of life in this state. It is such a horrifically complex thing. Mississippi politically remains a staunchly conservative state. The new Republicans are in power—the Governor, two U.S. Senators, right on down the line. I grew up a couple of blocks from Haley Barbour, who is the national chairman of the Republican Party. I once was asked to inscribe a book to Haley when he came to power as the national chairman of the GOP, which I said I would sign if he read my inscription before the audience. He agreed and my inscription in effect said, "Haley, congratulations. Good luck. Not too much good luck. May I remind you that whereas I remain a member of the party of Jefferson Davis, Stonewall Jackson and Robert E. Lee, you are a member of the party of Thaddeus Stevens, William Tecumseh Sherman, and Ulysses S. Grant." I did not mention Lincoln. So on the surfaces, this state has changed remarkably for the better, though there is still a hard-core racism here.

Bales: I think I remember seeing someplace, perhaps in the courthouse in Jackson, where you can still the words "Blacks Only" or "Whites Only."

Morris: Yes. As you know, I have just finished this book for Random House, a very personal book in the same vein as *North Toward Home*, *New York Days*, and *The Courting of Marcus Dupree*. One of its narrative threads is the making of Rob Reiner's movie, *Ghosts of Mississippi*, which is partly about the Byron De La Beckwith trial in 1994. My son David Rae, a photographer, was covering the trial at the courthouse in which Beckwith was finally convicted of murdering Medgar Evers thirty years earlier. He called me and said, "You better come on down here," which I did. The trial was quite a historical event and during a recess he took me up to the third floor of the Hinds County Courthouse and showed me the door, which is a real pentimento. The door to the restroom had been painted over, but beneath the coat of paint you could make out the outlines of the words "White Women."

Bales: Along these same lines, I sense many conflicting emotions about racial changes in your writings, particularly in some of your earlier essays, such as "Despair in Mississippi; Hope in Texas" [*Dissent*, summer 1963]. You are repelled by your native state, but you are still drawn to it. You are appalled by the race conditions, but are still hopeful. What else were you thinking back then? But more importantly, what led you to question this way of life after your youth spent in the Deep South during this troubled era?

Morris: Well, that's a good question. I was very embittered toward my native soil during that period when I wrote the *Dissent* article, but Mississippi had indeed descended into barbarism. That was the year that Beckwith killed Medgar Evers. That was the year after the James Meredith crisis at Ole Miss, which I always call the Last Battle of the Civil War. And it was also a period—I think I mentioned this in *North Toward Home*—in which Mississippi had produced a genuine set of exiles, almost in the European sense, and I was one of them. I was living in California at the time, but later I moved to New York, and in New York City there were just dozens of Mississippians who were exiles from their own land but who still loved the state and whose roots were there. It was truly a love-hate relationship.

I recall Faulkner's words vis-à-vis Mississippi: "One loves a place not so much because, but despite of." Not because of its virtues but despite its faults. I felt that very much back then. While living in the East and running a national magazine, and then writing and continuing to live on Long Island, I have always viewed my native ground from afar. When I eventually returned, I was just going to sort of "test the waters," I suppose, by being writer-in-residence at Ole Miss. I planned on just staying a year, but that was early 1980 and I have been here in Mississippi ever since. I want to see how it all turns out. I want to see what happens.

Bales: It all reminds me of one of your favorite phrases: "The old warring impulses of one's sensibility to be both Southern and American."

Morris: That's very much a part of it. As with a number of other writers from the South, I am asked this question a lot. I do not consider myself a southern writer. I consider myself an American writer who happens to be a southerner, and I have written a great deal about other places than the Deep South. I have written extensively about, for instance, Texas, about New York City, Long Island, Washington, D.C., and England. And in this latest book of mine, *The Ghosts of Medgar Evers*, I try to capture something of the southern California and Hollywood culture, which was an interesting diversion for me. So I have written extensively about places other than the Deep South.

Bales: You have also written about the humorous pranks you have played over the years ["Watch Out or You'll Get a Note from a Witch," *New Choices for Retirement Living*, April 1994]. So you have a wide spectrum here: from the articles on the Deep South to humor, to politics, to past romances, to many other topics, and published in a wide variety of periodicals, including *Esquire, New Choices for Retirement Living, Playboy, Car and Driver, Reader's Digest, Commentary,* and *New Republic.*

Morris: Even the old *Saturday Evening Post.* Back when it was a big media magazine it ran about twenty thousand words in advance of *North Toward Home* ["The Yazoo Years," *Saturday Evening Post,* October 7, 1967]. I have written for a lot of magazines, and you do have to do that when you make your living as a writer. And it's always very wise, as a writer who pays the mortgage from what he makes writing, to try whenever possible to have your magazine writing correspond in some way with a book in progress or a book you have in the back of your mind. It is just something most writers have to keep in mind.

Bales: You often mention your parents and how they were somewhat moderate politically. I recall your writing that your father said, pertaining to blacks, "If we are going to tax them, then they probably should be allowed to vote."

Morris: I remember as if it were yesterday when he made that observation, because he was decidedly in the minority in Yazoo City, Mississippi. His remark had a real effect on me and made me start thinking. There was also my beloved grandmother, Mamie, and her comments that she would make from time to time. She was a daughter of the whipped-down South, born in 1878, the year the federal troops withdrew from Mississippi. I remember once she said to me, "Well, when we all get to heaven maybe we'll be black and they'll be white." That got me to thinking too.

Bales: That quotation is from one of the more memorable parts of *North Toward Home.* And after reading *North Toward Home* and the article in *Dissent,* I can't help but wonder if you were a civil rights activist in other ways besides in your writing? This passion is certainly there, particularly in these earlier works.

Morris: Yes, I am a member of a generation of southern whites that passionately believes in civil rights and the importance of race relations. We came out of what we called "The Troubles" and were involved in the evolution of a somewhat more healthy society. I never marched in demonstrations. I was not, for instance, at Selma where some of my friends marched, but I felt that my writing was my main responsibility in that regard. The epilogue to my book I have just finished, *The Ghosts of Medgar Evers,* goes into my feelings a little.

Bales: You touch upon coming home in your first essay of the book *Terrains of the Heart and Other Essays on Home*, published in 1981. You write: "I have never denied the poverty, the smugness, the cruelty which have existed in my native state. Meanness is everywhere, but here the meanness, and the nobility, have for me their own dramatic edge, for the fools are *my* fools, and the heroes are mine too." You include similar statements in other works, such as the final chapter, "South Toward Home," in *New York Days*. Can you elaborate on these sentiments?

Morris: Being a writer, I have always agreed with an observation of Walker Percy that with some writers—I'm paraphrasing—it's very important eventually to live in proximity with the principal landmarks and events of one's own past. I find that important to me. One of my friends, William Styron, lives in Connecticut and on Martha's Vineyard, but he has never really left the South. All you have to do is read his writing to see that. So he (I'm just using an example) is a fellow writer who does not feel the way I did—that somehow I eventually had to repatriate myself in the land of my birth and my youth. It's important to me; you may have gotten a glimpse of that today going out to my family village of Raymond and seeing where my ancestors are buried.

Bales: I also sensed it when you gave me that lengthy and detailed tour of your hometown, Yazoo City. You even showed me where your parents buried your dog Skip—under the elm tree in the backyard of your childhood home.

Morris: I am glad you liked seeing where I grew up. I have a cat now named Spit McGee. Sometimes I think the Lord has made Spit the reincarnation of Skip, my dog. The Methodist Lord (I am convinced the Lord is a Methodist) sent Spit down to make sure I'm okay.

Bales: Speaking of your dog Skip, I'm reminded that after your black Labrador, Pete, died you said you would never get another dog, but that you would get another wife first.

Morris: Shelby Foote, for instance, among a number of people, is a big dog person. He and my dog Pete and I went to the battlefield at Shiloh once and watched Pete, a wonderful black Lab, wade in the bloody pond at Shiloh. When Pete died we buried him not terribly far from William Faulkner's grave in St. Peter's Cemetery up in Oxford, Mississippi. A lot of people came to the Episcopal service we had for him, and it was reported by NBC Nightly News and other media. Shelby Foote and other people kept asking me, "Will you get another dog?" I would reply, "No, I'll get another wife first," and I indeed had the wisdom to ask JoAnne Prichard to join me in holy matrimony. It so happened JoAnne was a cat woman, which explains my having these cats now. I dote on them as valet and servant twenty-four hours a day. So, I'm both a dog and a cat person.

Bales: Our conversation about your youth and remembrance reminds me of something else in *Terrains of the Heart*. In "Coming on Back," the same essay I mentioned previously, you maintain that a writer must always be a stranger to the place he loves and the people there, because there are too many ghosts. Are these the ghosts of your memory?

Morris: Exactly, it's the ghost of memory. With all that memory implies, I strongly believe in those words. A writer really has to be removed from the place from where he dwells, otherwise he would never be able to absorb its real contours. You have to have that detachment, a little grain of sand in your perception of things. Otherwise, you will just be so absorbed in that place that you would not be able to write. You have to have that sense of remove to understand it and to write about it.

There are so many things that pain me about where I live, but I have been able as a writer not only to live with these things and observe them but to write about them. I do believe we have a lot of heroes here and we have a lot of fools and I believe that both of them are mine. I'm a writer and they are my property.

Bales: In *Homecomings* you write that the "phenomenon of memory" pushed you along as a writer.

Morris: Yes, the most valuable asset that I think a writer has is memory. The memory embraces a lot of things and as time passes memory shapes your awareness of real events, real turning points in one's life. The things that you remember are the things you are going to write about. Someone who is very eloquent on this subject is Eudora Welty, here in Jackson. It's that quality one has in one's subconscious that goads you to memory, and memory goads you to writing.

Bales: Your growing up in the Delta has influenced you a great deal, just as much as your family and teachers did. Just how did the Delta affect you and what were the other major influences on your life? I'm particularly interested in this sense of isolation that you often write about.

Morris: I am one who very much believes that the land on which you live, whatever kind of land it is, shapes you as a person, as a human being, and as a writer. And the Delta is a phantasmagoric place. Anyone who grew up in the Mississippi Delta has been strongly shaped and affected by it, without exception—whites and blacks in different directions. It is the richest land on earth; it's richer than the Nile Valley. There is the violence of the elements. It is a place of enormous extremes, emotionally and otherwise. The Delta is myself. From my earliest memory I loved the Delta and I also feared the Delta. I still feel the same way about it—I love it and it frightens me. That is why it's just so important to my experience and to my writing.

As for the isolation, I grew up in a small, deep-southern town, right at the edge of the Delta. The town itself was half hills and half Delta and all crazy, as I think I once wrote. It was before television, that great silencer of conversation. It was just there for us. We had to make our own mischief and adventure, and those old people sitting on the porches were telling their stories. I would never have been able to articulate this at the time, but what they were really doing was trying to give us a way to see. It was a very unhurried time. There was pain and cruelty all around us of course, and you had to absorb that. In my growing up period, I felt the Delta not so much in my mind or I guess even in my heart, but in my very pores. It is a very, very complicated place. The Anglo-Saxon and African blood sources trying to live together on that stretch of the Lord's earth was volatile, very hard and strange, but just really at the core of us all.

Bales: I recall James Dickey saying that the sense of isolation fostered storytelling in the South. The old farmers got together at the churches and the meeting houses. They wanted someone to talk to, and it's not hard to imagine how this talking eventually evolved into storytelling.

Morris: Oral tradition in the South is still very much alive. Just get off the interstates. The southern oral tradition has been at the substance of the southern literary tradition. It is the storytelling and the listening to the stories when you are young, which gives you a way to see your way through things. This is vital, I think.

Bales: You often mention cemeteries in your writings and anyone who has read *North Toward Home* knows that the local cemetery there in Yazoo City was practically your second home.

Morris: It was probably the most civilized place in town!

Bales: That's what I figured. But in addition to that, I sense that for you, cemeteries represent not so much death, but of peace and tranquility through this whole idea of memory and remembrance.

Morris: Yes, I still feel that way. Among other things, cemeteries are marvelous sources of human history and reminders of life in its passing. One of the most interesting experiences that I have ever had in a cemetery occurred last year at the witch's grave in Yazoo City, where there was a dedication of a historical marker to the witch who burned down Yazoo City in 1904. The historical marker was to the witch and to me.

And then I had a book signing at night, by candlelight, in the cemetery. I would venture to say that that was a historical first. Please let me know if you find in your research that a writer has ever had a book signing at night in a cemetery! Also, in cemeteries you do not have telephones, no FAX machines that I know of, and you do not get e-mail in cemeteries. I find them tranquil places. I have often felt that what we should feel about the dead—which we will all be one day—is not pity or overwhelming grief, but rather gratitude that they lived.

Bales: Speaking of this sense of history, we certainly saw that today when we went to Raymond and saw your old family cemetery, with the stone historical marker that was erected some ten or fifteen years ago to your—who was it?—your great-grandfather?

Morris: Major George W. Harper, the founding publisher and editor of the *Hinds County Gazette* in Raymond, which today is the second oldest extant newspaper in Mississippi. That ceremony took place in the Reagan administration. Harry Truman had set up some kind of fund where federal money would go to tombstones for Confederate soldiers who had finally been identified. My great-grandfather was a Confederate major in the militia and mayor of the town, so we got a *little* federal money that paid for about half of it. My son David Rae and I put up this historical marker to my great-grandfather and his great-great-grandfather in the old family plot there in Raymond.

Bales: Your English teacher, Omie Parker, has taught generations of students in Yazoo City and you dedicated the new edition of *Good Old Boy* to her. She told me that you started writing up the "Pee Wee Teams" for your school paper when you were in the sixth grade. I don't remember reading about that in *North Toward Home* or *Good Old Boy*, and I'm kind of intrigued by it.

Morris: I think maybe I did. It was for my old high school newspaper, the *Yazoo Flashlight*. I guess I started doing some scribblings on sports for the *Flashlight* that early. But a little later on I started doing some sports stories for the city newspaper, the *Yazoo Herald*. The first story I did—the first byline I think I ever got in anything outside the school paper—was for a baseball game between (I believe) Yazoo City and Satartia. Lo and behold, the article came out, and I discovered that I had neglected to provide the final score. It was quite a debut.

Bales: You've been interested in sports all your life and even won some awards while at Yazoo City High School. You wrote the introductory essay to the *Official Souvenir Program* of Atlanta's Centennial Olympic Games.

Morris: I was very honored to have been asked to write that essay, "A Prayer Before the Feast," and I worked hard on it. I have received great reaction to the essay from people all over the country who picked up the *Official Souvenir Program.* The editors had asked me to try to set the South into the larger context of not just America, but of the world.

Bales: I know you follow sports and you've thrown out the first balls at games. You even correspond with President George Bush about sports. What do sports represent for you, particularly as a writer?

Morris: I have so many memories of sports. I grew up with them. I got through a lot of painful adolescent periods as I was playing sports. When you boot a ground ball in front of a whole group of people, you can't hide behind a tree; you're there. After you miss a free throw or a couple of free throws with half a second to play that would have won the game for you, you can't go hide. When you're growing up, especially when you're an adolescent, these are very painful moments that you chalk up to experience. They help you later with bigger crises. I've always loved the flair and drama of the best of sports. I was actually the sports editor of what I consider to be the greatest student paper in the country, the *Daily Texan* at the University of Texas. I was sports editor for a semester before I became editor in chief.

Last month I gave a talk at a fundraiser in Shreveport, Louisiana, for about three hundred people. There's a fellow who struck me out four times in the southern finals in youth baseball in 1950 at the Louisiana State University baseball field. *Four times!* His name was Seth Morehead and he later became a major leaguer and pitched for the Chicago Cubs and the Philadelphia Phillies. Jake Gibbs, the Ole Miss baseball coach who played with the Yankees for ten years, knew that Seth Morehead had struck me out four times way back then, and he got me a bubble gum card of Seth Morehead. Now Seth Morehead was at that speech in Shreveport. People told me he was going to be there, so I produced the bubble gum card before the audience, and Seth Morehead, whom I literally had not seen since that game *forty-seven years before*, was very pleased by it. He turned out to be a great guy and I said, "Seth, when this so-called literary speech is over, let's go out in the parking lot and you try that curve ball on me again. I can't promise that I'll hit it, but I'll sure give it another try!"

Bales: I think you mentioned in *North Toward Home* that you once saw him on television during a major league baseball game.

Morris: That's right. I had just gotten back from England. I was sort of displaced and I was headed to take over the *Texas Observer* in Austin and I was in my father-in-law's house in Houston. My son, David Rae, was about six months old, crawling around the floor, and I was about half asleep. It was the old television game of the week with Dizzy Dean and Pee Wee Reese, and I heard Pee Wee Reese say, "Coming in now from the bullpen, number thirteen, the left-hander Seth Morehead." I immediately woke up, of course. I had no one to talk with because only little David was in the room, so I shouted at him, "You see that fellow? That guy struck me out four times in 1950!" David looked up at me for a second and then resumed his peregrinations around the room.

Bales: When you mention sports helping you through life, I remember that you played against some tough teams, what with rough farm boy players and even drunken farmers yelling at you.

Morris: Tough boys, yes, they were tough boys. I showed you the old gymnasium in Satartia. That was a difficult place to play on Saturday night. They didn't like us big city boys. We came from a town of nine or ten thousand, and we had our photographs in the *Yazoo Herald* all the time. They were tough, but we were teammates in the summer on the baseball teams. Our summer baseball teams were kind of an all-star team of the county. Very uneasy teammates until we won the state championship, and then the country boys were not as hostile to us as they previously had been.

Bales: Let's talk about your autobiography. You mentioned in *North Toward Home* that you felt strongly that you had a story to tell about your life that would be a reflection of the experiences of other people your age. What else led a thirty-year-old to write his life history?

Morris: I still get many, many letters on that book, and I am glad to see that some are from members of the younger generation. There was a wonderful editor from Houghton Mifflin, Dorothy de Santillana, and she was in charge of the literary fellowship for an author's first book that is still being offered, the Houghton Mifflin Literary Prize. She encouraged me to apply for this (which back then was five thousand dollars) and to write a sample chapter with a rough outline of the rest of the book. So I just sat down and the first chapters of *North Toward Home* practically wrote themselves. I rarely had an experience like that.

I did not see a fictional work at the time; I just gravitated to the autobiographical form. As it unfolded, I thought that people might laugh about a thirty- or thirty-one-year-old guy writing his autobiography, but I tried to make it a reflection of one person's life and experiences that had broader implications for his generation and for various regions of America. I divided that book into three parts: Mississippi, Texas, and New York, and it just kind of flowed. Well, the first two-thirds did; the last part was most difficult because I was writing about real, contemporary things and where I was living at the time. Maybe part of the reason I chose that form had something to do with my newspaper background, covering real things, real events. I'm glad I wrote that book.

Bales: *North Toward Home* has such an array of conflicting emotions about race. In the Mississippi section of the book, which focuses on your youth, you mention that you and your friends felt unconscious affection and sometimes pity towards blacks, but also disdain and cruelty. Later on, while recounting your college years, you discuss your summer visit to Mississippi and how angry and disillusioned you became while observing your neighbors' unruly, mob-like behavior at a White Citizens' Council meeting. When did your attitude about race start changing? When you were at the University of Texas?

Morris: Yes, I think so. Austin is five hundred miles from Mississippi, and it was a university in transition then. It provided me with a perspective on my native ground, for I had great professors and I started reading a lot. For instance, I started reading Faulkner. I began reading some of the journalists, such as the great Mississippi editor Hodding Carter, who really had an effect on me. Faulkner did as well, but it was that immersion of oneself in history—the reading of history and the great literature—that gave me this understanding of the complexity of matters. I would come home in the summers and I could see that I was gradually changing my attitudes. And when I was running for editor in chief of the *Daily Texan* (this was in 1955 and not too long after Brown vs. Board of Education), I got to thinking more about social concerns and other current problems. The integration issue was very alive out

there, and I knew I had a huge responsibility as the editor of one of the
nation's largest student papers. I just started thinking things through and
talking to people. It was a gradual evolution.

Bales: I mentioned these conflicting emotions you had. In *North Toward
Home*—and I think in your other writings too—you state that courtliness and
kindness went hand-in-hand with violence. Can you expand on that a bit?

Morris: That is so Mississippi. You have on one hand this tenderness, and
on the other this nihilism. You still see it to this day, though not in such an
exaggerated form as one saw it back in those years. It's just part of the soil
and the psyche here. My friend, the historian David Sansing, has always
written eloquently on what he calls the two Mississippis: the Mississippi on
the one hand of violence and cruelty and self-destruction, and the Mississippi
on the other hand of literary tradition, of nobility, and of compassion. There's
always been those twin elements in the history and the psyche of this region,
and I suppose there always will be.

Bales: One of the most often-quoted lines in *North Toward Home* is that
you left your native state to go to college in Texas at the urging of your
father, who told you "to get the hell out of Mississippi." There were other
reasons, weren't there?

Morris: Yes, that's another thing I won't forget. My father was reading
the *Memphis Commercial Appeal* in the front room one day and all of a
sudden he just turned to me and said that. That was so atypical of my father.
I think he couched it in terms of economic possibilities. There were a number
of my contemporaries in Yazoo City who just gravitated to their fathers'
plantations or their business establishments. My daddy had none of these so
he expressed it in those terms. I think he saw some difficult times coming,
and I don't think he wanted me to be hurt. But of course there were other
reasons I went to the University of Texas. My big ambition then was to go
into radio and television, and I actually started my major that first year in the
university's radio and television program. But it just so happened that that
great student daily was there and I started writing for it. So I left the electron-
ics media for the print media, and I am glad I did it.

One of the biggest decisions I ever had to make was (I think) towards the
end of my freshman year at the University of Texas. The play-by-play announcer for the minor league team in Austin—it was a class AA team in the
Texas League—was retiring. They had auditions, both for a live play-by-play
and for the re-creations, and they offered me the job. I was certainly tempted,

but I just mulled it over and I said, "No, I'm not going to do it. I'm going to go back home this summer, take some courses at Millsaps College, and play some semi-pro baseball." That was a *very* big decision.

Bales: While editor of the *Daily Texan* at the University of Texas you often wrote about the "twin deities," the oil and gas interests that controlled the state. Can you summarize the problems?

Morris: We were very freewheeling back then as we were approaching the 1960s. It was 1956, the segregation issue was alive, Texas was still totally controlled by the oil and gas industry, and we were young and feeling our oats. The university administration did not like our editorials and tried to censor us, but we prevailed. About three or four months ago I was out in Austin to give a talk at the Lyndon B. Johnson School of Public Affairs, and the administration was trying to censor the paper again; in fact, in a worse way than the university had tried to censor it back in the 1950s. The young editor there, a very courageous and resourceful young woman, called me four or five days after my visit and asked if I would help them. So I wrote an article that she ran on the editorial page of the paper. She told me just last month that the *Daily Texan* prevailed and was victorious. The administration tries to censor that paper about every ten years. It takes a strong editor to defy that.

Bales: Did the president at that time, Logan Wilson, and the university's Board of Regents ever understand your position on the various issues?

Morris: Logan Wilson and the Board of Regents were all appointees of a rigorously conservative governor named Allan Shivers. I don't think the Board of Regents knew or cared. I think President Logan Wilson did, but he was caught in a wicked crossfire. But J. Frank Dobie, the folklorist and historian whom I adored, wrote a famous letter to the *Daily Texan* when the censorships started coming that is still being quoted out there. He said, "The University of Texas Board of Regents cares as much about intellectual enlightenment as a razorback sow about Keats's 'Ode on a Grecian Urn.'"

Bales: Looking back, if you could edit the *Daily Texan* all over again, would you change anything?

Morris: I would not change anything in the totality of it, but I think I would use more humor in little things. I did use some humor, such as running blank spaces where editorials were censored, and also running editorials under titles like, "Let's Water the Grass"—things like that. But I think I would use the sharp edges of humor and satire more than I was able to do at the time. But back then I was young and a little frightened, for this was big-time stuff. So as I said, in the totality of it I look back on my period with a certain amount of gratification and pride, and I do think the stand we took then has been of immense help to subsequent editors of the *Daily Texan*. They are about to celebrate their hundredth anniversary soon. I'm proud of that.

Bales: You went to college in Texas and edited the *Texas Observer* for several years. Do you have the same attachment for this state as you do for Mississippi?

Morris: It's an emotional attachment. No, I never did. I grew to maturity in Texas—kind of an intellectual maturity—and I love Texas. But although getting to know that huge state as a young man and as a writer was valuable and I owe it a lot, it never really tugged at my heart the way that Mississippi has in an intensely emotional way.

Bales: I always thought the *Texas Observer* was something of a political publication, but it had a literary side to it as well, didn't it?

Morris: It really did, and that was of tremendous importance to me in learning how to write. We could write anything we wanted under Ronnie Dugger, as we could later on, under my own editorship. Most of my favorite writing from my period on the *Observer* is that more literary kind of writing—about human beings and little towns and not directly political. The *Observer* has always had that tradition of Bill Brammer who wrote, in my opinion, one of the two great political novels in American literature, *The Gay Place* [1961], with the other being Robert Penn Warren's *All the King's Men* [1946]. Bill Brammer wrote wonderful pieces on the *Observer* in the period just before me, as did Ronnie Dugger, Bob Sherrill, and others. The writing that I did for the *Observer* that I'm the proudest of are those essays and pieces that are not directly related to politics per se.

Bales: You divided *North Toward Home* in three sections: Mississippi, Texas, and New York. Why not one on Oxford? Did you want this book essentially to be about America?

Morris: That, plus the fact that I was simply not ready to write about Oxford. I thought about it. If I were writing *North Toward Home* again now (if it were, say, 1965 and I had the experiences of a writer that I have now) I would include another section called "America From Afar" or something like that. I would have "Mississippi," "Texas," "America from Afar," then something like "Back to Texas," and then "New York." But the overwhelming consideration for me at the time was that I was not yet ready to write about that period, which was the most exotic time of my life. I was at Oxford University for three or three-and-one-half years—the first and last time I will ever live in a museum.

I once asked Robert Penn Warren, who was in my same college in Oxford years before, if he tried to write about that experience, and he said he was never even able to get a poem about it. But I knew that I was going to come back to Oxford. I have a substantial section in *New York Days* on Oxford, and I have written essays on Oxford and a little book called *My Two Oxfords* (Oxford, Mississippi and Oxford, England), and have written about playing basketball for Oxford University on the varsity team and winning the national championship. I do eventually want to get back to this novel of mine called *The Chimes at Midnight*, which is set in Oxford, England.

Bales: You mention *My Two Oxfords*. I recall you gave a copy of that to President Bill Clinton when he was in Jackson.

Morris: I did, indeed. He had a rally down here in front of the Old Capitol shortly before the 1992 election. I first met Bill Clinton when he was twenty-one years old. I took him around New York City the day before he was sailing to England to Oxford. I hadn't seen him in a couple of years, and Governor William Winter got me to be the emcee at that rally, but of course it didn't do any good. I think the Democrats got about 40 percent of the vote, despite the fact that Clinton was from Arkansas and Gore was from Tennessee and both were Baptists! The Republicans are in full swing here, but he saw me and came up and hugged me, and I had a copy of that book and I gave it to him. He immediately turned to an assistant and said, "Put this in the briefcase. I want to read it." And Bill Clinton whispered to me then, shortly before the election when he was holding on in the polls: "Willie, it's going to be a tough few weeks, but I *think* we're going to make it."

Bales: When you were in Oxford did you then have any ideas of what you wanted to do? Did you ever consider teaching?

Morris: No, I never considered teaching. As my time was coming to an end there in Oxford (I was married and my son, David Rae Morris, was born there), I had the strongest urge to return to Mississippi as a journalist. This would have been the late 1950s up to 1960. I remember I wrote a letter to Big Hodding Carter, the editor and publisher of the Greenville *Delta Democrat-*

Times. He had won a Pulitzer Prize and was a very fine, courageous man—liberal on race—whom I had met when I was at the University of Texas. He happened to be giving a speech out there and he defended me and the *Daily Texan* in our censorship troubles. We had stayed in touch and I wrote a column for him for a while from England for the *Delta Democrat-Times.*

So I wrote him a long letter and said that I was trying to figure out what I was going to do when I got home, and asked if he had a job for me. Hodding wrote me back a few days later. Actually, I had played so many tricks on my contemporaries in our college in Oxford that they got me back then for all of them. A guy named Roscoe "Rocky" Suddarth, who later became our Ambassador to Jordan, saw the letter from Hodding Carter in the mail box cubicles at the front gate. He took that thing and steam-opened it and forged a typewritten letter as if it were from Hodding Carter. He was just jumping all over me saying I was no good, and of course he would not hire me, and going on like that. For about an hour I was crestfallen, but then I figured it out.

But I got Suddarth back. Long before Rocky became big in the State Department I took a classified ad in the Oxford city newspaper saying, "Used, good condition, second-hand bicycles for sale at one pound six pence each. Come to room 223 at New College." There was a long line outside his room. I got him back good!

Then he gave me the real letter from Hodding Carter, which said that his son, Hodding III, who was my age, was coming back to help his father and he did not think the *Delta Democrat-Times* was big enough for both of us. Unfortunately, there were no alternatives then. If you were liberal and did not go to work for Hodding Carter in Mississippi as a newspaperman in the late fifties, there was nothing. So I went back out to Texas, as Dugger was leaving the *Observer* and he wanted me to take over.

Bales: After Texas and before you started work at *Harper's* you were in Palo Alto, California. Were you taking graduate courses there?

Morris: I was sitting in on courses, as my wife at the time had a Woodrow Wilson Fellowship. I wanted some time to write, and I was even toying around with getting a Ph.D. in history, but thank God that did not last very long. I actually wrote my first part of *North Toward Home* out there, the section on predicting the baseball scores. As you may remember from the book, in my youth back in Yazoo City I would pick up the real games on shortwave radio in advance of the same games that were literally re-created an hour or so later, and I would tell my friends what was going to happen next. No one knew the games were being re-created from an air-conditioned studio in Dallas by Gordon McLendon, the "Old Scotchman" on the Liberty Broadcasting System.

Bales: That was published in the *New Yorker* ["Memories of a Short-Wave Prophet," *New Yorker*, November 30, 1963].

Morris: It was, indeed. I had just gotten my first agent and I wrote that section—a long section of about twenty thousand words. It was the first transaction I had with my first agent, and she sent it over to the *New Yorker* and was just totally astonished when two weeks later the editors accepted the whole thing. That section in *North Toward Home* (I didn't even have the book in mind at the time) and that issue of the *New Yorker* came out on a very inauspicious date. It was November 23, 1963.

Bales: In chapter two in *New York Days* you mention how in 1962 your wife, Celia, and you were having breakfast and you received a letter from John Fischer asking you to come to *Harper's*. But you were interested in other periodicals, weren't you? I believe you went to New York for several interviews with various publications, including *Harper's*.

Morris: I almost went to work for the *New York Times*. Harrison Salisbury wanted me to go to work for the *New York Times*. The way the *New York Times* works with their young people whom they take on is that the editors work them up through the ranks, usually sending them out to cover the courts in the Bronx or Queens. The newspaper was opening up a new bureau in Texas and wanted me to be the Dallas Bureau of the *New York Times*, but I did not want to go back to Texas. I stayed in touch and again almost went to work for the paper about a year-and-a-half later.

I had interviews mainly with the *Times,* but I ended up at *Harper's*. I think one reviewer of *New York Days* said there was a disparity between *North Toward Home* and *New York Days* on how I hooked up with *Harper's* [Louis Menand, "Willie's Version," *New Yorker*, September 20, 1993]. The letter that I quoted or paraphrased from my memory from John Fischer in *New York Days* I could not have used in 1966 because of the situation at *Harper's* magazine. So I just glossed over that letter in *North Toward Home*. I could not reveal Fischer as having written that.

Bales: Larry L. King once recalled your *Harper's* years by saying, "You could hardly pick up the news mags or the newspapers or turn on a talk show without everyone saying what great things were happening at *Harper's*."

One surmises from *New York Days* that you and your staff believed that *Harper's* could influence, if not downright change, events in the United States. This is probably the same attitude you had at the *Texas Observer*, isn't it?

Morris: It was certainly an extension of it. I agree with Larry L. King that the magazine was being widely and deeply read in the United States; you could tell that from the mail we were receiving. And I suppose our attitude was something of an extension of the old *Texas Observer* days. I do not think it was a naive attitude. I felt strongly that when the very fabric of American society seemed to be falling apart in those turbulent years—the 1960s up until the 1970s—we at *Harper's* had to reflect those stormy times and at least shape events. It was certainly what we tried to do, and we had some truly great writers and contributors.

Bales: If everything had worked well at *Harper's*, how long do you think you would have stayed? You mention in *New York Days* that you told John Fischer that you would give it at least ten years. Did you always have in the back of your mind that you would get back to your own writing?

Morris: Yes, I did. If things had been moving along smoothly with the ownership I certainly would have stayed on a few more years. I recently saw Ben Bradlee on one of the national television shows when his big autobiography came out not too long ago [*A Good Life: Newspapering and Other Adventures*, 1995], and the interviewer asked him, "What is the most important asset of a great publication?" and he said, "the owner." John Cowles, Jr. was by no measure a Katherine Graham and never could have been. Let's say that if he had been running a vast media empire pulling in millions upon millions and had viewed *Harper's* as sort of the jewel in the crown (which I indeed think it was), I probably would have stayed on five or six more years. But the urge to do my own private work would have eventually stimulated me to leave the business.

Magazine editing is also a young person's calling. You constantly go through these coup d'états in book and magazine publishing. *Esquire*, for instance, has just changed hands and is going to make radical changes. It's in the nature of the beast.

Bales: You once said that it is impossible to be both a writer and an editor. Do you still believe this?

Morris: It was very, very hard for me. I was fortunate at the time to do my own work when I was running the magazine. William Dean Howells accomplished it many years ago—he was magazine editor and wrote his novels—but that was before a gadget called the telephone. I never could figure out how to deal with the telephone. It was a tyranny. Ninety-eight percent of the calls had absolutely no consequence on a monthly issue of the magazine. Howells did not have to deal with the telephone. Being both an editor and a writer is schizoid in a way. If I had had another four or five months on my book *Yazoo* it would have been a different kind of book and a deeper book, although I am glad I did it. I think it is a pretty good work, but I simply did not have the time to do it. It is an all-consuming calling, running a modern magazine, and it draws on many of the same resources as writing. It is even more exhausting than writing. It would be very hard to edit and write; I could rack my brain to think which magazine editors these days are doing any writing of substance.

Bales: After leaving *Harper's* you received many job offers but you ignored them all, preferring to move out to Long Island. Is it true that you just did not want to work for anyone else anymore?

Morris: Yes, it is true. The first offer was from Sargent Shriver. He was deeply involved in Senator Edmund Muskie's campaign for the Democratic nomination for President and wanted me to go to work for Muskie as his main speechwriter. I thought it over and decided not to accept it. Then almost immediately I received a very attractive offer from the President of Duke University, Terry Sanford, who later became a U.S. Senator. I decided against that too. I said to myself, "Just try to go on with your own work and dedicate yourself to that and see what happens."

Bales: You mentioned *Yazoo* a little while ago. One thesis I keep noticing in your books is that you talk about your own life but you also parallel your experiences to what is going on in the country. *Yazoo* is similar to *North Toward Home* in this respect. In your first book you parallel your life to what is happening in the United States. In *Yazoo,* you parallel the integration of your hometown with your segregated upbringing. Of course, even in *The Courting of Marcus Dupree* you do the same thing when you have the flashbacks back and forth. Did you deliberately write the books this way or were these unconscious decisions?

Morris: It's just the way the writing flowed. I don't know if it was a conscious decision on my part as a writer to use my own persona and my own experiences to reflect broader things that were going on in our society, although it certainly turned out that way. I do not think it was a conscious decision at first; it just came out. Later it probably became more conscious. In *New York Days*, for instance, I *really* wanted to reflect on those hazardous years of the sixties and early seventies through my own eyes and my own experiences and through living in the cultural capital of New York City. It is something that just evolved from my commitments as a writer.

Bales: After you left *Harper's* you moved out to Long Island. One of the books you finished out there has entertained Mississippi children for years: *Good Old Boy*. But that must have been a dismal time for you and I imagine that while writing it your mood was anything but light.

Morris: Oh, yes. I was out there alone living on an inlet of the Atlantic Ocean, though I do not think you necessarily have to be in a lighthearted mood to write lighthearted things. Maybe my lugubrious mood contributed to the dangers and risks of the Clark Mansion episode and the scary aspects of the cemetery where the witch lay buried.

But I will say this: I never for a moment thought when I was sitting out there alone writing this book (really for my son David Rae) that it would have such a fantastic effect on kids. I could *never* have predicted it. It is kind of a phenomenon. Down here everybody under the age of, let's say, forty has read it while growing up. It is in all the schools; it's in schools all over the country. I get these fabulous letters from kids ranging from eight, nine years old up to sixteen and seventeen. Often all the students in a class write individual letters. Many parents tell me that it is the only book their child ever read or ever liked. And in the responses I get from kids they ask me all these questions and invariably the first question is, "Was everything in this book true?" Second is, "Where is Spit McGee now?" Also "Where is Rivers Applewhite now?" "Could Skip really drive a car?" Right on down the list. That book has struck something in this country.

Sometimes I ask kids who come up to me or who write letters to tell me why they liked the book so much. A lot of them say, "Because I am not growing up this way, I never have any adventures." I received a letter recently from a little girl in a suburb of some big midwestern city who said, "I never go barefoot, and I have never even seen a lightning bug, and we don't even get moon pies up here."

Bales: And when they complain about this, don't you always tell them that they don't have to have this sort of adventure?

Morris: It all can be inside your mind or in your heart. You can make your own adventures, which is what we were doing anyway. I suppose it is harder to make your own adventures in a suburb of Chicago than it was in a small deep-southern town in the pre-television age in the 1940s and the 1950s.

Bales: And, of course, *Good Old Boy* was made into a movie. You were present for much of the filming and you even coached the children on the proper southern accent.

Morris: They were Los Angeles little actors and actresses, and they were pretty good. Two or three times they pronounced Yazoo "Yah-zoo," which is blasphemy. The little boy playing me was a Hollywood actor about ten years old. He and I struck up a friendship. We corresponded for a while. He wrote me about the first dance he went to, the first tuxedo—he was born on Elvis Presley's birthday. It was a great experience for the little Hollywood kids because they had never been to a swimming hole before. They had never seen crawdads. Some of them had never seen a cow, and certainly never seen a mule. You're not going to find a mule in downtown Beverly Hills, I can assure you.

In my concluding chapter of *New York Days* I wrote a section of watching the producers film that Disney movie of *Good Old Boy* down in Natchez. It was déjà vu for me of the most stunning kind because there I was, watching people playing my long-departed grandmother and grandfather and my great-aunts. My great-aunt Susie was played by Maureen O'Sullivan. It was so real watching people playing my long-ago chums and watching a Hollywood dog playing my dog Skip.

Bales: After *Good Old Boy* came your novel *The Last of the Southern Girls*. What gave you the idea for the plot of that book?

Morris: The Louisiana State University Press recently came out with a reissue of *The Last of the Southern Girls*, which had been out of print for a number of years. I wrote an introduction to the reissue of it, which I think is a funny essay about the circumstances behind my writing it and my mood at the time. When the book was first published it did not get many good reviews, but as some things go, it made more money by far than anything else I have ever written. I spent some time off and on in Washington during that period, and I got to know Washington as an outsider I think pretty well—certainly in a human way—and I wanted to invest that crazy book with some of the emotions I felt about the nation's capital and a lot of the things I had learned about it. It is a very strange book; some producers almost made a big movie of it and were looking at Faye Dunaway to play the role of the heroine. It did not come to fruition, but the book still could make a pretty interesting movie some day. I know people are buying it.

Bales: You mentioned Washington. I think it was in the first part of 1976 that you worked for the *Washington Star* for awhile.

Morris: That was an interesting time. The *Washington Star* was an afternoon paper, and it has since folded. It was the competition for the *Post* and was a pretty interesting newspaper. It did not nearly have the depth of the *Post*, but it had a roster of good writers and journalists, including my old friend Ed Yoder, who won a Pulitzer Prize for his editorials during that period on the *Star*. Also John Sherwood, Mary McCrory, and Jack Germond. Winston Groom, who later left, was a reporter and Pat Oliphant was the cartoonist. Winston Groom's desk was next to mine right in that grubby old newsroom. People who saw the movie, *All The President's Men,* and the newsroom of the *Washington Post* with its lush carpets and fine furnishings—that was not the *Washington Star*.

But the paper had a program called writers-in-residence, which enabled writers to come in for three months and do something like three columns a week. The first one was Jimmy Breslin. I succeeded Jimmy and I took over his desk in the newsroom (and as I was rummaging through the drawers in the desk I found old socks and several empty bottles and stubs of cigars, so I figured I was at home). It was exhausting work, for I was out of practice on deadlines, but I made good friends there. I did persuade Winton Groom to leave newspapering to write his first novel, his very fine Vietnam book called *Better Times Than These* [1978]. Of course, Winston went on to write the novel *Forrest Gump* [1986].

In my collection *Terrains of the Heart* I have a pretty lengthy section called "Vignettes of Washington" that includes some of my pieces for the *Star*. My articles were not all that political; they were on many different subjects.

Bales: You decided to come back to Mississippi in 1979 and you were a writer-in-residence at Ole Miss for about ten years, beginning in 1980. What led you to think the time was right for you to return?

Morris: I figured it was time to be getting on back. In retrospect now I think that I probably should have come on home about four years earlier, though I had so many dear friends there and in Long Island whom I missed after I left. That is what I missed the most—my friends still living there.

I could never live in New York City again as it's a young person's town. When a reporter asked James Jones if he would ever live again in New York

City he said, "No, I've served my stretch." But I would not take anything in the *world* for those years in the magazine industry. I just felt it was time to be getting on back home. All my people were dying off, and as I say, I had this deep heartfelt urge to go on back and do my writing from down here. I think it was a wise decision—a very, *very* wise decision—and I postponed it a little too long. There is something good about seeing from time to time the companions of your boyhood and driving through the town as you and I did today, and living around the landmarks of your own early years—close to the old family plot in Raymond, Mississippi. That means a lot to me.

Bales: When you were in Oxford you had classes on writing and the American novel. What did you like and dislike about teaching? Do you miss it right now?

Morris: No, I don't miss teaching, and I never particularly enjoyed teaching, per se. I did enjoy being around the students and the give-and-take with them. Often in my small writing class I just could not stand sitting in a seminar room for three hours on one night, so sometimes I would just take them to an inexpensive restaurant or to the bar. We would talk about writing and discuss their writing assignments. Some of them have done very well, such as Donna Tartt, who in 1992 published *A Secret History.*

Bales: Wasn't John Grisham in your classes?

Morris: No, John kind of sat in on those classes. He would come when I had visiting writers, such as William Styron, Shelby Foote, James Dickey, Peter Matthiessen, John Knowles, George Plimpton, Beth Henley, or Ellen Gilchrist. When Grisham was just getting started he was a law student at Ole Miss. It was an interesting and diverse group of people. I really liked the young people but I was just not cut out to be a teacher; I couldn't sit still long enough!

Bales: You mentioned *Terrains of the Heart* a few minutes ago. I'm sure a writer is somewhat critical of his past works, but many of those essays have stood up very well over the years.

Morris: Yes, one of the things I have been drawn to over the years is the essay form, which for one reason or another I have always been comfortable with. I think the essay form is a very effective literary form, just as a broader literary type—nonfiction—has appealed to me a great deal. And yes, I think a lot of those essays stand up; they were written often in passion and sometimes in anger and sometimes in detachment.

Bales: In fact, I think one of your essays was later produced by Maryland Public Television ["A Love That Transcends Sadness," *Parade*, September 13, 1981; "The Art of the Essay," part three of the *Literary Visions* Series, The Annenberg/CPB Collection, 1992].

Morris: It was produced by Maryland Public Television, but it was run nationally by PBS. The producers had a half-hour series that focused on three literary genres: short fiction, drama, and poetry. They talked to me about the informal essay and dramatized that essay of mine about death and graveyards.

Bales: And speaking of your essays, you wrote one a while ago in which you defended the waving of the Confederate flag at the University of Mississippi sports games ["The Ghosts of Ole Miss," *Inside Sports*, May 31, 1980; reprinted in *Terrains of the Heart*]. I know you have thought about this a great deal since then. Haven't you somewhat reversed your position on it?

Morris: I changed my mind. It was not a sudden reversal. I think writers have the prerogative to admit that at some point in the past they might have been wrong. I've been wrong on other things too, and I was wrong on this. I was newly arrived back home, but over a period of time I began to see that I was not on firm ground. I believe that any symbol that not only angers but inflicts hurt on a large percentage of a population in a democratic society should be reassessed. Mississippi has a black population of 35–36 percent. Our black brethren are offended by people waving the Confederate flag at Ole Miss sports events, and I can see why. I think it is harmful and also mindless.

Bales: In *New York Days* you not only reflect on your years at *Harper's*, but also discuss what was happening throughout the country then. What is your opinion of the sixties?

Morris: The 1960s in this country was a catastrophic period, a watershed period. The decade had some unpleasant sides to it, but also some good and healthy features as well. The women's movement emerged from the sixties, for instance. There was renewed concern for the environment, expanded freedom of expression, which are vital to a country like ours. The sadder aspects of the sixties were evident to us all back then: a lack of generosity of spirit, an exclusiveness, and far, far too much mindless noise. But the sixties were a profoundly complicated time in our history, and as I look back on them now, from the vantage point of X number of years, I see both the good and the bad of that period with an added clarity. I tried to invest *New York Days* with my own sense of that time—and with personal things.

Bales: I see very little bitterness or score settling in *New York Days*. Is this why you waited some twenty years to write it?

Morris: I postponed writing *New York Days* because I knew it was going to be so *draining* and difficult. Now I *am* glad that I waited those years to tackle that juncture in my life as an editor and as a writer. I do think it gave to that time and to my own life a retrospective (I don't know if I should call it wisdom) but certainly a view. As I said, it was a very difficult book to write, and I am glad now that I did it, and I'm glad I have it behind me.

Bales: *Homecomings*, published in 1989, received many positive reviews and it is certainly an excellent collection of essays. It's also a beautiful book from the purely physical viewpoint. How did it evolve?

Morris: From my future wife, JoAnne Prichard, who was a superb editor with marvelous taste at the University Press of Mississippi here in Jackson. I think *Homecomings* was the first in the Press's *Author and Artist* Series, and she had the good idea of bringing my writings together with the paintings of William Dunlap, who is just an excellent artist. It's a beautiful book, and it also got JoAnne and me together. John Langston, our art director there, also did a good job. I think that book has gone through two or three printings.

Bales: Yes, it has. Two of your other illustrated books are *Faulkner's Mississippi* and *After All, It's Only a Game*. How did you come to write those?

Morris: *Faulkner's Mississippi* had its genesis in *National Geographic* magazine. I had never written for *National Geographic*, and the editors asked me to contribute a long piece on Faulkner's Mississippi, which was their cover story ["Faulkner's Mississippi," *National Geographic*, March 1989]. And then Oxmoor House asked me to expand that into a book-length piece, to which were added the photographs of the great photographer, William Eggleston. (The Japanese camera industry not long ago chose Bill Eggleston as the finest color photographer in the world.) So from the beginning it was an act of collaboration with Bill. I had already done a great deal of research for *National Geographic* on the piece, and I just proceeded to expand it, working hard over a period of time. I actually wrote that expanded book in the Sun and Sand Motel here in Jackson in a room next to the one being occupied by the great black civil rights leader Aaron Henry, who recently died.

Bales: And *After All, It's Only a Game*?

Morris: JoAnne was certainly the editor of it, and she got Lynn Green Root, a watercolorist here, to illustrate it. Eudora Welty described Lynn Green Root's paintings as having the spontaneity and exuberance of a fireworks

display. A number of the sports essays in the book were ones I had already
written or partially written, with themes on the subjects of football, basketball, and baseball—about being young and being involved in sports.

Bales: Let's get a little current now. You have finished the multi-layered
The Ghosts of Medgar Evers, in which it is clear that you are focusing on
more than just a movie. This is a literary device that you seem to use in some
of your other books. *The Courting of Marcus Dupree* is not simply a football
book and *The Ghosts of Medgar Evers* is not just about a movie.

Morris: With *The Courting of Marcus Dupree* a lot of football people
thought it was literature and a lot of literary people thought it was football; I
guess it is both. *The Ghosts of Medgar Evers* is coming out in January,
published by Random House. It was *very* difficult to write. I covered the
Byron De La Beckwith third and conclusive trial for his murder of Medgar
Evers thirty years before ["Justice, Justice at Last," *New Choices for Retirement Living*, June 1994]. He had been released by two hung juries in the
1960s, but was prosecuted once more and convicted in 1994.

The trial was one of the most traumatic events I ever witnessed, with all
the elements of great drama. I later sent a memo to my friend, Fred Zollo,
the producer, about making a movie based on the trial and he went right to
Rob Reiner, and Rob took it. The movie *Ghosts of Mississippi* came to fruition much, much quicker than most big Hollywood movies. I watched a good
part of the filming, both here in Jackson and in Los Angeles. I got to know
Rob Reiner very well and some of the actors and actresses. The book, though,
is not a "making of a movie" volume at all, which was why it was so difficult
to write. I also include historical background on Mississippi and the life and
assassination of Medgar Evers.

The reception to the movie earlier this year really got caught up in political
correctness, and it did not do well at the box office. James Woods was nomi-
nated for an Academy Award, but the movie did not win any Academy Awards.
I think it is a fine movie and was destined to have been caught up in some of
the tensions and vagaries of our contemporary times. The vast majority of
people nowadays see movies in video store rentals and on television reruns,
so there is a huge audience out there. I have no doubt that the so-called average
viewer cared for that movie a lot more than the political correctness reviews
would have indicated, although it did get some great reviews.

Another one of the reasons *The Ghosts of Medgar Evers* was so hard to
write is because the story constantly kept changing as I got more and more

into the book. But again I tried to use my personal experiences to reflect events and attitudes about modern America, about what we think heroes should be or should not be. One of the threads of the movie is the history of the Beckwith-Evers case. I go deep into history and personal memory. Another thread is the actual making of the movie itself. So as a writer it was a fascinating diversion from the essentially private calling of a writer, because a big Hollywood film is nothing if not a very communal exercise. I learned a great deal about movie making. I'll never be involved in a movie again, but I consider it an important book. I'm glad I spent those months on it and on the movie itself, because I learned a lot about that strange subculture of Hollywood and about how far, far removed Beverly Hills is from Mississippi. There are no two more disparate places in America than Mississippi and Beverly Hills, and I tried to go into that in the book.

Bales: Aren't you working on some fiction now?

Morris: I've been putting off a Korean war novel, *Taps*, of which I have a very long and somewhat rough draft that took me about a year or a year-and-a-half to do in a cabin on the Bogue Chitto River in Pike County, Mississippi. It will take more work. I have put it aside and I'm gradually getting back to it now.

Bales: That's your current project?

Morris: Yes—not right this moment, but I'm getting into it. I still have this short novel set in Oxford, England, *The Chimes at Midnight*, that has been bothering me for a long time. I have both of those on my mind.

Bales: Wasn't *Good Old Boy and the Witch of Yazoo* inspired by some sort of witch scare near your cabin on the Bogue Chitto River?

Morris: Yes, it was in a way. I wrote that book so quickly. It's kind of a sequel to *Good Old Boy*. It did not make the splash that the first one did, but the kids like it. It involved a satanic cult and modern-day witches down there outside of McComb, Mississippi. The story was in all the newspapers and it was more funny than evil to me, but it gave me a push to get into that book.

Bales: I see that you are involved in various arts programs in Mississippi. Tell me about some of your activities and non-literary pursuits.

Morris: I go to a lot of sports events, and I give occasional lectures around the country. I don't particularly enjoy speaking but it helps pay the mortgage. I have a beautiful wife and three cats. I am not so much involved in an organizational way in cultural events, but I try to encourage young people in this regard. I enjoy living in Jackson, Mississippi. I enjoy cooking, both outdoors and indoors. I try to combine these things with my writing. I do want to add that because of my dog Skip (not the book, but my real dog Skip), the Hartz Corporation named Skip one of the ten greatest animals in the world. The company's officers sent me a framed scroll and I have to pick out my favorite animal charity as they are sending a sizable donation to it. So Skip has gotten around.

Bales: I just have two more questions. Your books often include your childhood friends. We saw Henjie Henick's grave today in the Yazoo City cemetery. What about Bubba Barrier, Billy Rhodes, Honest Ed Upton, and Muttonhead Shepherd? Where are they now?

Morris: It's funny you mentioned Muttonhead Shepherd. It just so happens that two weeks ago JoAnne and I were in the mountains of North Carolina at the High Hampton Inn at a very laid-back literary conference that Winston Groom has had for the last three or four years. Gay Talese was there, as was Nan Talese, Pat Conroy, and John Logue—and Muttonhead Shepherd just showed up with his wife. We grew up together and played ball together. He runs all through *My Dog Skip* and *Good Old Boy*, and there he was in the mountains of North Carolina. He had moved to a little town up there and coached football and baseball and taught in the high schools.

Bubba Barrier and Billy Rhodes are still living over here in Yazoo City and Honest Ed Upton is in Dallas. They have all kind of scattered around, but Spit McGee still lives out in the swamps in Yazoo County. He comes into town about once a month to pick up his flour and bacon. Henjie Henick is dead, of course. He runs through all of my books. I visit his grave every time I go over to Yazoo City.

Bales: My last question. You mentioned your wife, JoAnne, several times. There is that old adage that says that behind every good man—or every good writer—stands a good woman. Is that true for you?

Morris: More, even more than that. JoAnne is not only one of the best human beings I have known, she is one of the smartest and just a highly talented editor. It helps to have an editor in your house—one whom you trust—who happens to be your spouse. She's also one of the *funniest* people around when she is in the mood to be, and she's from the Mississippi Delta, as am I. We share the same kind of past and memories of people and things. Life would be very different without her. She is also wonderfully encouraging about discipline—getting back to that next book. So all these things add up. I'm very fortunate.

An Interview with Willie Morris
Rebecca Bain / 1998

From *The Fine Print*, WPLN-FM, Nashville Public Radio, Nashville, Tennessee. Published by permission of Nashville Public Radio.

Bain: Welcome to *The Fine Print*, WPLN's program about all things bookish. I'm Rebecca Bain. Thomas Wolfe may have felt you can't go home again, but writer Willie Morris doesn't exactly agree. He's been back home for awhile now, and he likes it just fine. Born and raised in and around the Mississippi Delta, Willie Morris graduated class valedictorian of his Yazoo City High School in 1952, and he left the state to attend the University of Texas in Austin. There he joined the student newspaper and immersed himself in journalism, books, and social consciousness, writing scathing articles on segregation, censorship, and the improprieties committed by the Texas legislators. Four years later, Willie Morris left for Oxford, England, to study history as a Rhodes Scholar.

Upon his return to the United States in 1958, he worked for a number of publications, eventually landing at *Harper's* magazine in 1963. By 1967 he was editor in chief, and his first book, a memoir titled *North Toward Home*, was published soon after. *North Toward Home* was a huge critical success, winning the Houghton Mifflin Literary Fellowship Award for Nonfiction. Perhaps even more important to Willie were comments like this one by author John Kenneth Galbraith, who said: "No one at age thirty-two should write his memoirs; Willie Morris is the only exception. This is the most sensitive, amusing, and generally enchanting book I have read this year." Willie left *Harper's* in 1971, saying in a press release, "It all boiled down to the money men and the literary men, and as always, the money men won."

But Willie Morris won too, because now he could devote himself full time to his writing. He moved to Bridgehampton, New York, and the books poured out. Books like *Yazoo: Integration in a Deep-Southern Town*, *The Last of the Southern Girls*, *A Southern Album*, and *James Jones: A Friendship*. But in 1979, Willie Morris decided *writing* about the South wasn't enough. He wanted and needed to *live* there again. So he accepted the job of writer-in-residence at Ole Miss, a position he kept for the next ten years. Willie Morris was in town recently and it was my great pleasure to get to talk to him again.

He has a new book, *The Ghosts of Medgar Evers*, which will be coming out next month. But it was an essay he wrote on getting older that brought him to town. It's titled "As the Years Go By, Do We Grow Crankier or More Tolerant?" and it's included in the new Reader's Digest anthology *Are You Old Enough to Read This Book?: Reflections on Midlife* [1997].

Morris: I've been reading this Reader's Digest book with much pleasure. It's a wealth of riches and I think it's going to be a national bestseller. When the editors asked me to contribute to it they gave me the list of distinguished writers and public figures who were going to be included, and I was certainly drawn to it—and to the subject: as you grow older are you crankier or more tolerant? And I really think I am more tolerant. I was a lot crankier, I think, when I was in my thirties, as an editor and a writer in Texas and later in New York during a very grueling period of American history. I really do think I have mellowed. My wife thinks so and my cats think so.

But I think a lot of it, Rebecca, for me as a writer and as a man has had to do with the good decision I made a number of years ago to return home after many years in the East. Having been divorced and a single man for over twenty years, a good marriage really helps. And spirited cats help. But also returning to one's roots as a southerner and a Mississippian; living on the banks of Purple Crane Creek, which overflows in the rains; renewing childhood friendships; and going back to my hometown Yazoo City a lot has kind of brought things together for me—certainly as a writer. I find myself happier now than I have ever been in my life, and I never thought this would be true. The aging process is suffused with surprises, and it affects one's writing.

Bain: You mention in this book that one of the things you have been doing for several years now is that instead of sleeping heavily, you wake up early and spend sometimes up to three hours reflecting on life.

Morris: It's usually from about 6 A.M. until 9 A.M. I sleep till noon (I'm an afternoon and night writer) and I've never had any problems sleeping. I'm a very heavy sleeper with bizarre dreams. It's a kind of subtle reverie where it's a half-dream and I'm reflecting on my past and many of my transgressions. Not so much major transgressions as semi-transgressions. And it's been the most bizarre experience for me and I still have it—almost every morning. I tell my wife about all this, then I go to work in the afternoon within this context of memory and evocation, and I truly think it helps my work. I've talked to other people my age who have had this same strange experience. It's not painful, but it's also not comfortable. Later in the day, however, once you wash your face and shave, take a bath, feed your cats, and go to work, it becomes a kind of context for your own writing. I really feel this. This has been very, very important for me, and I tried to put it in the essay for this book.

Bain: I think you did so very successfully. One of the things that I found most interesting about this particular process is that it allows you to put other people's actions in context too. You don't take a bad review so personally. If someone says something about you that you find hurtful or offensive, you are able to step back a little bit and think, "There is a lot more going on here than just someone saying something nasty."

Morris: And in my thirties and forties I would have responded to things like this quite differently. I think that's probably a step forward.

Bain: That sounds like a great step forward! Since you've mentioned that you have gone back home, I would like to talk about that now. You grew up in Yazoo City, Mississippi, a town that straddled the demarcation line between the hills of Mississippi and the Delta. And of course you've written so eloquently about that place and that time in your books. But what is it about the Delta that makes it so unique?

Morris: I don't think there is any other region in America that is so hypnotic and so complicated and so brooding as the Mississippi Delta. I think I was fortunate to have grown up in this town (half hills, half flat land) which just totally shaped me as a person and as a writer. I've taken a lot of outlanders through the Delta—Yankee journalism writers, civil rights activists, and lately Hollywood people—and they greet the Delta with kind of an amalgam of fear and titillation. It is the most unusual place in America, and I don't think I'd have become a writer if I hadn't grown up in the Delta.

Bain: It fed something in you, right?

Morris: The power of the land, and the complexity and the tragedy of that land. I love the Delta, but I've also always been afraid of it. For me it's evoked a combination of love and fear. I even felt that as a boy, and I feel it even more now. It's a beautiful and scary place, and it's produced such wonderful writing.

Bain: It's like what Faulkner said: it's an area we love not because of its virtues, but despite its flaws.

Morris: Faulkner was not from the Delta; he was from the hill country of course, but he wrote some of his best works in the Delta. And also Eudora

Welty, about whom I'm writing a piece for *Vanity Fair* on the occasion of
her ninetieth birthday ["Mississippi Queen," *Vanity Fair*, May 1999]. I love
Eudora Welty. She may be our greatest living American writer. She did not
grow up in the Delta; she grew up in Jackson, but some of her great writing
is set there. Richard Ford spent a lot of time in the Delta. Shelby Foote, of
course, and Ellen Douglas and Elizabeth Spencer are from there, and right
on down the list. It really elicits a power of memory, which is what writing
is all about, I think.

Bain: I hate to detour into something when we are talking about a topic
like this, but I have to ask you . . . is it really true that you met Eudora Welty
for the first time at the Jitney Jungle [a grocery store chain] when you were
eight years old?

Morris: Absolutely true. I was born in Jackson, a block-and-a-half from
Eudora's house in the Belhaven neighborhood. We moved to Yazoo City
when I was an infant, but I'd spend my summers with my grandparents and
eccentric spinster great-aunts in Jackson. And Eudora knew my grandparents,
my great-aunts, and my mother. My Great-Aunt Maggie Harper introduced
me to Eudora when I was about eight or nine (during World War II) in the
Jitney Jungle. Eudora recently reminded me that my great-aunts crossed the
street to use the Jitney as their private pantry. They'd go in several times a
day for an onion or a muskmelon. Aunt Maggie introduced me to Eudora
when I was eight or nine, and as we were leaving, Aunt Maggie whispered in
my ear, "She writes those stories her *own* self."

Bain: Her own self! That's good. Another quick look back if you don't
mind. Would you tell listeners about the Witch of Yazoo?

Morris: The Witch of Yazoo! The town put a historical plaque on her
grave a couple of years ago. The witch was poisoning fishermen on the Yazoo
River, and they hated her so much they didn't even give her a name. She was
chased into the swamps where she became trapped in quicksand, and the last
thing she said was, "I will return . . . burn down Yazoo." They buried her in
the Yazoo City cemetery and put sturdy chain around her grave. Twenty years
later, in 1904, the witch broke out of her grave and burned down the town,
the whole downtown area that had to be rebuilt. The day after the fire a few
people visited the witch's grave, and they found one of those chain links
broken.

One of the strangest book signings I ever had was at night about a year
ago, around the witch's grave by candlelight. Yazoo City has a "Witch Way

to Yazoo" festival every year. Kids come from all over the South to look at
the witch's grave.

Bain: And you come too and read, don't you?

Morris: At night, and sign books at night in the cemetery. That's a historical first!

Bain: Well, you have just been saying so eloquently why the Delta is such
an incredible, rich region, so special you grew up there. You could have
married your high school sweetheart, you could have spent your whole life
in Yazoo City, but no, your father said, "Get the hell out of Mississippi."
And you got out.

Morris: That's right. Well, it surprised me. It was my senior year in high
school and he was reading the *Memphis Commercial Appeal* one day. It was
so unlike him; he said, "You really ought to get the hell out of here." He
pitched it in terms of opportunity, for I think he saw troubles coming, and he
thought I would get into trouble politically. He went out to the University of
Texas by himself on a Southern Trailways bus to look it over for me. I was a
baseball player (we had a state championship baseball game in Jackson my
senior year in high school), and editor of the school newspaper, the Yazoo
High *Flashlight*. He was playing poker in the firehouse soon after he came
back home and said to me, "You better go to school out there. It's got a daily
newspaper, and the *Yazoo Herald* only comes out once a week. It's got a
main building thirty stories high. It's got the most beautiful baseball stadium
I ever saw." I think he gave me good advice, but I'm glad I came home.

Bain: But it was a necessary step, wasn't it? Getting out? Going away?

Morris: I think so, I really do. I wouldn't take anything in the world for
it. Young fledgling writers often ask me for advice about such things, and I
think it helps to get away from home for a while. It gives you a perspective
on your own heritage and lineage. I wouldn't take anything in the world for
having run *Harper's* magazine in the tempestuous 1960s. It was a *basic* experience. We were very representative of and caught up in those extreme times,
and we were all using words to deal with what was happening to our beloved
America then. I was glad I was in New York in that period. Now I'm glad
I'm back home.

Bain: I know people tell you all the time about how your words have
affected them, about how the things that you've written have touched them
in some way, changed them in some way. I wanted to tell you this story. Your

work as an editor changed me politically. I was a junior in high school. It was May of 1970 and *Harper's* published Seymour Hersh's piece on the My Lai massacre ["My Lai 4: A Report on the Massacre and Its Aftermath," *Harper's*, May 1970]. I read that article, and I went from being someone who just bought everything anybody told me politically to someone who began to question everything politically. It was a huge turning point in my life, and I too was editor of my school paper the next year.

Morris: Seymour Hersh's piece gave me such special pride, and it was the one that evoked the most intense response among readers. That and Norman Mailer's "The Steps of the Pentagon" [*Harper's*, March 1968], which was the longest magazine piece in history and became his Pulitzer Prize-winning *The Armies of the Night* [1968]. Those two articles—such a fantastic response in terms of letters and phone calls. I'm glad that got to you.

Bain: You're always identified (in addition to "Willie Morris the writer"), as the "youngest man to ever be editor of the oldest magazine in America." As you look back on those times, of what things are you most proud?

Morris: Of catching much of the essence of our beguiling and tortured society of that era. Of coming up with really great writing and reportage (the best of our day, I think, looking back on that). Making close, lifelong friendships with people ranging from William Styron to David Halberstam to Larry L. King, just right on down the line—friendships which have endured. But I think the thing I'm most proud of is really being part of our American civilization of that period and, I would hope, having shaped it somewhat for the better.

Bain: I think you can make that claim.
Morris: Well, they were complicated times.

Bain: They were, but you and the magazine helped us to try to understand them. There you were—you had spent all those years as editor of *Harper's*, and then you and the money-grubbers had a parting of the ways. You left the magazine and began writing full time. At what point did you decide that you wanted to return home?

Morris: Because my people were dying down in Mississippi. I would return home to the strains of "Abide with Me" at the funerals. I had this neighbor up in Long Island, Truman Capote, and at Bobby Van's saloon one day we were talking and he said, "All southerners go home sooner or later . . . even if it's in a box." I thought about that, and I was rather reluctant to wait that long. It was some kind of strange and interior pull that brought me back. I was a little scared at first. I ended up being the writer-in-residence at Ole Miss for ten years.

Bain: I have to interject here. I would have given anything if I could have come to your classes.

Morris: I wish you had. John Grisham did. I read John Grisham's first book; gave him his jacket blurb [*A Time to Kill*, 1989]. Winston Groom wrote the book *Forrest Gump* [1986], and he would come over. I was the first person to read the manuscript of *Forrest Gump*. I'm about to go to Grisham and Winston Groom to collect my 20 percent finder's fee. I've always wanted to buy Arkansas.

Bain: I believe with 20 percent of those gentlemen's sales you *could* buy Arkansas.

Morris: At least part of Arkansas. But it was fun at Ole Miss. I was there ten years and Donna Tartt, who wrote *A Secret History* [1992], was one of my students. In fact, I've got about eight of my students in those classes who have written books. But then I got married and moved to Jackson. I married a cat woman and I've got my three cats and I just keep on writing. I got good news the other day. The last time I was on your show, Rebecca, was for my book *My Dog Skip*. Hollywood is making it into a big movie. This is absolutely definite. They are going to film for two months in the spring. The producers include Mark Johnson, who did movies like *Diner, Rain Man*, and *The Natural*. And this is definite. They are beginning to audition all over the country now for a dog who can bark with a southern accent.

Bain: That's wonderful! Absolutely wonderful! Well, since you mentioned Hollywood, I want to talk about the new book you have coming out. Because it's not published yet I have not been able to read it, but I'm dying for it to come out. It's called *The Ghosts of Medgar Evers*, and the subtitle is *A Tale of Race, Murder, Mississippi, and Hollywood*. What has Hollywood got to do with race, murder, and Mississippi?

Morris: Good question. This was a tough book to write. It took about a year longer than I thought it would, but I'm rather proud of it. The movie *Ghosts of Mississippi*, which Rob Reiner of Castle Rock Entertainment directed, was my idea, and Myrlie Evers, the widow of Medgar Evers, and I were the consultants on it. My wife, JoAnne, and I spent a lot of time in Hollywood. I probably will never do this again. It was kind of a dalliance into a subculture that I knew little about, and I found it intriguing. I've always loved movies. I've been a lover of movies since I was a kid.

The kind of narrative thread of this book *The Ghosts of Medgar Evers*, which is coming out the first week in February, is the filming of the movie *Ghosts of Mississippi*, but it's not about the movie itself. It's really a very personal book, and in a funny way it's kind of about Medgar Evers and me. Of course, most of it is set in Mississippi and Hollywood. It's a rather difficult book to describe, which is why we had so many problems with the title. I'm glad I did it. I think the reception of the movie itself (the responses) ranged from adulation to just total criticism. It suggests a lot about contemporary American society. I think it got caught up in the contentions and nuances of our present-day society, particularly as things pertained to race, which I consider the central thread in American history and in present-day America. We have all the complexities of race and how it touches people so *The Ghosts of Medgar Evers* is about a lot of those.

Bain: There's something else I wanted to ask you about. You hear all kinds of comments these days about how the South has changed. It's much more like the rest of the country is one thing you hear. People from other regions of the country are moving here and that is changing it. You're someone who grew up in the South, moved away, had a good, long time away, could stand back and take a good, long look, and then move back. What do you think? Is the South different these days?

Morris: It's both different and abiding. Sure, it's different in terms of a lot of the physical landscape and the shopping centers. It's the Americanization of Dixie. You have a lot of outsiders who are moving here for the climate and for a slower pace, and I think they are smart to do so. The obvious manifestations of change are before us, but you get off those interstates and there's still an indwelling vein of memory, storytelling, and of being pushed back into your past. As a writer I feel this is essential and is of enormous importance. I think the South will always have that incredible sense of the past that no other part of the country has, with the exception, of course, of New England. And this has been so crucial to our writing.

My friend Richard Ford, the novelist, and I recently spoke at the ceremony honoring Eudora Welty's childhood house in Jackson, Mississippi, as a historical landmark. Richard said, "Wherever I go people ask me, 'Why has Mississippi produced such an august array of writers?' I always try to answer that Mississippi, as with the larger South, is so complicated it takes that many writers to interpret it." I've never heard that before but it kind of makes sense to me.

Bain: It does to me too. I think you're right. I don't think we ever will lose our sense of the past. Incidentally, it was a pleasure to get to reread *North Toward Home*. When I knew you were coming in I thought, "Oh, good. An excuse to reread a book I love." And I laughed all over again. There's a scene where your mother and grandmother are going to Jackson, and you stop and pick up a couple of soldiers.

Morris: That's right. It was during World War II and they were Yankee soldiers.

Bain: Your mother asks them where they are from—one's from New York, one's from Massachusetts—and your mother and grandmother immediately begin verbally beating them up for being so bad to us during and after the Civil War.

Morris: Exactly. I was about five years old and of course, none of this was lost on me. Those poor kids! They were hitchhiking from a little ordnance plant into Jackson and did not know what hit them when my mother and grandmother descended upon them. I had never heard such vitriol, and of course this was almost a century after the Civil War. I've never forgotten that, and I bet those two boys haven't either. It all has to do with this phenomenon of memory, which engulfs us. It engulfs me as I get older. I tried to write a little bit about that in this Reader's Digest book—those strange reveries I have and all the rest. It goes with the territory, I suppose.

Bain: Now your first book was *North Toward Home*. As you told us in this Reader's Digest book, you're now having all these reveries. You say that you know that's changing you as a writer and it makes me wonder. The sequel to *North Toward Home* was *New York Days*. Are we going to have another book, *South Toward Home*?

Morris: If not, it will be something like it. I'm not quite sure how I'm going to write it. I've got to finish this short novel that's been bedeviling me for years. It's set in Oxford, England, in the late 1950s.

Bain: Look at your body of work. I hear about all these things that you're thinking about doing and wanting to do. You must write all the time. Every afternoon? Every day?

Morris: When I'm really working on something I put in about four hours a day, which is enough. I really have no choice; I have no alternative to words. I don't know what I'd do without words. I've also found that as I've gotten older (and this also is a surprise to me) I kind of enjoy writing more than I used to. I don't have that kind of angst, which a lot of writers put on themselves—that it's such a burden and all that. I don't feel that way anymore the way I used to. It's very strange and hard to describe. It's not that it's the apex of pleasure to write, but it's more fun than it used to be. I think that may have something to do with wanting to put things down, trying to have something that might endure.

Bain: I had read you'd said that, that you had no alternative to words.

Morris: Yes, well, I don't. I couldn't keep down an office job, I can't wear a tie and a coat (my neck itches), and I hate the telephone, so I guess I'm in the right line of work.

Bain: As far as we, your readers and fans, are concerned, you're definitely in the right line of work. Willie Morris, thank you.

Morris: Rebecca, thank you.

Bain: Willie Morris, the author of more than a dozen books, including *North Toward Home*, *My Dog Skip*, and the latest, *The Ghosts of Medgar Evers*, which will be published next month. And that concludes our program for this week. I hope you enjoyed it and I hope you will join me each Saturday at noon, or Sunday morning at nine, to check out *The Fine Print*. For Nashville Public Radio, I'm Rebecca Bain.

An Interview with Willie Morris

Leonard Lopate / 1998

From *New York and Company*, WNYC, New York Public Radio, New York, New York. Published by permission of WNYC Radio and Leonard Lopate.

Lopate: For many of us in the North, Mississippi is a mysterious and inscrutable place. It's the *Deep* South, marked by its extremes: rich and poor, cruel and gentle, and of course, white and black. Medgar Evers was born in Mississippi and in 1963 he was murdered there. The trial of Evers's murderer was the subject of the film *Ghosts of Mississippi*. Medgar Evers, the film, and the complexities of Mississippi itself are all integral to Willie Morris's latest book, *The Ghosts of Medgar Evers: A Tale of Race, Murder, Mississippi, and Hollywood*. It's published by Random House and I am very pleased that it brings Willie Morris back to *New York and Company* today. Hello.

Morris: Good to be on your show again, Leonard.

Lopate: You refer to the "ghosts" of Medgar Evers, which mirrors the "ghosts" of Mississippi. Can one person have more than one ghost?

Morris: Medgar Evers does. This is not a book about Hollywood or moviemaking per se. The organizational thread that runs through it is the background of Rob Reiner's movie *Ghosts of Mississippi*, the making of it, and the subsequent national response to it. It is a very personal book and it was a very tough one to write. Medgar Evers, in my opinion, has manifold ghosts, and that's why I deliberately use the plural in the title. During his life he was relatively unknown, which is sad. When my friend, the young, white assistant district attorney in Jackson, Bobby DeLaughter, played by Alec Baldwin in the movie, started the reinvestigation almost thirty years after Byron De La Beckwith murdered Medgar, the layers of emotions were so complicated and so deep.

Lopate: Medgar had headed the NAACP in Mississippi and actually had been nationally prominent in some ways. But obviously Martin Luther King, Jr. was the towering figure and maybe there was no place for anybody else.

Morris: Medgar was the field secretary for the NAACP in Mississippi during what we still call "The Troubles"—the late 1950s and the early

1960s—but he was not particularly visible nationally. His death was the first of the 1960s assassinations, and six months after it President John F. Kennedy was killed. One of the things that touched me the most, which is in my book, is that following Medgar Evers's burial in Arlington National Cemetery with full military honors (he fought in combat in France in World War II), President Kennedy comforted his widow and children in the Oval Office. Kennedy himself was dead six months later. Then came Martin Luther King, Malcolm X, and Robert Kennedy.

But what I've always felt about Medgar was that he did not really reach any kind of national prominence until his death. After all, his early efforts for civil rights came before sit-ins, before Freedom Riders, before Rosa Parks and Montgomery, and before Dr. King in a place of abandoned repression— Mississippi. He only had his wife, Myrlie, and a handful of others who were wholly behind him. King had his Montgomery congregation and later, of course, a much larger web of support and a national forum. To me, in writing this book, implicit in these circumstances were questions of greatness that transcend race, which are even more unimaginable because Medgar was black in Mississippi in the first half of the twentieth century and basically alone. He was on the death list; he knew he was going to die.

Lopate: Now Mississippi, as I said earlier, is a place of great mystery for people in the North despite the fact that it's produced some very famous sons and daughters: William Faulkner, Eudora Welty, Elvis Presley . . . and Willie Morris is a sixth-generation Mississippian. Why do you think we see this as a dark and dangerous place?

Morris: Mississippi has always been the crucible of the national guilt. My friends and I always like to speak of the *other* Mississippi—not the Mississippi of cruelty, but of nobility; not the Mississippi of illiteracy, but of perhaps the greatest literary tradition in the United States; not the Mississippi of nihilism, but the Mississippi of the better angels of our nature. It's very complicated. I would go so far as to say, "We've got a long way to go down there, but the state of Mississippi is a hell of a lot more of an integrated, biracial society than New York state."

Lopate: It's interesting when you talk about the nobility because the man who killed Medgar Evers had one of those names that almost sounds genteel: Byron De La Beckwith.

Morris: He always called himself Byron De La Beckwith VI. I covered his third and final trial in 1994 for a magazine, thirty years after the murder

["Justice, Justice at Last," *New Choices for Retirement Living*, June 1994].
There were two hung juries in 1964.

Lopate: Wasn't that significant at the time? Acquittals were expected in
trials of that sort, so this was an indication that even then everybody knew
that Byron De La Beckwith had done it, or that he was more vulnerable to
public sentiment than some other Ku Klux Klan member or sympathizer.

Morris: He shot Medgar in the back in front of his wife and three children
in the driveway of their house in Jackson. The two juries in 1964 were all
white and all male, but on them a total of eight white men voted to convict a
Ku Klux Klan hero for murdering a black man. There is no statute of limita-
tions on murder. If one of those two juries had not been a hung jury, he
would still be drinking mint juleps in Tennessee under his Confederate ban-
ner, rather than languishing in jail for life.

Lopate: Because of double jeopardy—you can't try a person twice for the
same crime if he's acquitted. But the hung juries made it an open case until
something was finally done.

Morris: Exactly.

Lopate: That trial was covered by your son who is a photographer. He's
the one who got you down there in 1994?

Morris: Yes, my son, David Rae Morris, who is a wonderful photographer
based in New Orleans. This was 1994. I was pushing a book deadline, and I
was not going to go down to the Hinds County, Mississippi, courthouse until
the closing stages. David called me up and said, "Daddy, you better get down
here. This is something." It was probably the most bizarre and stunning event
that I had witnessed in a long, long time.

Lopate: Why?

Morris: It was the whole past, the accumulation of the past over thirty
years. It was dead witnesses called back to testify with other people reading
their words. All the evidence was gone. Bobby DeLaughter (with the eventual
help of the widow, Myrlie Evers, who was a co-consultant with me on the
Rob Reiner movie) did not have the murder weapon, they did not have the
original autopsy reports, they did not even have the transcripts.

Lopate: Bobby DeLaughter seems like an unlikely prosecutor here. We're
talking about a white assistant district attorney who was not an activist for
racial equality. He described himself as a conservative and he eventually
switched from the Democratic to the Republican Party.

Morris: That's right. It took a man of that personality and character to finally convict this cowardly assassin thirty years later.

Lopate: If he had been perceived as a liberal he might not have had as good a case simply because of suspicion towards him?

Morris: Bobby is a very conservative man and there were suspicions of him that he was a do-gooder. DeLaughter was anything but a do-gooder. He's moralistic. He believes in right and wrong. He's deeply, deeply religious. Eventually he reminded the widow Myrlie of her late husband, Medgar. They were both workaholics with a strong sense of right and wrong and a mutual love for our native ground of Mississippi.

Lopate: Let's talk about the film that was made down there in Mississippi. You mentioned director Rob Reiner, and there was Alec Baldwin playing DeLaughter, James Woods playing De La Beckwith, and Whoppi Goldberg playing Myrlie Evers. That involved an invasion from the North into this town, didn't it? What was the reaction of the people?

Morris: The people from Castle Rock Entertainment were embraced warmly, and the media dealt with them with great respect and affection. There was a lingering hangover, however, from several years before over producer Fred Zollo's movie *Mississippi Burning*, which was attacked for various reasons from a veritable popular front, including white liberals, black civil rights activists, reactionaries, and racists.

Lopate: The liberals complained that in a story that dealt with racism in the South, all of the heroes were white.

Morris: Or FBI men.

Lopate: And the FBI had been notorious for *not* getting involved in the case until very late. There was the feeling that the film was skewed toward white heroes and that there could have been at least one black hero in it.

Morris: With the difference being that *Mississippi Burning* was largely a work of fiction. It was very loosely based on the Neshoba County killings of 1964, which I wrote a book about called *The Courting of Marcus Dupree*. The movie *Ghosts of Mississippi* was a true history. I think it's a good movie. I defended it as being 100 percent faithful to the spirit of the truth and 80 percent to the spirit of accuracy. But nationally the reviews got caught up in a lot of political correctness and the clashing voices of our contemporary America. Rob Reiner knew he wasn't going to make a cent on it. I remember he came in while we were viewing dailies out in the Culver City Studios and he had just seen my buddy John Grisham's movie *A Time to Kill*. He said, "We don't have any of this. We don't have half-naked women tied to trees, we do not have pyrotechnics, we do not have modern day Ku Klux Klan members shaking their fists at NAACP leaders in broad daylight on the court-house square in Canton, Mississippi. We have none of this. This is about vigilante justice."

Lopate: He had a great performance by James Woods. Everybody agreed with that.

Morris: Oh, absolutely great. Leonard, one of the things that struck me the most were the emotionally wrenching moments in the actual filming. Alec Baldwin played DeLaughter (a very fine actor; I think this is his best role). The three children of Medgar and Myrlie Evers were in the movie. Van and Darrell played themselves, Reena Evers played a juror, and Yolanda King, daughter of Dr. Martin Luther King, played Reena. The actual jury consisted of eight blacks and four whites. Beckwith, of course, did not think he would *ever* be convicted in Mississippi. As he said, "All it would take is one."

While they were re-creating the genuine court scene in the Culver City Studios, Alec Baldwin was doing the first take of the word-for-word summa-tion that had actually been given by DeLaughter in the real trial. Reena, playing a juror, just broke down, sobbing uncontrollably. They had to com-fort Reena and there were perhaps twenty-eight takes of that scene. Another time Myrlie Evers showed up on the set, and Reena introduced her to the actor, James Woods, who was in his complete Beckwith makeup. Myrlie Evers visibly cringed and said her first reaction was to choke him. All these layers of intense emotion during the filming itself.

There was also the re-creation of the assassination at the Evers house. I was told that only two other movies in history had ever been filmed at the actual house where a murder had occurred: one was *In Cold Blood* and the other was about that *Playboy* pin-up, *Death of a Centerfold: The Dorothy Stratton Story*. That filming of Evers's murder was a very moving moment, and it really got to all of us. I mean, where does truth end and Hollywood begin?

Lopate: You mentioned that this film was not a success and Rob Reiner didn't expect to make any money on it, but do you think that people like Reiner—people with clout—are less likely to make films like this because of the critical reaction? You're damned if you do and damned if you don't.

Morris: You're damned right, what with the response to this movie, the fact that not only did it not make a cent, but that it lost millions and millions. You're damned right!

Lopate: But he thought he was doing something important, and then when you get beaten up as well . . . .

Morris: Rob's a tough guy and a very admirable guy, and he views the reaction to it with a great sense of philosophy. But it hurt Rob; it really hurt him.

Lopate: In some cases the criticism was really crazy. A critic from *Variety* complained about details which were in fact true. For example, he claimed that John F. Kennedy's civil rights speech did not occur on the night of Evers's murder. That actually happened.

Morris: That actually happened. *Variety*, which has great power in the industry, said that here's an example of how Hollywood lied: that Hollywood depicted President Kennedy giving his great civil rights address—the most emphatic by any American president up to that point—on the night of Medgar Evers's murder. Well, of course it took place on that night.

One of the reasons, Leonard, I got into this book was that John F. Kennedy, Jr. phoned me one day back during the filming, asking me to do a piece for his magazine, *George*, on Jesse Helms. I told him I couldn't because of my involvement in this movie, *Ghosts of Mississippi*, and he was intrigued. I told him—he did not know—that his father did give his famous civil rights address on the night that Medgar Evers was murdered, just a few hours before Medgar was shot in the back. John Kennedy, Jr. said, "Why don't you do a piece for *George* on all of this, not just your own involvement in the movie, but the history of Evers and Beckwith?" I did write this ["Back to Mississippi," *George*, January 1997], and in doing it I got involved in the piece and thought, "Maybe there's a book here."

Lopate: A number of people felt that there *were* problems with the movie. The film did pass over Myrlie Evers's role in keeping the case alive. Jerry Mitchell, the reporter for the Jackson *Clarion-Ledger*, complained that his role in the story hadn't received enough attention in the film (he had reported possible jury tampering in the first two trials, which had sparked interest in this case). Bobby DeLaughter felt that he shouldn't have been made into such a noble hero-type. So maybe those are things that we should be concerned about, but it's impossible to make movies without leaving some things out.

Morris: This is all in my book. The whole Mississippi caldron, the strange paranoia of my beloved native state, contributed to this.

Lopate: Do you think it's just Mississippi? When Spike Lee makes a movie about Malcolm X, people complain that he's going to distort it, and he does. But whoever made a movie about Malcolm X would have been accused of skewing things one way or another. I wonder if it is possible to make a film about race in this country. And is it possible for a white director to make a film about race in this country?

Morris: Rob Reiner said he could not. He said from the beginning that he, as a white man, was not qualified to direct a civil rights movie with a black person as a hero. He saw his entry into this whole complicated area of race in America through the white hero Bobby DeLaughter. The thing to remember, I repeat, is that the movie is about a true story.

Lopate: White directors sometimes are wary of making films featuring blacks because they don't want to get the facts wrong, and they can be accused of being patronizing. On the other hand, if they focus on white figures from the civil rights movement, then they're accused of skewing the story.

Morris: If I were worth a hundred million dollars I would have made this a three-hour movie with the first hour on Medgar and Myrlie Evers. I would then have immediately switched from the hung juries of 1964 to 1989, when DeLaughter—later with the great help of Myrlie Evers—began this fantastic investigation into the past. But Rob wanted to do a two-hour movie, and I think it's a good movie.

Another one of the salubrious things to come out of this conviction of Beckwith in 1994, thirty years after he shot Medgar Evers, is that it's focusing attention on these old, languished civil rights murders. There's the one in Hattiesburg, Mississippi, where these killers did not serve a *day* in jail after murdering a wonderful civil rights black leader named Vernon Dahmer. These cases are coming back!

Lopate: But it's still a tense situation. You said that the movie producers were embraced, but the fact is that they had trouble getting cooperation from some people, especially for using locations during filming. The governor surely was not cooperative.

Morris: Well, we've got a neo-Dixiecrat right-wing governor. He's to the right of Mussolini, except he doesn't believe in public highways.

Lopate: And there were a lot of white people who just didn't like the subject of the film.

Morris: That's right. It's a very complicated society. As I said, this is not a book about Hollywood, but the response to the movie is part of how I feel about what I consider to be the greatest issue in America, racism.

Lopate: Do you think that Mississippi has a very right-wing governor because it doesn't want to give up the ghost? Is there still a nostalgia for the past?

Morris: That's part of it. We've had a string of very progressive governors. This is all very flawed and complicated, but the current governor has come on the heels of three or four really fine progressive Democrats.

Lopate: *The Ghosts of Medgar Evers: A Tale of Race, Murder, Mississippi, and Hollywood* is published by Random House. My great thanks to Willie Morris for being my guest today on *New York and Company*. This is Radio New York, AM820, WNYC. I'm Leonard Lopate.

Morris: Thanks, Leonard. It's always good to be here.

Index